Beatrice Webb

Beatrice Webb

A Life, 1858-1943

K·ITTY MUGGERIDGE

& RUTH ADAM

Academy
Chicago
Publishers

© 1967 by Kitty Muggeridge and Ruth Adam
Published in 1983 by Academy Chicago
by arrangement with Alfred A. Knopf, Inc.

Academy Chicago, Publishers
425 N. Michigan Ave
Chicago, IL 60611

Printed and bound in the U.S.A.

Library of Congress Cataloging in Publication Data

Acknowledgments

The authors wish to thank the following for permission to quote: The Passfield Trust, for permission to quote from the writings of Beatrice Webb; the Public Trustee and the Society of Authors for quotations from the writings of Bernard Shaw; the executors of the late Mrs G. B. Shaw; (National City Bank, Ltd) John Farquaharson Ltd for quotations from Edith Nesbit; the executors of H. G. Wells; Frederick Muller, Ltd for quotations from *The Webbs and Their Work*; the executors of William Beveridge; Laurence Pollinger, Ltd for extract from the work of D. H. Lawrence; Odhams Books for the use of a photograph; the Chamberlain Trust for extracts from the letters of Joseph Chamberlain.

We wish to thank Rachel, Lady Clay, most gratefully, for the help she has given us by making available various family papers and photographs; and also Miss Anne Holt for her kind permission to quote from her private collection of family letters and from her grandfather's journal. We also thank Lady Hobhouse for permission to quote the letters of Margaret Hobhouse; and the late Colonel Richard Meinertzhagen to quote from the *Diary of a Black Sheep*. We are much indebted to Mrs Beatrice Mayor for providing us with firsthand information concerning the life and character of Beatrice Webb. We also thank Lord Parmoor and the Hon Frederick Cripps for the loan of several photographs and Mr Thomas Ponsonby for allowing us to publish the photograph of Bernard Shaw and the Webbs from his private scrapbook; Mr Alan Chappelow for his photograph of Beatrice and Sidney and Mr Richard Russell for supplying us with reminiscences about them.

We are extremely grateful to Mr Kingsley Martin, for his advice and his permission to quote; to Mrs Margaret Cole for the opportunity to discuss with her various aspects of Beatrice Webb's career, to Professor Robson for his friendly interest and to Mr

ACKNOWLEDGMENTS

Leonard Woolf for all he told us about Beatrice and Sidney and for
the time and trouble he spent in reading and commenting on our
manuscript.

We want to thank Mr Collison, the B.B.C. librarian, for his help
in allowing us to consult records and advising us on research, and
Mrs Enid Moore for her inexhaustible research in finding and
verifying the pictures. We wish also to express our indebtedness to
Mr C. A. Allen, the Keeper of Manuscripts at the London School of
Economics, who, from the time we first launched on this book,
helped and encouraged us by his kindness and attention which
made our research easy.

Our grateful acknowledgment is also due to those authors whose
works we have studied.

K.M.
R.A.

Note—Except where otherwise stated, in the reference notes at the
end of the book, all quotations are from the diaries of Beatrice Webb.

Contents

CONTENTS

Illustrations

Beatrice Webb

Descendants of

Richard Potter = Laurencina Heyworth
1817–1892   in 1844   1821–1882

Lallie	*Kate*	*Mary*	*Georgina*	*Blanche*
1845–1906	1847-1929	1845–1923	1850–1914	1851–1905
= *Robert*	= *Leonard*	= *Arthur*	= *Daniel*	= *Willie*
Holt	*Courtney**	*Playne*	*Meinertzhagen*	*Cripps*
in 1867	in 1883	in 1870	in 1873	in 1877

Richard		William	Daniel	William
Catherine			*Barbara**	Julia
Robert			*Richard**	Alfred
Elizabeth			Margaret	Richard
Philip			Frederick	Rosy
Edward			Laurencina	Henry
Mary			*Beatrice* (Bobo)*	
Laurence			Louis	
			Mary	
			Betty	

       *Lord Courtney   *Barbara Drake
         of Penwith   *Colonel Dick
                           Meinertzhagen
                           *Beatrice Mayor

Note: Characters who are referred to in the book are set in italics.

Theresa	Maggie	Beatrice	Dickie	Rosy
1852–1892	1854–1921	1858–1943	1862–1864	1865–1949
= *Alfred Cripps**	= *Henry Hobhouse**	= *Sidney Webb**		= 1 *Arthur Dyson-Williams*
in 1881	in 1880	in 1892		in 1888
Seddon	*Stephen**			*Noel*
Ruth	*Rachel**			
Fred	Eleanor			
*Stafford**	Arthur			= 2 *George Dobbs*
	Esther			in 1898
	John			
	Paul			
				Patrick
				Leonard
				*Kitty**
				Richard
				Bill

*Alfred, Lord Parmoor of Frieth
*Sir Stafford Cripps

*Rt. Hon. Henry Hobhouse
*Stephen, C.O. in 1914–1918
*Rachel, Lady Clay

*Lord Passfield

*Kitty Muggeridge

My Aunt Bo

MY MOTHER was Beatrice Webb's youngest sister, and the family, impatient of her improvidence and critical of her bohemian ways, was relieved when my parents took themselves off to live abroad. They went to Switzerland. Neither of them suffered much from a social conscience, and my father settled down happily to organise the amusement and diversion of the other guests in the mountain resort we had come to, which was chiefly patronised by people of means and leisure, an enterprise which later developed into the huge tourist concern it now is.

At that time, however, it was not the kind of occupation the Webbs would have considered useful, or productive, or even moral. However, my father, a man of slight ambition, was well content to earn the modest livelihood it brought him. True, he made no contribution to the family expenses. My mother paid the bills. But it enabled him to live in luxurious hotels, exercise his talent for sport, and hob-nob with the rich, whose company he loved. I think it was when the hob-nobbing got out of hand that she brought up her favourite topic of the Webbs most often.

My mother's tastes were altogether different, though no more acceptable to her sister Beatrice. She loved water-colour painting, beautiful scenery, the company of what she called "interesting" people—often referring to such names as her friend the painter Walter Sickert, or her friend the author George Gissing, or H. G. Wells, or A. J. Spender—and a bohemian way of life which meant a hit-or-miss kind of existence, complete disorder, and the dropping of everything at any time of day or night to consider a metaphysical point. We shambled round after my father in disarray, renting chalets as we moved from winter to summer resort.

Wherever we went, I can remember my mother telling people in a loud upper-class voice about her sister, Mrs Sidney Webb. On a terrace overlooking the lake of Geneva, to a company of mountain-climbers, landscape-painters, rich single travellers of both sexes,

Russians with names like Bariatinski, and Dolgorouki, she would suddenly remark, "My sister, Mrs Sidney Webb, does not believe in unearned incomes." No one paid any attention, and continued to watch the view as though it reflected back to them a comforting image of incomes unearned. Up in the mountains, her voice came echoing across the rink, as she struck out on her skates with long, sweeping curves, "My sister, Mrs Sidney Webb, thinks that the playgrounds of the idle rich should not exist!" E. F. Benson and his handsome valet continued to circle unconcernedly around the orange they used as a marker, making intricate figures on the ice in the English style of skating. Or, crossing a glacier in summer, the phrase would ring out in the thin air: "My sister, Mrs Sidney Webb, says the rich should be abolished." And the ladies, roped, continued to peer curiously into the crevasse, and the gentlemen to hack another step in the ice as a precaution against a more immediate danger. At home, to my father, it was simply, "George, Sidney and Beatrice would not at all approve. . . ." and he would continue preparations for tomorrow's fireworks.

The image of my disapproving aunt, so frequently conjured up by my mother, was too remote for me to understand. It would greatly have astonished me to learn that, in fact, we ourselves were living on unearned income in the company of the idle rich, and even on their playgrounds, which she seemed so much to dislike. I loved the life, full of friendly hotel-keepers, merry peasants and English people all smiles, and the world around me so beautiful. I was blissfully ignorant of such things as politics, socialism, local government, trade unions, the poor law, upper or working classes or the Fabians, and indeed would never have qualified to become what my aunt often referred to as "an active citizen."

Moreover, my annual visit to England did little to enlighten me. I was sent to stay with my rich uncle, Alfred Cripps (father of Stafford). On arrival, he would present me with a golden sovereign, which he flipped from a metal case. My cousin Ruth, my godmother, would call me a little gipsy (which I rather liked), give me new clothes and get her maid to curl up my rats' tails, hoping, I suppose, to remove at least the outward traces of my unruly upbringing. But I did not conform easily to the well-regulated household, and on one occasion dismayed the company by kicking my cousin Stafford during afternoon tea, for trying to make me say grace. Actually, I didn't know what to say. I enjoyed my stay in the fine house, flowing with milk and honey and servants and horses, and afterwards compared notes about it with my brothers who had been sent to various other of my mother's sisters. But I was always delighted to get back to my hugger-mugger, nomadic family.

Our life in the Alps came to an end in September 1914, after the declaration of war against Germany. Together with a host of other anglo-continentals, fleeing from internment, we entrained for England. We landed at Folkestone and there we stayed, not bothering to move on, flitting from lodgings to lodgings in a permanent state of impermanence.

It was here, in the spring of 1915, when I was eleven years old, that I first set eyes on the relation whose name had so often been on my mother's lips. The Webbs, on one of those rare holidays they allowed themselves from their self-appointed task of pulling down the old order to make way for the new, were cycling purposively through the lanes of Kent, by way of recreation. When we heard that they had decided to call on us, we were excited and a little apprehensive. My mother immediately informed the landlady that her sister, Mrs Sidney Webb, would be coming to lunch and ordered vegetarian food. We hung expectantly out of the window, watching for her arrival, and presently there sailed into view, pedalling vigorously, a small beetle-like figure, crouched over the handle-bars of a bicycle made for two, and, perched majestically behind him, what appeared to be a large grey bird. It was them! And they alighted at our front door. "Ah, there you are!" shouted my mother, and my aunt shouted back, "Ah, Rosy, here we are!" There was something brave and nautical in their call, like sailors calling to each other in a high wind. My aunt swept into the living-room of our rather shabby lodgings and embraced us all, unaffectionately, with a politician's kiss; a greeting with rather less in it than met the eye.

She was a slender woman with what was then called a "beautiful carriage." Her dress was elegant—a charming bell-skirt of grey cloth, a belt with a silver buckle, a pretty jacket and a large hat tied on with a flimsy veil—that is, after she had removed a nondescript dust coat, which she flung impatiently aside. She had huge black eyes, set wide apart, a delicate Roman nose and arrogant mouth. But her beauty was marred by a lack of tenderness, a kind of domineering masculinity and in the end could only be described as handsome. She walked with the swinging stride of a gipsy and something untamed in her gave her an air of breeding and "race" unwarranted by her lineage. Coming up behind her, as though for air, was Uncle Sidney, a figure of derisory contrast. He was as short and thick as she was tall and slender, a very small man with a very big head, pretty little hands and feet which looked as though they would screw on and off, and wearing thick-lensed pince-nez. He arrived bathed in perspiration from his recent exertions. ("Sidney sweats, you know," my aunt delicately pointed out.) On this occasion he had on his head a white handkerchief knotted at the corners, such as he always wore when it was hot. His countenance was expressionless and he spoke with a lisp, in a voice which was little more than a husky whisper. After the vegetarian meal and some exchanges with my parents, the nature of which I forget, Aunt Bo turned her attention to us children. "And what are you going to do with your young life?" she questioned. One of my brothers was going to be a doctor, another going into the Indian Civil Service and a third into the Navy, to all of whom she nodded approval. When it came to me, I told her I thought of being either a shopkeeper or an actress, whereupon she sniffed up one of her nostrils and directed her alarming eyes and aquiline features to my youngest brother who, fortunately for him, was too young to have decided on a future career. The visit was short and we were decidedly relieved when it came to an end. We had all been awed by her presence and yet as we watched them ride off on their tandem, pedalling in unison, there seemed to me something ridiculous and even slightly forlorn about the pair of them as they vanished into the distance, raising a little puff of dust as they went.

It was not until after the war that I again met my aunt. It was in the early twenties and the first Labour government was in office. Uncle Sidney, who had become a member of Parliament, was President of the Board of Trade. I had completed my education, such as it was, and having abandoned my early project of becoming a shopkeeper or an actress, was training to be a secretary, so that I might escape the otherwise inevitable fate of drifting round with my parents who had resumed their nomadic life abroad.

Perhaps it was because she had no children of her own that Aunt Bo took such an active interest in her many nephews and nieces, seizing every opportunity to indoctrinate them with her ideas. I quite often visited her, in their house at 41, Grosvenor Road, on the Victoria Embankment overlooking the Thames. Those visits were astringent rather than pleasurable and no warm intimacy developed from them, only a kind of cool affection, as though tenderness were against her principles. But her greetings and farewells were curiously eager and demonstrative, as though her feelings were struggling for expression against a rigid self-imposed discipline. I used to feel that there must be something in the family legend about gipsy blood. I remember arriving one evening for dinner and having the impression that the front door had opened of its own accord. Aunt Bo, her large eyes glowing like hot coals, appeared to leap at me from the dark passage behind her, like some wild animal. No doubt the explanation lay in a chance reflection of light. Nevertheless, those red animal eyes haunted me for some time afterwards. On another occasion, I remember her showing me a pretty piece of jewellery, a necklace of gold and cornelian, a copy of some old piece by a famous Italian jeweller, given to her by her father. She laid it out and offered it to me, temptingly. I had the impression, I don't know why, that accepting it would involve me in some obligation, and so, priggishly, I refused it. She took no offence, but packed it off to my sister-in-law. Seeing it round her neck, afterwards, I reproached myself for being such an idiot. No doubt I was meant to.

The house in Grosvenor Road was not very attractive, and many people have recalled its lack of charm. Occasionally I would stay the night there. The evening meal was always frugal, with a special vegetarian dish for Aunt Bo. But, had it been sumptuous, her habit of intently watching her guest eat each mouthful took away all appetite and one often rose from her table hungry. This habit of watching one eat was a peculiar family characteristic, shared by many of her sisters.

After dinner we would go upstairs where my aunt would smoke a number of herbal cigarettes with a child-like relish, and she and my uncle Sidney would conduct one of their famous dialogues with an occasional "We think . . ." addressed to me and I would marvel that two minds should have so many single thoughts. When the time came to retire, she would show me to my room in the attic with great courtesy, explaining as we passed the second floor, "Sidney snores, you know. So I put him in the spare room."

There were two occasions when Aunt Bo guided my feet into the way of Socialism. She had started the Parliamentary Labour Club, which was to provide inexpensive club facilities for the newly-elected labour M.P.s and their wives, and, among other things, the services of a secretary. This job she gave to me. I was delighted. My first duty was to take down a number of letters for Hugh Dalton. I got them down famously, but when it came to reading them back—alas!—no word was decipherable. (I have aways held it greatly in his favour that he just smiled and chivalrously let the matter drop.) Thenceforth I concentrated on the social side of my work and my aunt understandingly ignored the gaffe. After the Parliamentary Labour Club, at her suggestion, I enrolled as a student at the London School of Economics, her own pet educational institution, one of her brain-children. But I had no talent for sociology and my academic career was undistinguished.

In spite of her busy public life, her fame and her fact-finding, Aunt Bo always somehow found time to preside over important family events. I have a vivid memory of her at a family share-out of my Aunt Kate's (Lady Courtney's) treasures, after her death. We were all—about a hundred of us—invited to come to the pretty house in Cheyne Walk, where Aunt Kate lived and died, and there to pick out one object by which to remember her. It was a strange sight to see all my cousins—(oh yes, I was there, too)—closely examining carpets, books, furniture and pictures, estimating what was most valuable. "Shall I have the Chippendale chair or the Watteau drawings?" we asked ourselves. The effort of deciding was too much for me and I asked Aunt Bo to send me a small memento. She did. It was a Woolworth's paste brooch.

No one could have been more delighted than Aunt Bo when I married Malcolm Muggeridge, the son of one of her fellow-Fabians. She liked him immediately and they became firm friends. She shrewdly foretold his brilliant future. It was on one of the many weekends we spent at Passfield Corner, their cottage in the country, that she invited me to go on an Intourist trip to Russia, where, they felt, their dreams had all come true. The idea fascinated me and I accepted her generous offer eagerly. When I arrived in Leningrad, the Webbs were there. They were staying as guests of the Soviet government, in the Astoria hotel, in the lap of propagandists. I had travelled Intourist (third class) and was staying in a hostel and eating on a third-class Intourist meal-ticket. Even so, I got a small pat of butter on my black bread and shreds of meat floating in my soup, while in the Workers' Restaurant they were lucky to get dry black bread and cabbage-water. I said to her that back in Manchester you could eat better on the dole. She would hear of no such thing. I insisted that there was hunger all round us. "My dear Kitty," she replied imperiously, "if you don't care for what is provided, you can always order rice pudding. I do."

But she was old by then. At the time of life when most people begin to look towards the shores of eternity, she was determined to find the rainbow's end in Stalin's Russia. Even then, on parting, she said to me endearingly, "Ah, my dear, old people are sometimes mistaken."

This was my Aunt Bo, imperious, intimidating—and unexpectedly disarming. My aunt Mrs Sidney Webb, the legend of my childhood and the famous sociologist, was just as real, and it was the image she herself liked best. But the two images were different depths of the same woman.

I have always wanted to put them together, so that they focus into one.

K.M.

I

Youngest but One
1858–1865

BEATRICE POTTER WAS BORN into a happy family, as the eighth daughter of an ideal marriage. "They appear to me the most admirable pair I have ever met," said the Victorian philosopher, Herbert Spencer,[1] delighted by the Grecian profile and lovable amiability of her father, and awed by the perfect femininity, combined with an independent character, of her mother. Both came of north-country stock, from families which had risen to industrial power early in the nineteenth century. Their fathers had had the adventure of making a quick fortune, between youth and middle age, leaving the second generation with the agreeable problem of learning how to spend it, by moving south and cultivating good society, a little hampered by their northern consciences reminding them that it was virtuous to make money but wicked to be lavish with it. Like the newly-affluent society of a century later, they made a cult of family life and took a passionate interest in every detail of their children's upbringing. But whereas the professional parents of the nineteen-fifties put their faith in psychiatry, those of the eighteen-fifties put theirs in religion, and were concerned with their children growing up good rather than well-adjusted. All the same, the Potter household was a kind and tolerant one with a full, satisfying nursery life. The eight little girls were free to roam about the grounds of the large country house, provided for their benefit; to ride ponies, make pets of the cats and dogs, have their own particular chickens and look after them, go for eleborate picnics and read what they liked. When two of them, whose birthdays fell close together, celebrated them, their elder sisters made them crowns of red and pink roses and blue larkspur, and organised a procession, with all the rest carrying wreaths of flowers. The servants were sent for, so that they, too, could watch the charming scene, and the butler proposed Hip, hip, hooray for the queens of the May, and their mother was so moved that she wrote a poem about it all in her journal that night.[2]

Yet Beatrice insisted, all her life, that she had had an unhappy childhood, and looked back on her early years with the same kind of self-pity with which Dickens described the boy David Copperfield and George Eliot the little Maggie Tulliver. In spite of having so many sisters she was always playing by herself. In spite of being petted by the maids and watched over by a saintly and benevolent nannie, she brooded about being neglected. Alone in the woods, she made herself secret grottoes and built muddy dams to divert the stream into leaky pools. But even while she was absorbed in these satisfying occupations, she was building castles-in-the-air in which she lay on her death-bed, and all those around her wept and begged her forgiveness for not having appreciated her earlier. The psychiatrist of today, looking at the record, would diagnose some hidden anxiety, and would probably ask, first, what kind of a relationship this troubled, withdrawn child had with her mother. The answer is that her mother admittedly loved her less than any of the others, and that Beatrice hungered, hopelessly, for her mother's attention in the years when she needed it most, and, as a grown woman, after her mother's death, built up a fantasy that her mother's spirit had come back to watch over her, wanting to make up for the past.

Laurencina Potter, Beatrice's mother, was generally admitted, by her family and friends, to be as near perfection as it is possible for a human being to be, and owned it herself, without disguise. The conviction had first been planted by her father Laurence Heyworth.

His family had been domestic manufacturers, who wove cotton on their own looms, at home. When the machines came, and the spinning and weaving moved into factories, most of the displaced ones took jobs as factory hands, but Laurence left his home-town of Bacup, in Lancashire, and went to Liverpool and set up as a mill-owner and eventually took to trading with South America and became a rich merchant, and a power in politics as well. But he was a down-to-earth Radical, a friend of Cobden and Bright, and chose his wife from the humble people he had left behind, and for love. She was gentle-hearted and beautiful, but frail and unstable. Her family suffered from constitutional melancholy and suicidal mania. She died of consumption when her children were still babies, and her husband transferred his whole affection to the only daughter,

Laurencina, and insisted that everyone around her, including her brothers, should regard her as a paragon of virtue, beauty and learning.

In her early twenties, when she was making the Grand Tour, accompanied by a younger brother and a Bacup relative as companion-cum-attendant, she met Richard Potter in Rome. They fell in love as they wandered among the ancient monuments, talking of Shakespeare and of Shelley. He was, as she observed in an autobiographical novel which she wrote about their love-affair, a man of intelligent and upright nature, capable of enjoying pleasure to the utmost, yet delighting in activity and on the look-out for duty. He was also extremely attractive physically, and rich.

Richard Potter's father had made a cotton-fortune and was— like his father-in-law—one of the radical, dissenting, reforming manufacturers of the north, and one of the first members of Parliament after the Reform Bill. In the year of Waterloo, he had married a strange black-eyed girl, reported by some to be descended from an aristocratic old Norman family, by others from the gipsies, and by herself from the Jews. Richard was born in 1817 and almost died then because (said his father irritably) none of the females attending the birth had the sense to pull off her flannel petticoat and wrap him in it.[8] But he survived—fortunately for the Labour party of the twentieth century which owed much to his descendants—and so did the three sisters born after him. After the birth of her fourth child, the fey young mother ran away from her husband and never came back to him. She wanted to lead the Jews back to Palestine, and got as far as Paris, but was recovered and put in an asylum, from which she was removed by Richard after her husband's death. In old age she became an amiable and popular grandmother and died of laughing at an anecdote related to her by her son.

Richard Potter, throughout his life, was successful, happy and beloved by his family and his friends. Himself the child of a broken home, he became a devoted husband and a model father. Brought up a Unitarian, and mixing with agnostics, he became a conventional and contented Anglican. His background was north country Radicalism; in later life he was an influential Conservative, moving easily in London Society, a friend of the intellectual giants of his day. In the heyday of Victorianism, he gave his daughters the freedom usually allowed only to sons and wanted the vote extended to women householders. A ruthless and prosperous capitalist, he loved poetry, studied Dante in the original and taught his daughters to appreciate the eighteenth-century humorists. He could travel all night and ride all day without fatigue; enjoyed rich food and choice wines and also evading the rules of diet imposed on him by his womenfolk. He could drive a hard bargain involving thousands of pounds and coax a fretful baby into good humour, with equal diplomacy. He enjoyed life, and it was his infectious optimism that made him so valuable to those who loved him.

His grandfather had been a farmer and shopkeeper, but he was educated at public school and university, was bored at the idea of going into the family business and meant to make the Bar his profession. At the time he met Laurencina, his father had just died, leaving him with a comfortable income and he had decided to travel for a year before settling down to work. He proposed to her in Rome, and they came back to England, and were married immediately.

Marriage to Richard Potter offered Laurencina the two things she wanted most: unqualified adoration and the kind of life for which she felt most fitted. She believed that she was unique, not with the ordinary girlish vanity of a pretty and accomplished young woman, but as a simple fact, obvious to everyone. In the novel which she wrote about herself, *Laura Gay*,[4] the heroine was so brilliant and well-read, so saintly and above all so utterly original that naturally all the men worshipped her and the young women were consumed with jealousy and a friendly older one felt obliged to warn her to conceal her fluency in Latin, because men tended to think that if a woman had plenty of brains she must have no heart. Laura Gay even had a private line to God and "suffered neither priest nor veil to intervene between her spirit and the holy of holies."

Laurencina, like most women who feel themselves superior to their sex, despised the rest of it, and preferred the society of clever men. John Bright said that she was "one of the two or three women a man remembers to the end of his life as beautiful in expression and form." She wrote political essays and lectures and was a zealous supporter of the anti-corn-law agitation. The married life she visualised with Richard was one of close intellectual companionship, a circle of distinguished friends and herself as a scholar and writer—the old-fashioned pattern of "learned leisure" favoured by the cultured rich before the Industrial Revolution threw up a new plutocracy. In many ways, she belonged more to the eighteenth century than the nineteenth. Richard amiably gave up the idea of a profession and they settled down in a house in St John's Wood. But two pregnancies, in rapid succession, left her nervous and delicate, and the financial crisis of 1848 swept away most of their money. At the age of twenty-six she found herself badly-off, for the first time in her life, with two daughters and a third child on the way. Richard, at thirty, found himself obliged to start making a liveli-hood, not from choice, this time, but of necessity.

Fortunately, he had influence. A school-friend offered him a partnership in a timber firm in Gloucester, and his father-in-law got him a directorship of the Great Western Railway. Richard discovered new abilities in himself. He raised storms at the G.W.R. about the inefficiency of the Board, resigned when his protest was over-ruled and was coaxed back, with new powers, later on. He made the fortune of the Gloucester business, during the Crimean War, by suggesting to the British and French governments that they should buy up the depreciated timber lying in his yard and make huts for the soldiers currently dying of exposure. The British government mislaid his letter, had to ask for a copy, and then mislaid the timber on its way to Balaclava, but paid the bill promptly. Louis Napoleon agreed to Richard's proposal instantly, and left him in his private cabinet at St. Cloud (littered with secret documents) to write out the contract, but it seemed impossible to get the money out of the French government. One of Richard's many friends, a more exper-ienced tycoon than himself, advised him to try bribery. Richard cashed a cheque for £1,000 and distributed it as recommended, starting with the porter at the Ministry (20 francs) and ending with the Minister himself (£500) who promptly pocketed it and signed the papers authorising immediate payment. The profits to the timber-yard added up to £60,000.

The change in the Potter circumstances altered the whole balance of their marriage. Now that Richard had tasted the satisfaction of making a fortune for himself, as opposed to inheriting one already made, he knew that this was what he really wanted of life. He enjoyed everything about it; the excitement of speculation; the sense of being part of the dynamic march of Victorian progress; the planning, the diplomacy, the comradeship with other captains of industry and the sense of personal power. But it was a man's world, in which the husband installed his wife in comfortable quarters, to produce and bring up a succession of babies and to run a home to which he was welcomed back whenever he could spare the time to be with his family. Laurencina found herself, after all, condemned to the ordinary domestic round of the well-off nineteenth-century wife, occupied with a country house full of servants and children, expected to spend her time supervising nursery, schoolroom, kitchen, house and garden; to entertain her husband's business acquaintances at the weekends and to live with an eternal grievance about his being so often absent, punctuated by gloomy speculations about the kind of social life he was leading, out in the world.

Her novel was published and was not well received. "The political sketches are not very vivid. The dialogue is stiff with the starch of pedantry," said the *Leader*. *The Sunday Times* remarked unkindly, "A strong satire may be painful but a weak one is ridiculous." Laurencina copied the reviews into her "Journal" and added sadly, "I did not feel sure of being an author and doubted the continuance of my own profession," and resigned herself to domesticity.

She was a perfectionist, and she did it extremely well. The establishment ran on oiled wheels, not a penny was wasted, and staff were kept up to the mark. Shortly after Beatrice was born, when Laurencina was still weak from a difficult confinement, she nevertheless sent for all the excercise-books of her six eldest daughters and went through them, noting in her journal that Lallie and Kate, though strong on Latin and Greek, were weak on other subjects; that Mary and Georgina had made little or no improvement and that Blanche and Theresa, though passable in reading and sewing, were behindhand in everything else. She resolved that from now on she would have to inspect their work regularly, herself, and dismiss governesses as required. At this time, the eldest of the schoolroom group was only thirteen and the tail of it under six. Maggie, at four, was still in the nursery, with no duties beyond being good and refraining from being jealous of the new baby.

At a time when only two girls out of every three survived long enough to grow up and get married, the Potters had had eight children in thirteen years and kept them all, but they were all daughters, and Laurencina longed for sons above everything in the world. When Beatrice was four years old, Laurencina's prayers were answered at last, and she had a boy. As soon as she was allowed to sit up, she confided exultantly to her Journal:

A son has been given to us, now eight days ago, of most promising appearance, exceedingly healthy, strong, full-sized and like his papa, placid beyond all my former infants. May we have wisdom and self-denial enough to train the child in the way he should go, always setting his religious and moral culture before every other, and carefully guarding him from insidious influences; and please God to give him health and a portion of the Divine Spirit, and to accept him as a servant and son for Christ's sake. Amen.[5]

(When Beatrice was born, the entry had been shorter—"My strength much impaired by having little Beatrice, my 8th daughter.")

Nothing was too good for little Dicky, who, from the first, was clearly "a genius" and an angel of unselfishness as well, though his splendid health and gay disposition did away with any suggestion of precocity. Laurencina had, up till now, been a severely undemonstrative mother, but she was openly affectionate with this child, caressing him constantly, making excuses to keep him close to her, letting him play on her bed in the mornings, and taking him out with her when she went for a drive, while Beatrice was left at home. She could hardly bear to be parted from him and when she went away on a visit had him to sleep in her bed, and woke him to share with her the beauty of the moonlight on the Severn outside her window. A highly-trained nurse was engaged specially to look after him. She was resentful if expected to include the youngest-but-one in her duties, and the first memory of Beatrice's life was of finding herself outside the nursery door, naked and astonished, with her clothes flung out after her, while the nurse went back to attend to Dicky.

Laurencina began to notice, with severe disapproval, that Beatrice was giving way to one of the cardinal sins of the Victorian nursery and showing jealousy of her little brother. It made Dicky's extraordinary sweetness all the more noticeable. He was always so unselfish and loving, and when Beatrice was in disgrace (as usual) he was personally distressed about it. Sometimes, Beatrice made a desperate effort to get back into favour. When her mother was away (having torn herself from her youngest in order to present her eldest at court) and Beatrice was five years old, she wrote Laurencina a painstaking letter:[6]

Dear Mama,

   I am quite well and very good. I shall be very glad when sister comes home. I love dear little Dicky very much. Give my love to Uncle Laurence. With my best love to Pap, Lallie and you,

        I am, dear Mam,
          Beatrice.

This was the happiest time of Laurencina's life. In the autumn of 1864, she wrote in her journal:

It is more than two years since the birth of our little Richard and now all things have prospered with us. My dear husband has nearly doubled his property and he has much enhanced his social position by the zeal, honour and ability with which he has managed the Great Western Railway during the last year. His position as chairman of it has brought him into contact with many persons of every degree and I hear his praises on all sides, not only for ability and the sterner virtues but for genuine kindness and sympathy.[7]

Her happiness ended abruptly a few days before Christmas, when Dicky's nurse woke her before dawn with the news that he was very ill. Two doctors were sent for immediately. The first suspected a severe shock to the system and gave him a purge; the second diagnosed scarlet fever and regretted that a purge had been administered. Laurencina never left the nursery, through seven days of alternate hope and despair, of Dicky begging for water and being refused "for fear of diminishing the tone of his stomach" and being made to take food which he did not want—"but whatever I wished him to do he did with beautiful obedience. Alas! I fear that all he took only went to nourish the fever and augment his sufferings." At night, Laurencina lay on the bed beside him,

trying to soothe him to sleep as he lay tossing and restless yet perfectly sensible and resigned. Indeed he never uttered an irritable word or cry throughout his illness. At daybreak on Thursday morning he said earnestly, "Oh, I love you so very much," and that he repeated in the most heartfelt way many times over and then he said over and over again in the most earnest way, "I will never be a naughty boy again." I could not relieve his little heart until I had assured him that he was a good boy because he earnestly wished and tried to do right, and that God our father in Heaven loved him too and would either cure his illness or give him another beautiful body which could not suffer instead of the one which was suffering so much. This soothed him and for a few minutes he slept calmly. When my breakfast came up he was pleased to have a saucer full of my tea—"Mama's tea out of Mama's saucer,"... Throughout Friday, Saturday and Sunday he grew gradually weaker and more suffering. He seemed to like me near him and to feel my hand. On Christmas Day, Monday, at 11.30 p.m. he entered into the rest and joy of our Lord.[8]

Richard Potter, with the authority which came naturally to him, but was seldom applied to his wife, insisted that she should join with him, at once, in "a solemn act of submission to the will of God" and made her vow to dedicate herself, with him, to the nurture of their remaining children. But after the funeral, Laurencina shut herself up and poured out her bitterness to her journal, reproaching herself for not taking better care of Dicky, recalling every detail of his life and perfections and, inevitably, making damaging comparisons between him and the last daughter whom she could have spared so much more easily. In her self-imposed solitude, the great problem of her whole life—how to reconcile her longing for the mystic consolation of religious orthodoxy with the iconoclastic intellect inherited from her father—obsessed her more and more. When she despaired of solving it, she distracted herself by study for its own sake—learning Greek grammar from a French book, Latin grammar from an Italian one, making a collection of learning, which she had no idea of putting to any use in her own life, like a miser hoarding coins. She hoped to know twelve languages before she died, and almost succeeded.

"Creeping up in the shadow of my baby brother's birth and death," was Beatrice's own bleak summing-up of these years. She became a sickly little girl, continually developing the kind of non-organic complaints—such as neuralgia, indigestion, insomnia and inflammations of all sorts—which are characteristic of children who feel neglected and are making a silent bid for attention and love. Once when the wretchedness of being herself pressed on her harder than usual, she stole a bottle of chloroform from the medicine-chest, with a vague idea of killing herself and thus escaping from the ennui of existence, but found later that she had left the bottle uncorked, so that the contents had evaporated. In time, she learned to come to terms with her mother's rejection of her. (In later life, recalling Laurencina's appearance, she described her as ugly and hard-looking when her face was turned away, but beautiful when it was turned towards you.)[9] She learned to regard her mother simply as a source of arbitrary authority whose rare interventions in her own life she silently resented. "Beatrice is the only one of my children who is below the average in intelligence," Laurencina noted coldly at this time. Beatrice learned to circumvent her mother's authority, to be cunning in watching and humouring her, so that she might lead her own life without interference, and to look elsewhere for the affection she needed.

The outsize Victorian household—unlike the small, shut-in family of today—did at least offer a lonely child the chance of making relationships because among so many people there was always someone to whom she could attach herself. Standish House, the home into which she had been born, was a complete community, with the front part (heavily carpeted and comfortably furnished) for master and mistress, guests and the elder girls, and the back part (with bare rooms and stone corridors) for the younger ones and the staff. Across the yard was a laundry, fully staffed and working full-time, and beyond that the stables and harness-room, also with their own personnel. It was a rented house, one of the three (later of four) between which the family divided their year. They were a restless group, always on the move, like gipsies. Standish, which had been chosen because it was near Richard's Gloucester business, stood on the Cotswold Hills, looking across a broad valley. Twice a day, when the tide was up, you could see the silver streak of the Severn estuary, ten miles away. Behind the house, on the hillside, was an immense park-like field, and behind that a half-circle of beech-trees. Beatrice used to spend lonely hours wandering about the grounds, sitting in the leaf-filled hollows of the woods, or in the crevices of the quarries and "conjure up the intimacy and tenderness lacking in my life". At other times, she would take refuge in the laundry, which was sunny in the summer and deliciously warm in the winter, where the laundry-maids welcomed her, and let her curl up, to doze and day-dream, among the rough-dried sheets and table-cloths, or perch on the ironing-board and explain to an admiring audience that when she grew up she meant to renounce the world and be a nun. Sometimes she drifted into her sisters' schoolroom and was tolerantly received by the governesses, but as soon as the business of tackling lessons became serious, she was apt to retire to her bed, with one of her indefinable complaints, when the family doctor would conveniently prescribe fresh air and exercise instead of work. She preferred to educate herself, to read books from the library, of her own choice, and to write down her reflections—including confessions of her own guilt and inadequacy—in a private notebook.

The mainstay of the whole complex organisation of the Potter home was Martha Jackson, nicknamed "Dada", who was the poor relation from Bacup whom Laurence Heyworth had first engaged to accompany Laurencina to Rome, and who had stayed on with her, acting as nannie to the first babies, and later as a kind of regent when Laurencina went back to her books and her meditations about God. Dada mothered everyone in the household, whether servants or children, nursed them when they were ill, comforted them in trouble and spoke up for them when they were in disgrace. She was also the only person who could deal with Laurencina in one of her difficult moods. To Beatrice, she was "a saint, the one and only saint I ever knew". By creed, she was a Particular Baptist, but she never tried to convert her charges. To her, religion was a state of mind, an overpowering consciousness of love, which dominated everything she did. She loved and served those around her without ever judging them, because she believed that this was the nature of Jesus of Nazareth.

One scene with Martha was, as Beatrice wrote sixty years later, "cut deep" in her memory all her life. She had done something wrong and then denied it; which, in the theology of the Victorian nursery, was a mortal sin. She faced Martha, tempted to tell another lie to cover it. There was "a moment of silence and then, as the sole response, a flash in her grey eyes of mingled amusement and love." What impressed Beatrice so deeply was not so much that Martha forgave her, but allowed her to get away with it.[10] Twice, in Beatrice's subsequent life, when she was a public figure, on the crest of the wave of her career, she had a traumatic experience in which she lived through this moment again, believing, both times, that she was about to be publicly and shamefully exposed, and had to fight the temptation to lie a second time to save herself. Very early in her childhood, the sharp, critical child realised and noted the difference between her mother's religion, with its interminable intellectual arguments, and that of Martha, who seldom spoke of it, but lived in communion with an outside spiritual force, and it was Martha's faith which haunted the grown-up Beatrice through a lifetime of intellectual agnosticism.

These years in the wilderness laid the foundations of her personality. Always afterwards, she was hampered by insomnia and nervous illnesses. The idea that she was an unlovable person dominated her relationships for a very long time, linked with the belief that it was wicked to wish so much for love and attention. But it was not all loss. The very oddities she developed, as the left-out, non-conforming one of the family, helped to make her the brilliantly original woman she became. Her aloofness and her self-education meant that she always persisted in finding out everything for herself, instead of accepting what other people said. She had to study, desperately, because unless she was mentally occupied, the terrible cloud of lonely boredom came down on her again. Her habit of confiding her thoughts to her journal—and the sleepless nights which she occupied by writing it—made her the outstanding diarist of her time. Her gratitude to Martha and to the domestic servants who had comforted her when she needed it most, and the warmth of her relationships with them gave the working-classes a special aura, for her, ever afterwards. They were her people, her tribe by adoption, and she could talk with them and make friends with them as though they alone spoke her mother-tongue.

If she had ever thought, dimly, that her mother would turn back to the surviving youngest, some time after Dicky's death, the hope was short-lived. The following year, Laurencina was able to report in her journal:

The birth of our 9th little daughter, whom we propose calling Rosalind Heyworth Potter, the 5th July at 19, Kensington Palace Gardens. She is apparently very healthy and placid and promises to be handsome. We were very much disappointed that she was not a son, for it seemed that a little son might in some measure have consoled us for the angel we have lost. Alas! my darling, no present infant could withdraw my mind from dwelling most constantly on your dear life and your untimely death. May it please the Lord to unite us all together in the hereafter. May our dear little babe walk in your lovely steps and be spared to close our eyes if we live to old age.[11]

Laurencina did, in fact, transfer much of the special affection she had lavished on her one son to her ninth and last daughter. Beatrice, inevitably, transferred all of her old resentment to the newcomer.

Philosopher on the Hearth
1865—1873

AFTER ROSY'S BIRTH, Beatrice moved up into the schoolroom, to join Georgie, Blanche, Theresa and Maggie, pursuing the customary Victorian routine for the daughters of rich men: the nursery, the schoolroom and a spare diet, leading up to "the Season", which had already been reached by Lallie, Kate and Mary. The children were now taught by an English and a French governess, a music teacher, and—for Latin—by a Canon of Gloucester. Their teachers —apart from the parson—ranked, in the household hierarchy, just above the servants. Laurencina now visited the schoolroom regularly to examine progress, and there was consequently a constant shifting of tutors and governesses. Otherwise the Potter girls—apart from "Little Rosebud"—saw very little of their mother. Once they left the schoolroom, each one in turn was expected to take over the entire running of the household for a year, but apart from that they had freedom to amuse and educate themselves which few girls of their time were allowed. Long before Beatrice drifted into the schoolroom, she had been accustomed to spend most of her time in solitary reading, and the first entry in her diary, in 1869, deplores the harmful effect of this on the young mind:

I am quite confident that the education of girls is very much neglected in the way of their private reading. Take, for instance, a girl of nine or ten years old, she is either forbidden to read any but child's books or she is let loose on a good library. Sir Walter Scott's novels are recommended to her as charming and interesting stories—"books that can do no possible harm", her adviser declares. But the object of reading is to gain knowledge. A novel now and then is a mere recreation to be offered to a growing mind, it cultivates the imagination, but taken as the continued nourishment, it destroys many a young mind. The whole of their thought (for a child of nine or ten spends little

[32]

or no thought on her lessons) is wasted on making up love scenes or building castles in the air where she is always the charming heroine without a fault. I have found it a serious stumbling block to myself. Whenever I get alone I always find myself building castles in the air of some kind, it is a habit that is so thoroughly inured in me, that I cannot make a good resolution without making a castle in the air about it.

Beatrice got on well enough with those around her, apart from her mother. One of the governesses—who, she says, "did not trouble me. For the most part I liked them and they liked me"— described her as "Bebo la vif"; the other sisters being summed up as "Georgie la fière, Blanche la sensible, Thérèse l'aimable and Marguerite la remarquable,"[1] and in the letters which this restless, itinerant family was always exchanging, when half of it was parted from the other half, she is included just as warmly as anyone else. Maggie wrote to her father from Standish:

Little Rosy sends her love to you and wants you to tell Beebo that she has her brown bantam hen which agrees very well with the white one. I suppose Bee feels quite a grand lady and shows you all about the place as if it were hers.[2]

When some of the girls were spending a holiday at Grandpa Heyworth's house near Liverpool, Maggie wrote to Theresa:

You can't tell how very busy we are, studying natural philosophy—(you may laugh at us, but I can tell you it is very interesting)—and in making a bathing gown for Beatrice. We have made a resolution never to be idle, for in this place there is a great temptation to be so. We also take constitutional walks round the field and jumps over the ditch. Give my love to dear Kate, Mary and Georgie and accept treble the same yourself.[3]

When Richard Potter took a party to stay at Llandudno, Maggie wrote home, "Today Papa is going to take us to the Methodist Chapel. ... The bathing is very jolly on the whole. I can swim now a little, and Beatrice is learning..."[4] When Laurencina was away and the family at home, Maggie wrote:

Standish, July 25th, 1870. Dearest Mama....... I do hope you are not anxious about us, dear Mother, for we ourselves are quite well..... Little Rosie is in remarkable health and spirits and does not mind the heat much, though of course she stays in the house from 11 to 5 o'clock. On Saturday Bee and I spent the afternoon in making her a doll's house, with which she is quite delighted. Poor Bee heard with great disappointment that she is not likely to go to Scotland. . . . . On Saturday Papa arrived with four huge lobsters and a large turbot, all of which we managed on Sunday; Kate was quite horrified. Kate is really an excellent manager, only second to you, and I think it would be safe to leave us with her for any length of time. . . .[5]

An autocratic disposition and a vein of irony can be detected in Beatrice's earliest letters. When she was only eight years old she way already issuing orders to her nurse:

Dear Fanny, I am fearfully disappointed about not going to Standish (the pens are so bad that I must write in pencil) on Saturday which I expected to have done, and also have you spoken to Copner about my chickens. Tell him to keep them up at the farm until I come back, tell him also please to send down my hen without-a-tail. If you have not forgotten the stones you said you would try and get me, and been fortunate to give them in the care of Miss Margaret and tell her to put them in the shelf where my cristels are for me, take care you say these exact words else you may be sure I shall have some difficulty in getting them for she will naturally think they are for herself.[6]

Her account of two Conservative candidates for Gloucester (in a by-election of about 1866) in a letter to her mother indicates the interest she was already showing in politicians:

Dear Mama, Thank you for your kind letter. I hope you and Lallie are quite well and grandpapa and cousins. The two Conservative Candidates were here yesterday, one of them is very short and finely dressed; he had his top coat trimmed with sealskin; he had also silver buckles on his boots and his hands were covered with rings, with a very stylish blue tye which covered his vastcoat; He also saied he spoke Italian and French perfectly. He played on the piano and sung; he seemed not to now what mony words ment, for he asked papa what was the meaning of Demonstration and Major Lees asked the meaning of Hustings and Nomination. Major Lees is very tall and very fat, with a great beard, mustache and whiskers, with an eye glass which he satisfied his curiosity in staring at everybody. I must now say goodbye, dear mama, I remain your dutiful child, Beatrice.[7]

Laurencina governed by remote control. She seldom spoke directly to any of her servants and left the management of the establishment to her daughters whom she brought up never to feel rich. Their penurious housekeeping seemed unreasonable to a brother-in-law who groused over the frugal breakfast they gave him—"You girls have neither the habit nor the desire for comfortable expenditure." She broke her rule of solitude only on rare occasions, to debate in the evenings with Herbert Spencer her "unsettleable controversies" about religion, or to talk to a favoured guest. The French historian Taine, in his *Notes on England*, quotes a description of a visit to Standish by his friend Michel Chevalier:

M——, being invited to the country, discovered that the mistress of the house knew much more Greek than himself, apologised, and retired from the field; then, out of pleasantry, she wrote down his English sentence in Greek. Note that this female Hellenist is a woman of the world, and even stylish. Moreover she has nine daughters, two nurses, two governesses, servants in proportion, a large, well-appointed house, frequent and numerous visitors; throughout all this, perfect order; never noise or fuss; the machine appears to move of its own accord. These are gatherings of faculties and of contrasts which might make us reflect. In France we believe too readily that if a woman ceases to be a doll she ceases to be a woman.[8]

It was natural that Beatrice and her sisters should turn for warmth and affection to their handsome, exuberant, extravagant father. "Generous and tolerant almost to a fault, he was the soul of genial kindliness and had at any rate with his own family one of the sweetest tempers I have ever known."[9] He was their dearest companion and they were all a little in love with him. His third daughter Mary described the "rush when he returned from one of his business trips down the drive at Standish, when we were children, to meet his home-coming and of the breathless interest with which we listened to the graphic words which told of all he had done or thought during his absence from Mother and us."[10] When he was home he joined with childlike enthusiasm in their games. He helped them construct a dam in the woodland stream near the house to form a "nymph's pool" for Rosy. He whisked them off on impromptu fishing expeditions taking along lavish picnics of salmon and champagne. He read to them the works of Sir Walter Scott. When they were older, he treated them as equals, discussed business with them, encouraged them to voice their opinions and allowed them to smoke, ignoring the silent disapproval from the boudoir.

The Potter girls considered Gloucestershire "County Society" dull and conventional, and, although they rode and danced and flirted with them, had little to say to their fox-hunting "swains". Only one of them, Mary, who was perhaps less critical than her sisters, married a local squire, Arthur Playne. He was a mild-eyed slightly peevish young man who lived a few miles from Standish on a charming estate called Longfords. It looked on to a gloomy lake surrounded by beautiful beechwoods in which Mary, in later life, often gathered faggots like an old gipsy, which she instructed her butler to kindle on the drawing-room fire. Arthur owned cloth mills at Nailsworth near Stroud, was devoted to fox-hunting and country pursuits, disliked foreign travel and sat on the board of the local lunatic asylum. It was the least turbulent of the Potter marriages. It was also less fruitful than most of them, with only one son, William.

The family never established themselves as landed gentry. They saw little of their neighbours except for the Bishop of Gloucester and his wife. Richard Potter could never resist an ecclesiastic. He and Bishop Ellicot became close friends, and there was a good deal of coming and going between Standish House and the Cathedral Close, especially during the Gloucester Music Festival. It was an annual event celebrated by the Potters with house parties and banquets attended always by the Bishop and his wife. With their guests, they would drive over to Gloucester to listen to the music in the cathedral.

Except when the family had migrated *en masse*, Standish was never empty. A variety of guests were perpetually trooping across its hospitable threshold. There were Richard Potter's business associates, railway magnates from America, opulent, unscrupulous and witty, who seemed infinitely glamorous to Beatrice. There were the dull Scandinavian timber-merchants who were, however, no less important, and the common-sense British business-men. There were philosophers and Richard Potter's ecclesiastical friends. There were guests such as Tyndal and Huxley, who represented his interest in science, and John Bright his political friend from the old days in Manchester. Finally, there were the sisters' suitors who Beatrice decided were a queer lot. Added to this restless coming and going were her father's frequent business trips abroad. After he had been made president of the Grand Trunk Railway, he visited America and Canada five times, taking with him two of his daughters "to keep him company". He never took his wife, and Beatrice suggests, in *My Apprenticeship*, that he needed the girls as a protection against any "undesirable associations" he might be tempted to make during his travels.

"We lived in a perpetual state of ferment," Beatrice wrote, looking back. Darwin's *Origin of Species* had launched all kinds of philosophic controversies, and the steam-engine generated a kind of alarmed exhilaration. There was as much speculation about new railway enterprises, the opening of branch lines, and about rising land values as there was about evolution and the existence or non-existence of God. Everyone had his own train-disaster story, just as everyone has his car-accident one today. Richard Potter himself had a narrow escape. He had obligingly changed seats with the passenger opposite, who was unable to tolerate travelling with his back to the engine. When the accident happened, Richard was thrown out of the window and landed on the railway-embankment unhurt, while his fellow-passenger was killed outright. After that, the railway-magnate personally advised all his friends to travel with their back to the engine.

For a child growing up, it was a stimulating mental climate. Beatrice did her best to join in the discussions, and to draw the attention and admiration of the company—especially of the men —to herself. She talked to them with assurance, as though she was one of them, putting on "affected airs and a posturing manner" and perpetually showing off in an attempt to outshine her elder sisters. If, when bedtime came, she felt miserable, and resolved once and for all to renounce going into company for fear that her "silly vanity" might diminish her chance of becoming "a good and useful woman in this world and a companion of our Lord in the next," somehow, in the morning, her good resolutions were all forgotten in contemplation of the triumphs of the coming day.

Lallie was the first one to leave home. When she was twenty-three she married Robert Durning Holt, a Liverpool shipping merchant. At midsummer in 1867, after a week of tears in which everyone joined, she walked dry-eyed up the aisle of the church at Stonehouse wearing a very long white satin dress, a plain tulle veil and orange-blossom, and a magnificent pearl necklace which her mother-in-law had given her. She was followed by her sisters in the pink-and-white and green-and-white dresses she had made herself. Her mother looked frail but "resplendent in blue satin and Brussells lace"—not colours she would have chosen herself, commented Lallie's future sister-in-law, describing the wedding to her mother, but—

> —those Potter girls with their short hair made a very pretty and original group. . . . I am rather in love with them all, with their rough black heads and so like Joshua Reynolds' pictures . . . and (they) are so simple and nice and yet with so much in them from Lallie down to Beebo . . . All was so nicely arranged, and nobody in any fuss and with apparently nothing to do but receive their guests and make themselves agreeable.[11]

Lallie was good-hearted but inclined to manage people and never quite left off being the "eldest sister". She lived in Liverpool for the rest of her life and had eight children.

The Potters' eccentric old friend, the Liberal philosopher Herbert Spencer, often came to Standish—so often that Beatrice called him "the philosopher on the hearth". This singular man became the dominant influence in her life. He trained her mind when she was a child and formed her thought when she was a young woman. When she began to lose her faith in Christianity she found, for a time, his ethical creed a satisfactory alternative; and his theory of the Social Organism directly inspired her to devote her life to the scientific investigation of social institutions. When Beatrice was first aware of him, he was the most famous Englishman of his day, an implacable opponent of the State and a fanatical upholder of individual liberty. His books had been translated into such out-of-the-way languages as Sanskrit and Mohawk and he was so popular in America that, when he had only just turned from professional journalism to writing about philosophy, and was not yet famous, his admirers there, indebted to him "for work by which they knew he had been the loser", sent him 7,000 dollars and a gold watch. In

England he was recognised in the streets and often hailed by passers-by.

Spencer owed his popularity to the fact that he provided the mystique needed by an age whose fundamental beliefs had been undermined by Darwin's theory of evolution and the fantastic assumptions of science. He had hit upon a formula which made sense of everything, a new scientific creed, in which the words "I know" replaced "I Believe". His doctrine of the "Survival of the Fittest" gratified a generation dumbfounded to find themselves "no longer children of God, but members of a brute creation". He assured his disciples that the future promised unlimited progress, that its aim was pleasure and its end universal happiness "hitherto undreamed-of". The harsh prospect of a godless universe was softened by his concept of "the Unknowable"—which conveniently covered everything which could not be explained by science. His most original contribution to Victorian thought was his Science of Sociology (Carlyle called it the dismal science). Spencer declared that human society was a social organism and that the evils of society could therefore be diagnosed and cured by scientific investigation. Riding on the high tide of mid-Victorian optimism, Spencer could sing with conviction that there was a happy land not far away, and drown the gloomy prophecies of his denigrator Carlyle.

Portaits of Spencer show a fine head, close-set eyes, a prominent nose, a long upper lip and an obstinate mouth. He was vain of his small hands and feet, which he took to be a sign of good breeding and a proof of his theory about acquired characteristics, over which he had split hairs with Darwin. Beatrice remembered his tall spare frame, his bright eye, his precise speech and ridiculous pedantry, his irascibility and his elegant but unusual costume. The eccentricity, for which he was renowned, amounted almost to hysteria. It took the form of a kind of parody of the scientific method, as though he wished to ridicule it all. For instance, his cure for feelings in his head and insomnia, which he called "cerebral congestion", was to wet his skull with brine on retiring, covering it first with a flannel nightcap and then with a waterproof one to prevent evaporation, and so to bed. Another cure was laughter. In order to induce it, he engaged in an elaborate frolic reminiscent of Lewis Carroll's mad hatter. He lined a friend's hat with paper each day until eventually the friend cried out with a puzzled air: "My hat's too small!" "No, no," cried the philosopher, overcome by the required dose of mirth,

"Your head's too big!"[12] The spectacular ceremonial of his departures from London to Standish, as described by the ladies who kept house for him in St John's Wood, also belonged more to *Through the Looking-Glass* than to every-day life. He would arrive at the station bearing under his arm his current manuscript, which was attached to the end of a long piece of string tied round his waist. The string hung like a tail from under the hem of his coat at the back. He was followed by his amanuensis (bearing his chair, hammock, rug and air-cushion), who was followed by a female friend brought along to wave farewell. A porter carried the luggage. The party made straight for the waiting-room, where Spencer would take his temperature and count his pulse. At the appointed hour of departure four obsequious officials would arrive to carry him to his reserved saloon compartment. If his temperature was normal and he was feeling well, he indignantly brushed them aside, and, leading the little procession, stepped out briskly for the platform. Here the obsequious officials would help him into the carriage, sling the hammock under his supervision and be dismissed. Finally, having shaken hands with his amanuensis and waved farewell to his farewell-waving friend, he climbed into the hammock with some difficulty and settled down to endure the discomfort of the journey.

Herbert Spencer never married, but—like many other eminent Victorian bachelors—he loved little girls. In those days (Spencer was a middle-aged man by the time Freud was born), mothers were merely touched and amused if an elderly unmarried friend fell in love with their pre-pubescent daughters, confident that the prevailing sexual code was strong enough to protect them. It was an entirely allowable *tendresse*, openly expressed in—for instance—the sentimental photography of Lewis Carroll, and Spencer never hesitated to admit his affection for female children. He said they served as "vicarious objects of the philo-progenitive instinct", and would caress them frequently and claim "the forfeit" of a kiss when he answered their questions.

The bevy of little girls growing up at Standish was specially dear to him. He had first met the Potter parents in the days when he himself was young and unknown, over a flying-machine he had invented. Richard Potter was astonished and fascinated. He explored the possibility of making one, and would have financed the project, only Spencer could never get his machine off the ground.

Their friendship lasted for life. It was like that of Dr Johnson
with the brewer Thrale and his wife, except that when Richard
tired of his wife's interminable talk with the philosopher, he did
not get drunk in protest, but yawned and went to bed. The
Potter family was impressed by Spencer's ingenious mind and intrigued by his eccentricity, but Richard himself never accepted
Huxley's view that Spencer was "the most original of thinkers".
"He has no instinct, my dear," he told Beatrice, and was more
inclined to agree with Carlyle that Herbert Spencer was "the biggest
ass in Christendom", although in general he had an exaggerated
esteem for men of intellect. He never tired, for instance, of repeat-
ing to his daughters every detail of the afternoon on which Froude
had invited him to join the procession of eminent men solemnly
walking behind Carlyle as he took his ceremonial constitutional
along the Chelsea embankment. But Spencer's philosophising bored
him. "Won't work, my dear Spencer, won't work," he told him,
when Spencer was obstinately making his way against the tide of
parishioners flowing into church in an effort to demonstrate the
truth of some "natural" law that had just occurred to him. Nevertheless, he had an affectionate regard for the philosopher, and,
when he visited Standish, the two would fish the quiet reaches of
the river Severn, exchanging philosophical dissertations on fish for
economic dissertations on business.

The Potter children looked forward to Mr Spencer's visits, and
listened gleefully when, as an upholder of the principle of liberty,
he tiraded over the breakfast table against discipline. They approved
of his axiom, "submission not desirable", and were triumphant
when because of his theories of education, which he based on
Rousseau, their normal curriculum was thrown overboard (to the
great annoyance of their governess) and they were allowed to learn
"the natural way". This meant that they could escape from the
schoolroom and watch the great philosopher erect swings for them
and get up what he called "vivariums", and abandon their dull
lessons in favour of science; in other words, delightful country
rambles with him, hunting for fossils and plants and water beasts.
He initiated them into the mystery of natural history and explained
how the specimens they collected for him illustrated his various
theories. Once the science lesson developed into horse-play. The
boisterous tomboys all set upon him, threw him to the ground and
pelted him with rotten leaves and he came indoors grumbling. But

as he had preached a doctrine of revolt, neither Mrs Potter nor the governess were very sympathetic.

Beatrice never found these lessons interesting, but she was fascinated to watch the way in which Mr Spencer used the specimens brought to him to prove this or that theory. Her sharp eyes were quick to spot that he only noted those which endorsed the point he was making. The rest were discarded. All his theories were built up in this way. He began with his proposition or principle and found the facts to prove it afterwards. His method of writing a book was unique. Beatrice based her own method of research on it. He would arrange his title headings on foolscap paper on the floor in a semicircle about his chair. Seated in the centre, he threw, from a pile collected by his secretary in order to prove his point, each "fact" on its appropriate chapter. Any unwanted ones fluttered away to oblivion. It was a method he recommended to all writers.

The philosopher was on excellent terms with all the children, but with little "Beebo" he established a special relationship that blossomed into a warm friendship, and although in the end their views clashed violently, she never forgot the debt she owed him and cherished a tender affection for him to the day of his death in 1903.

It seemed to Beatrice when she was young that Herbert Spencer was the only friend she had, the only person who took any notice of her, who was interested in her studies or who was concerned when she was ill. He told her that she was a "born metaphysician", and that she reminded him of the woman whom he was supposed once to have loved, George Eliot, whom he described as "the most admirable woman he had ever met—mentally", adding regretfully that her masculinity of intellect showed in her build, and "with me beauty is a *sine qua non*". Beatrice, who was young and considered good-looking, fell for Spencer's flattery and became his most ardent disciple. She struggled to understand his books. In order to win his esteem, she set her mind to "discover, and where observation failed, to invent, illustrations which would prove his laws." Later on, when she was carrying out her sociological investigations, Beatrice found this early training in the art of casuistry invaluable.

The philosopher was inevitably a figure of fun to them all. His reply to the question, are we descended from monkeys, Mr Spencer? —"About 99 per cent of humanity have descended and one per cent have ascended"—brought delighted giggles and the little girls always pounced on an opportunity to ridicule his reputation as a famous scientist. On one occasion he proposed an excursion to Tintern Abbey, which he declared should be seen by moonlight, since its effects on the ruins were so exceptionally fine. Accordingly they set off by boat down the river Wye and reached the Abbey in the evening. Patiently they waited in the appointed grove expecting at any minute to see the moon shining through the trees, but no moon rose. At last the mystery was solved. The moon had risen in a state of eclipse and the "scientist" had not known it would take place and everybody laughed. "The truth is," he solemnly concluded, "that the wide grasp of the general is not necessarily connected with the great aptitude for the special."[13] It was not only the children who teased him. Mrs Potter herself was sometimes in an impish mood. He once arrived at Standish in order to recover from a particularly sharp attack of "cerebral congestion" and Mrs Potter quietly announced that she was putting him up in a haunted room where her brother had recently seen a ghost and which he had refused to sleep in ever again. Signs of a disturbed night were expectantly looked for at breakfast next morning, but the philosopher seemed more rested than usual and merely speculated upon the possible origin of the illusion.

In 1872 Maggie and Theresa went to America with their father. Her sisters had all "come out" and as Beatrice was the only one left in the schoolroom—Rosy being still in the nursery—the governess was dismissed and all formal lessons came to an end. From the age of thirteen she was left to educate herself, except for the philosophical dissertations of her guide and friend, Herbert Spencer. She proceeded with her usual zeal and industry to read everything she could lay her hands on, probably spurred on by her sister Maggie who wrote from Toronto:

To Bee, my old chum, ... Since our long companionship over French and the small looking glass.... I have formed quite a romantic affection for my dear little sister of fourteen and describe her eyes, music and all in the most glowing terms. Only I beseech you not to turn my present happiness into green-eyed jealousy by taking a mean advantage of my absence and becoming most awfully and scornfully learned, and looking down upon me as quite beneath your notice. If you do, I shall certainly come back to the schoolroom again—which perhaps won't suit you, my dear![14]

What Beatrice could not find in her father's library, she ordered from Mudies'. She studied French and German philosophy, the Bible, the life of St Paul and she translated *Faust*. She revelled in the novels of Walter Scott, George Eliot and Jane Austen and Fielding. "Read him my dear," her father told her. "If you were a boy I should hesitate to recommend him, but a nice-minded girl can read anything."[15] And Beatrice, whose nature was passionate rather than sensual, who had never felt much curiosity about sex, read and reviewed *Tom Jones* with the same detached and critical eye as she did Paley's *Evidences*.

By this time, Laurencina Potter had ceased entirely to emerge from the boudoir. There were at this time only four daughters of marriageable age for whom husbands had to be found, and she let them go up to London and manage the Season for themselves, insisting only, for the sake of good manners, on being told the names of any visitors they invited to stay at Standish. Long before she was old enough to "go into society", Beatrice joined her sisters on their annual pilgrimage for the Season. They had all been brought up to take an interest in politics, and Beatrice would wheedle tickets for the Ladies' Gallery out of the young men who came to court her sisters, and, while they were out dancing, she sat for hours in the House of Commons listening to the debates. She fell in love with Disraeli and hated Gladstone. On one occasion she returned from Parliament in the early hours of the morning and let herself into their house in Prince's Gardens "ravenously hungry". No one scolded her for being out so late, or indeed even noticed that she was.

3

"Only a Schoolroom Girl"
1873–1876

WHEN BEATRICE WAS FIFTEEN her sister Georgie fell in love with and married a young man whom their father had invited to Standish as a possible suitor for one of his daughters. He was enterprising, prosperous, substantially connected and all that Richard Potter desired in a son-in-law. Georgie's son, Dick, thus described their first meeting:

> In the autumn of 1872 Richard Potter announced to his daughters at Standish, his home in Gloucestershire, that a charming young man had been asked down to stay and that the daughters must be nice to him and behave themselves. My father arrived, a man of thirty years, full bearded, with Dundreary whiskers, and a monocle, and he did not go down at all well. The critical Potter sisters disliked his name, his manners and his face. They thought him a ridiculous fop. My father was taken out hunting, had a bad fall, and was put to bed at Standish, where he lay for some weeks with broken bones. It was during the period of convalescence that my mother and father were first attracted to each other.[1]

His name was Daniel Meinertzhagen. He was a merchant banker and the two were married after Richard Potter had coerced the family firm into increasing Daniel's share of the proceeds of their merchant-banking business. Georgie, like Lallie, had a conventional but elaborate wedding at Standish.

> Mendelssohn's wedding-march was played at the conclusion of the ceremony [the *Gloucester Journal* reported]. The couple left along a path strewn with flowers by the villagers. . . . the wedding-guests indulged in a dance in the evening and at nightfall there was a display of fireworks. The school-children were feasted in the afternoon and the villagers were not forgotten.[2]

Georgie wore a white-corded silk dress and a wreath of orange blossom and clematis, and her unmarried sisters were bridesmaids. The happy pair were "showered with slippers" as they set off on the first stage of their journey through life together, she to have ten children and an almost equal number of miscarriages, and he to make a fortune.

But to the fifth bridesmaid, Beatrice, Georgie's wedding-day was remembered as the one on which she herself "passed through the hall at Standish, feverish with excitement and with longing to see the world, with sisters kissing us and giving us a tearful goodbye, with a file of wedding-guests on each side, looking on with amusement and interest." As far as she was concerned, they might have been there to celebrate her departure, rather than that of her sister, for she too, was off on a voyage—going with Kate and her father to America.

On his last visit he had taken Theresa and Maggie who had sent home graphic accounts of all their experiences. The private railway carriage for the use of the President of the Grand Trunk was a

> most sumptuous affair, quite a little palace with every imaginable convenience, two sitting-rooms, two bedrooms fitted up with everything wanted in washing and dressing, including scents and delicate pomades.... Then there is a most excellent "Richot" (the president's chef) who provides us with cold woodcock and peaches when we are hungry, and who in general looks after everything.[3]

Niagara Falls had been terrifying and nerve-shaking:

> Not one of our gallant cavaliers dare to accompany us. They stood at the top laughing at our adventures particularly when the guide dipped poor Theresa into a rushing stream ... Going under the Falls is no joke, groping one's way breathless and blinded by the water, along a ledge of rock only a yard wide, with a precipice above and a whirl-pool below![4]

In her last letter Maggie had summed up her general impressions of America:

> Our American trip is almost finished.... quite sorry to leave such an interesting country. I long to know more about it, with its great West, its unexplored coalfields and its inexhaust-

ible supply of metals. Theresa and I have determined, if we are alive then, to go for a second trip in about twenty years' time. There will be a wonderful change in everything, for the country is growing like wild-fire. I expect there will be complete communism by that time. You will have to drive your coachman and wait upon your servants if you are foolish enough to have any.... A free-born Yankee would not degrade himself by service. Even the Irish, lately arrived from their native bogs give themselves great airs, serve for twice to three times the wage they would get at home ... This is the country for workmen, and England for those who wish to enjoy their ease and wealth. If I were a labourer, I wouldn't stay one day in our poor little used-up country. But for the higher classes, equality is not so pleasant.[5]

Ever since her father had been connected with the Grand Trunk, Beatrice had been accustomed to reading the letters sent home from such trips. Now it was her turn. She was fifteen, leaving home on a voyage for the first time, childhood behind her.

Three days after saying good-bye to Georgina and her new husband they embarked on a ship belonging to Robert Holt, Lallie's husband. Besides Beatrice and her elder sister Kate, they were accompanied by Arthur Playne, Mary's husband, who was to act as escort for the girls, and by Richard Potter's fellow-magnate, the original Mr Pullman whose name is now part of the language. Kate —who had found it so impossible to get on at home that she was now living in London on her own—immediately made friends with everyone around her, and was soon walking up and down arm-in-arm with the most popular man on board, while Beatrice looked on with surprise and envy at the ease with which her elder sister could "draw clever people out" and make them "talk to her as though she was their equal". She herself had looked the passengers over but her critical eye could not spot "anything in particular". It eventually lighted on an impressive, sombre-eyed Mr Hall, a popular presbyterian preacher from New York, who took her fancy because of a likeness to her favourite hero, Dr Arnold, although, she thought, he would "probably not be half so charming to live with". She spent the thirteen days at sea pacing the deck with him, speculating about her favourite subject, religion.

When they landed at New York, they went on almost immediately to Niagara Falls, and Beatrice was only able to catch a glimpse of Central Park and a clean elegant city with delightful tree-lined streets. She and Arthur both developed bad colds. He was a depressing and ineffectual escort. "The poor fellow," she complained, "is very low spirited when he is ill . . . he persuades himself and other people he is going to die." Undaunted by her cold, she went and stood over the American Falls but somehow they failed to thrill her as they had Maggie. She merely found herself wondering why she should be overwhelmed with a desire to hurl herself over the rapids into the whirlpool below. From Niagara Falls they went on to Chicago. Here Kate retired with a bad tooth-ache and Beatrice had her beloved father to herself. They wandered together through the streets of the town, recently burned to the ground in the great fire of 1871. Charred elevations of old buildings were joined like shadows to imposing new ones, and the ruins of a burnt-out church seemed to Beatrice to be quite up to anything in the way of ruins to be seen in England. They looked at the fine shops, and visited the exhibition of machinery, which seemed to them perfect and beautiful. They drove to a public school and were very amused to see "a common little negro girl sitting between two well-dressed bankers' daughters and learning the same things". When the time came for Beatrice to join Kate and Arthur on a lightning tour of the States, in the president's car, in charge of Richot as cicerone, she was sad at having to leave her father behind, and watched with a heavy heart his grey hat disappear into the distance as he stood waving goodbye on the platform.

They thundered across America, past prairie fires and prairie dogs, stopping briefly at the gold-mining towns of Omaha and Ogden where Beatrice observed that the miners were "a very intelligent set of people quite able to talk politics, both European and American." When they arrived at San Francisco, Richot took them to a respectable hotel overlooking the bay, from whose verandah they could watch the seals at play on the rocks. But their escort Arthur, having recovered from his cold, organised a daring visit to China-town to see a Chinese play. Beatrice thought the play tedious and sitting so close to "John Chinaman" distasteful. From San Francisco they made a hurried visit up the Yosemite valley. The beautiful valley inspired her with the ambition to become a great artist and the belief that "if I could copy nature with an immense deal of patience and perseverance and time devoted to it", she might end by being really successful. But the day-dream faded and left her sadly hoping that "perhaps some day I shall find a solution to this great difficulty of how I ought to occupy my life". The physical discomforts of the excursion were exhausting. They spent two nights on a ranch unable to sleep on account of the bellowing cattle, and returned to San Francisco tired out. But there were still the Geysers to be seen. Kate stayed behind because of a carbuncle that had to be lanced, but Beatrice followed a rather irritable Arthur on horseback and by carriage, through hot and uninteresting country, in order to reach the "Witch's Cauldron", the "Devil's Kitchen", and the "Devil's Lemonade". They looked at the hot water spouting out of the ground for a while until curiosity had been satisfied and then retraced their steps to San Francisco. Beatrice was so tired that she could scarcely talk when they were taken to visit a grand-niece of George Washington.

On their way back they stopped at Salt Lake City, where Brigham Young had set up his tabernacle. Beatrice had heard about the Mormons and their many wives and was eager to inspect their city, but by this time Arthur had fallen into low spirits again and was complaining disagreeably about everything and "had no power of making himself and his party considered". So Beatrice, impatient with her feeble brother-in-law, took matters into her own hands, and sent Richot off to find someone to show them round. He came back with the local Grand Trunk representative, who turned out to be an efficient guide and a pleasant change from the homesick Arthur. They were shown the Tabernacle and Brigham Young's chair, and where his children sat. Beatrice noticed with scorn that there were no seats alloted to his wives, who had to be content to sit scattered among the congregation. The party were introduced to General Munro and his wife, who came in wearing a "servant's print", and Beatrice was surprised that such important citizens should live on such a modest scale. They attended a service, but Beatrice, used to the high dignitaries of the Anglican Church, was not impressed by the preaching. She decided that the Mormon wives looked dejected and overwhelmed by their own inferiority and that Mrs Eliza Young, Brigham's seventeenth wife, was decidedly coarse. But the wide streets, with beautiful crystal streams on either side, the white houses with their green shutters and gardens, all set in the salt plain, gave the city a celestial appearance, utterly different from any other town Beatrice had ever seen.

On the last stage of the strenuous journey, Beatrice collapsed. When the president's car steamed into Chicago on November 6th, she fell half-conscious into her father's arms, stricken, according to her account, with rheumatic fever, scarlet fever and an attack of measles thrown in for good measure. Her illness could well have been fatal, but Beatrice, who had an unconquerable will and an iron constitution, survived the ordeal. To those at her bedside she was a formidable patient, but she fought her way back to life "nursed by Kate, spoilt by her father and feared by everyone but strangers", as she put it. At the end of four weeks, although still frail, she was well enough to undertake the voyage home.

On their last evening in New York, Kate and her father dined out, while Beatrice sat alone in her hotel bedroom, brooding. Her severe illness had left her with only a fading memory of all she had seen and done during the past two months. The trip had been a delightful adventure, but she had been too preoccupied the whole time day-dreaming about the purpose of her existence for the outward scene to have left a lasting impression. She was thinking of home and wondering how much she had changed since she left it, and whether she had improved. Touched by Kate's gentle nursing, she reproached herself about her other sisters. She had lived so much in a world of her own and kept so much aloof that her sisters were scarcely more than strangers to her. She resolved in the future to get to know each of them more intimately, especially Maggie, who was closer to her in age than the others. As soon as she got home, she decided, she would cultivate a warm intimate friendship with Maggie and they would have a delightful relationship.

During the Spring of 1874 she busily resumed her studies, read German novels and—in order to please her mother—dutifully practised the piano although she had little interest and no talent. Driven by her recently inspired ambition to become a great artist, she painstakingly "copied and corrected with rule and compass" patterns from her school of art book. She read Shakespeare aloud to Rosy's governess, Miss Mitchell, hoping to draw to herself some of the attention lavished on her little sister. Theresa, Blanche and Maggie were all at home too, but the delightful intimacy she had promised herself on that last evening alone in New York somehow failed to materialise. Blanche was absorbed in household affairs, never a subject with much appeal for Beatrice and although Maggie seemed more approachable than before, Beatrice still could not over-come her own pride and aloofness. Theresa, everyone's favourite, was deeply involved with a suitor who had fallen passionately in love with her. It seemed impossible to Beatrice for anyone to resist such ardent attentions, but just as the young man was on the point of "carrying off our dearest sister", Theresa unaccountably refused him. "He attempted to gain a jewel. . . . who can blame him for failing?" Beatrice sympathised, and did her best to persuade her mother to allow Theresa to distract herself by working as a nurse in the cottage hospital recently founded by Laurencina herself.

But Beatrice did not find it easy to settle down again to the quiet life at Standish. In America she had been spoilt by her father and Kate, and during her illness had ordered everyone about. She had been the important person then and now she was just one among many. With nothing to stimulate her active mind and no distractions Beatrice fell into a kind of apathy and drifted into what she herself condemned as "lazy habits", about getting up in the morning, about her drawing, and about her religious duties. She had no method, she told herself, and could not concentrate. One moment she was entirely absorbed in politics and hotly in sympathy with the Radicals—"but I don't think their time has come yet. . . . But who am I to talk of politics?"—and the next, her imagination was fired by a novel about a noble savage who was closer to God and less degraded than a civilised man. Perpetually, she was obsessed with thoughts about men—"impure thoughts"—and warned her-self against the danger of becoming like Rosamund in *Middlemarch*. Most serious of these moral lapses, she felt, was the fact that, for the first time, she began to find herself in a state of doubt about religion, the widespread Victorian *malaise* which Beatrice considered to be a sin, and decided that it was her duty to discover the cause and to find a firm faith for herself.

This discontent and doubting vanished for a short while. When the sisters once again migrated to London for the season, this time Beatrice, to her immense gratification, although still "only a school-room girl", was allowed to join in the fun.

The season of 1874 was not one of their most successful. Last year Georgie had been queen of the balls and it had all ended in her being carried off by her merchant banker.. This year, it was Blanche's turn. Her undoubted beauty, with her white skin, red lips and black hair, was a sensation until, half way through the season, swinging out into the ball-room in the arms of her admirer, guests noticed beneath the hem of her beautiful ball-dress the old red felt slippers she had absent-mindedly forgotten to remove. Possibly because of this kind of absent-mindedness in Blanche, the Potters suddenly found themselves unaccountably cold-shouldered by the admirer's family, and the young man, who was deeply in love with Blanche, turned, according to Beatrice, "grave, severe, gloomy and yellow". Theresa, too, had been put out of looks and spirits by the announcement of the engagement of the very man who a month before had so desperately sought her hand in marriage. The fact that she had twice refused him did not prevent her from suffering over it. Maggie, although she still had plenty of time in hand, was already on the look-out for a good match. Beatrice was quite shocked by her cynical behaviour and scarcely recognised the sister she knew at home. Maggie was frivolous, serious and sceptical in turn to each of her partners, and did not scruple to snub suitors young or old who fell below the standard of wealth and birth she had fixed on. Perhaps the cynicism did not suit her, and that was why no one proposed that season.

Beatrice, untroubled by thoughts of suitors, was able to abandon herself to the giddy round of excitement, enthralled by being allowed to help in the preparations for private theatricals. When Maggie fell ill with measles and she had to learn the part of Kate Hardcastle in *She Stoops to Conquer* with the prospect of playing it before a large audience, she could scarcely contain herself, although in the end Maggie recovered in time to triumph in the part. Best of all was the ball the Potter girls gave at Prince's gardens. "Oh, how I did love the dance!" Beatrice confided to her diary. Although only sixteen, she had as many partners as her elder sisters and often had the satisfaction of turning one away.

This enchanted interlude was brief, and by Autumn when she found herself once again in the depths of the country at Rusland, alone with her Mother, Blanche and Rosy, the self-esteem—the glow of satisfaction—from her success in London faded away. Her doubts and discontent returned. She worried about her health and was distressed about her soul. She prescribed the following diet for her health: "Breakfast—Bread and bacon or whatever there is. Dinner —meat and fruit. Tea—tea and bread and butter. Supper—one dish.' But ministering to her soul was not so easy. Blanche bored her, she was jealous of Rosy and the efforts she made to win her mother's approval and affection were rebuffed. She was "too young, too uneducated and (worst of all) too frivolous", according to her mother, to be a suitable companion. Beatrice was overcome with despair. "No God, no health, no love," she cried. "Nothing but wounded vanity and desperation." She found some consolation during that spring, in the solemn preparation for confirmation, and when she received the Holy Sacrament for the first time on Easter Eve, in 1875, she did so with every intention of becoming a good Christian. "I wish my aim in life to be the understanding of and acting up to religion," was her solemn declaration. There was only one thing in the way of this pious intention. She could neither understand nor tolerate the Doctrine of Atonement.

Beatrice was now seventeen and at a loose end. She had out-grown adolescence and yet was not considered old enough to "come out". Eighteen was the official age for this event. It was therefore decided that she should spend the coming year at Stirling House, a smart finishing school in Bournemouth, where it was hoped the sea air would restore her health, and the society of fashionable girls of her own age would be a suitable preparation for her launching into society. She did not take to her new surroundings and was like a fish out of water in the unfamiliar company into which she was suddenly thrown. The tedium of gossiping conversations and the unpleasing sound of incessant piano practice got on her nerves. She found the other girls unsympathetic and in self-defence took to lying and boasting and exaggerating the importance of her family and the grandeur of her home. It was not until she was given a room to herself that she became serene enough to tolerate her new surroundings.

Her life at Stirling House, solitary by choice, was more like that of a nun than a parlour boarder at an establishment for "finishing" young ladies. Only two of her father's old friends, Admirals Sullivan and Grey, were authorised to take her out. A distant cousin—Maggie Harkness—was a fellow boarder, and sometimes the two walked on the downs talking and dreaming of a future with their little ones around them. At other times she listened to her music master playing his favourite pieces. He had given up trying to make a musician of her and was turning her inaptitude for music into a mutual pleasure by reversing the usual role of pupil and teacher, through which she learned the valuable lesson of musical appreciation. Otherwise she lived the life of a recluse, devoting herself to study, fighting to overcome her faults of vanity and untruthfulness, and to profit spiritually from the enforced idleness imposed on her when— as often happened—she was ill. She earnestly struggled to strengthen her dwindling faith, without which mystical satisfaction life held no meaning for her. She read the Old Testament carefully for enlighten- ment about God from the prophets. For a time, she put aside puzzling over questions of doctrine and simply tried to live a truly Christian life, until she discovered to her dismay that she could not even achieve the very first Christian principle of either truth or charity. Would she ever again, she wondered, believe in the sacra- ment or the Doctrine of Atonement? Oppressed by her growing lack of faith she decided she must see Mr Eliot, the clergyman, who every Sunday preached such a beautiful sermon. He had spent a lifetime in the study and practice of Christianity, she argued, and should be in a position to offer her spiritual guidance. Feeling very nervous, and not quite sure what to say, she asked him to explain the puzzling Doctrine of Atonement. Mr Eliot pointed out that since it was in the scriptures it was her Christian duty to believe it; they were the only source through which a knowledge of God could be gained. Beatrice replied that she had failed to find many refer- ences to the doctrine in the gospels, and scarcely any in Christ's own words. Mr Eliot then asked her whether she did not think the Epistles as infallible as the gospels. "No," replied Beatrice, "The gospels are a record of Christ's own words, and the Epistles writings of good men," whereupon Mr Eliot closed the interview after press- ing into her hand a book on the perplexing doctrine.

The term at Stirling House came to an end without achieving its purpose. Beatrice returned to her family as chronically ill as ever, suffering from her usual headaches, indefinite pains, attacks of fever and boils. Nor was she better prepared for the London season. With a mixture of religious fervour and girlish defiance she insisted that she could not venture into the adult world until she had dis- covered a true religion, and that, in any case, the Potter family were already over-represented in London Society. Her parents wisely did not interfere and Beatrice was left alone.

It was Christmas and the usual family festivities were being held at Standish. Lallie and Dick Holt came from Liverpool, Mary and Arthur Playne from Longfords, and Kate from London. Kate brought her new friends, Canon Barnett and his wife, from St Jude's in Whitechapel where she worked. John Bright came, and

Herbert Spencer who, throughout the festivities, kept an insanely watchful eye on his appetites, indulging them with knife-edge precision, raising his spirits sufficiently to enjoy the revels and yet not over-stimulating his cerebral congestion. The fashionable craze for spiritualism had spread from London to country houses all over England, and everyone was "table-turning". At Standish, experiments were conducted enthusiastically in every room in the house. "Theresa has just returned from staying with Florence Jeffreys," wrote Georgina to her husband, "and is holding communication with the invisible world in darkened chambers all day long and as the process seems to agree with her appetite there can be no harm in it. She persuaded me to sit over a table for half an hour yesterday, in the hopes of raising or turning it, but nothing happened except our hands went to sleep and pricked pins and needles."[6] Theresa had the calm serenity of the credulous, but Beatrice was more sceptical. She examined the phenomena "scientifically", and after three sittings during which such messages as "Not you sit" and "Now dear Beatrice in Texas for signing of abolition year 1855. Sit saturday" had been violently rapped out, she decided that spiritualism was nothing more than a subconscious action of the brain, dismissed it as rubbish, and returned to her own bewildering speculations.

She turned from Christianity to examine Buddhism in the hope that it might be a religion in which she could believe, only to discover that, like Christianity, its doctrine, though beautiful, was based on a falsehood and wrapped in mystery. She deliberated with her mentor, Herbert Spencer, and in the end it was through his teaching that she was able to shake herself free from the gnawing doubts which had assailed her for so long. At first she hesitated, asking herself testing questions such as, "Do I look on death and trouble with less calmness than before?" and "Am I like a newly-liberated slave unable to decide which way to go?" but then, gathering conviction, she persuaded herself to believe in the "New Religion"—the "Religion of Science". Its doctrine was based on Herbert Spencer's *First Principles* and wrapped in the mystery of his *Social Statistics*:[7]

Even in the evils the student (who has learnt to look for the secret forces by which are upheld the great laws of existence) learns to recognise only a struggling beneficence.... Above all he is struck with the inherent sufficingness of things, and with the complex complicity of principles. Day by day, he sees further beauty. Each new fact illustrates more clearly some recognised law, or discloses some unconceived completeness; contemplation thus perpetually discovering to him a high harmony, and cherishing in him a deeper faith. . . . . Not as adventitious, therefore, will the wise man regard the faith that is in him. Not as something which may be slighted and made subordinate to calculations of policy; but as a supreme authority to which all his actions should bend. The highest truth conceivable by him he will fearlessly utter and will endeavour to get embedded in fact his purest idealisms knowing that, let what may come of it, he is thus playing his appointed part in the world, knowing that, if he can get done the thing he aims at, well; if not, well also; though not *so* well.

"Who could wish for a better faith than this?" demanded Beatrice defiantly.

She was searching for a faith which she could base on reason. If she had lived in the seventeenth century she might have accepted the sceptical flavour of Pascal's belief in God, and certainly both she and Laurencina would have found themselves at home among the ladies of Port Royal, with their austere virtues, the climate of power in which they lived and their exquisite piety—the things which both Beatrice and her mother valued above all others. Beatrice described her dilemma as a conflict between the "Ego that denies" and the "Ego that affirms" and she never resolved it.

4

Coming-out
1876–1882

BEATRICE'S PIOUS RESOLUTION not to come out was forgotten before the Season began. Standish was having one of its lively periods,
with her father at home and a round of house-parties and dances.
Georgina, on a visit with her first baby, wrote to her husband;

> The invalids are beginning to pick up and the house looks
> quite cheerful and I think there is less arguing going on than I
> have ever known, which fact you will be glad to hear of.
> Maggie is in a state of agreeable excitement, having a most
> ardent admirer here in the shape of a young Vernon, who is
> everything to be desired in the way of person and fortune, only
> Maggie considers him too much of a boy, being a very youth-
> ful specimen of twenty-four,[1]

—that is, two years older than Maggie herself, but the Potters
preferred their suitors to be sophisticated men of the world. To
them, their father was the ideal of male perfection, and the naïve
young Vernon, like others before him, was sent away disconsolate.
The "come-out" group, when Beatrice joined it, consisted of
Blanche, Theresa and Maggie. Kate, who had been "out" for ten
years, had electrified the family by leaving home and joining
Octavia Hill. Looked at objectively (a thing the Potters seldom did)
her social work was not a particularly eccentric bid for independence.
"Slumming" was as much a feature of Society life as private
theatricals or skating. Even the prototype Society girls of Du
Maurier's Punch drawings—those tall, dark, stately goddesses, whom
the Potter daughters so much resembled—were constantly involved
in it. But the Potters, up till now, had been original only in their
own particular way. For the last twelve years, there had always
been one or more of them "doing the Season" and they had established a tradition that they did as they liked. Maggie, on a visit,
wrote to her mother that her hostess had been giving her

plenty of good advice, that you would thoroughly approve,
about young ladies not becoming theoretical in their opinions
and set in their views; and keeping a modest reticence about
things of which they cannot be capable of judging. She thinks
that we as a family have adopted lately too decided opinions,
and above all a too decided way of expressing them.[2]

They knew the kind of thing that was said about them in conventional drawing-rooms—"most strong-minded, blue-stockinged
young ladies who could argue down the greatest arguer in the
world"—and saw no reason to change their ways. They never
softened their schoolroom habit of brutal frankness and went on
saying exactly what they thought, on all occasions, without reference
to the feelings of anyone involved. To them, reticence was a kind of
insincerity, and none of them (with the possible exception of
Maggie) was capable of being even moderately tactful. Their
admirers—who were many—found this transparent honesty attractive. (Leonard Courtney, whom Kate eventually married, was first
drawn to her by her burst of noisy laughter during a supremely
awkward silence at a party.) Their enemies—who were also many—
found it intolerable.

They were more sophisticated than the average debutante and
had already seen more of the world than most of their contemporaries could hope to see in a lifetime. They had associated since
childhood with popular philosophers and politicians and industrial
tycoons. Dinner-party neighbours, whose distinction was liable to
freeze the shy beginner into terrified silence, were old acquaintances
to them. In "this most gigantic of social clubs", as Beatrice described London Society of the day, where thrusting your way upwards was a virtue, it was impossible to despise the Potters, whose
grandparents had been shop-keepers and weavers.

It was, Beatrice summed up, "the complement, for its womenkind . . . of the masculine world of big enterprise with its passion
for adventure and the assumption of power". It was unique among
social aristocracies because it had "no fixed caste barriers, no recognised type of exclusiveness based on birth or breeding, personal
riches or personal charm". To foreigners, it all seemed absurdly
tolerant. "One never knows who one is going to sit next to, at a
London dinner-party," said a visiting diplomat, wonderingly. But
beneath the surface, there was a desperate struggle for position. The

first condition of membership was some kind of power over other people. It could be the obvious kind—wealth or aristocratic birth. If you had both, you were absolutely secure. Other kinds of power gave you at least a temporary foothold.

A great industrial administrator, not himself endowed with much capital, so long as he could provide remunerative posts for younger sons or free passes on trans-continental railways could, if he chose, associate on terms of flattering personal intimacy with those members of the British aristocracy, and there were many of them, who desired these favours.[3]

You could get provisional admission to the top drawing-rooms by being adopted as one of the current "lions". It was a shifting, uncertain world, in which success was ephemeral. The wife and daughters of a celebrated man would be dropped by hostesses, with indecent haste, on his death. Bankruptcy or a marital scandal were fatal, unless you were part of the impregnable top layer, in which case they were blandly overlooked. Sometimes you got promoted in error—for instance through a rumour of approaching marriage to some great political personage; and there was a deluge of invitations, which stopped instantly if the rumour proved false. The uncertainty of it all was nerve-racking, because the score was kept on an underground grape-vine, operated among leading hostesses.

The Potter girls came into this arena well equipped for the battle. Their father was one of the railway magnates who held a fairly steady position in the hierarchy, just below the permanent Establishment of birth and breeding and riches. Since childhood they had been with him behind the scenes, where the strings were pulled in the jockeying for personal power.

Cousin Peter has been here. He has been sent for by Hart Dyke—the party whip—and Roland Wynne, who are going to offer him the Grimsby seat (Maggie wrote confidentially to her father). He will refuse, but wished to ask you whether you will stand or whether he might use your name in accepting the candidature. I told him not to do so until he had heard from you, as I know you had not quite decided what you would do... The girls are all anxious that you should go in, but what about Mamma?[4]

It was their familiar world, the element in which they moved confidently, and in which they expected to remain—preferably at a slightly higher social level—when they married. But they were in no hurry to do so. At a time when the average girl's dream of triumph was to get settled for life during her first Season, only four of the Potters married before they were twenty-five, and two waited until they were well in their thirties. "You are quite mistaken if you think thoughts of marriage take up most of my time," Maggie assured her mother. "Only sometimes one laughs with sisters about our being all. . . . dear, charming old maids."⁵ They were attractive and amusing; and they were heiresses. They could afford to joke about the unlikely possibility. But they knew that however good a match they might make—and all but two of the nine eventually made "good" ones—once they were married their best time of all would be over. From then on, the future was entirely predictable— pregnancies and confinements and miscarriages, the nursery and the country house, while the husband went on pursuing his career and his social round, unhampered, just as Richard Potter had done ever since his daughters could remember, while Laurencina languished, grumbling, at home. "It's frightfully dull here," Maggie, staying with Georgina, confided to Beatrice. "I should take the first train back to Standish were it not for Georgie, who, poor girl, would really be too terribly lonely . . ." At Georgie's country seat, where the burning topic was horses, and which was rather happily named Wallop House, each day was "uncommonly long to get through. Here is our bill of fare, varied by a frequent wet day, which cuts off our most exciting course. Breakfast, children, walk; dinner, children, walk; tea, children, supper, talk, bed."⁶

The daughter of a wealthy home looked forward to the years between schoolroom and marriage in the way that a son thought of going up to the university—as the first step into the adult world. But Beatrice knew it already, thanks to her indulgent father and in-different mother, and had no need to be nervous. Within a few weeks of being presented, she was visiting the home of a "wicked earl" and listening to the cries of "Messieurs and Mesdames, faites vos jeux", along with the seasoned gamers. As the most fledgling of debutantes, she went for an unaccompanied walk—in those days of strict chaperonage—with a married man of fashion, trusting to her upper-class voice and manner and her dauntingly "bookish talk" to safeguard her against unwanted attentions. In spite of her scruples, she thoroughly enjoyed the full-time pursuit of pleasure—

the calls, the lunches and dinners, the dances and crushes, Hurlingham and Ascot, not to mention amateur theatricals and other sham philanthropic excrescences..... as one form of entertainment was piled on another, the pace became fast and furious; a mania for reckless talking, for the experimental display of one's own personality, ousted all else from consciousness.[7]

But afterwards, in sleepless nights, or during the long dull weeks in the country when the Season was over, she writhed at the memory of so much self-exhibition, castigated herself for her vanity, and counted up the small snubs she had received and the careless lies she had told. Then she would preach to herself about the futility of the social round, and take the languor and ill-health which came down like a cloud, once the feverish activity was over, as a just punishment for frivolity. She would torment herself, as she had for years, about not having a real aim in life. But for all her lofty moral attitude, and although in later life she condemned the whole system which produced "Society", she spent six years pursuing the ordained ritual and was regretful when she missed any of it. It gave her the chance to shine and it also gave her what she needed even more—the first "intimate friendship" of her life.

Beatrice had always wanted, above all, to be the close friend of Maggie, who was the sister she admired most. Maggie was the only one of the Potters who had inherited more of her father's sanguine cheerfulness than her mother's melancholy. Alone among them, she was capable of criticising her mother with enough tact for Laurencina to accept it. She quarrelled with her—as they all did—but where Kate was stubborn and Beatrice silently resentful, Maggie went her own way and then apologised charmingly. "I hope, dearest mother, that you are not still angry with any of your naughty children. I am improving rapidly and Beatrice is very contrite,"[8] she wrote on one such occasion. When Maggie was in Canada with her father, and he was cast down by one of Laurencina's reproachful letters, Maggie reasoned with her, "You yourself would hardly have wished him just in the middle of the battle to give up the command of the Grand Trunk, and perhaps to lose success, or at least to lose all the credit," and suggested that people "who believe thoroughly in religion" were supposed to welcome trials; "So I hope, dearest Mother, you won't allow yourself to be so miserable."[9] Apart from the petted baby of the family, Maggie was Laurencina's favourite daughter.

Soon after Beatrice came out, Blanche married William Harrison Cripps, a rising young surgeon who was well received by the Potters, and settled down to her inevitable destiny, beginning with a premature baby the following year. After she left home, Maggie and Beatrice, doing the round of the Season together, developed the close intimacy for which Beatrice had always longed. Maggie, like herself, had a passionate intellectual curiosity and could meet her on her own ground. She liked to discuss books and ideas rather than personalities, and her cheerful cynicism shook Beatrice out of the gloomy introspection of schoolgirl years. Above all, Maggie was someone to love who also loved her. While they were both young and unmarried, there was a bond between them unlike anything Beatrice had experienced before, combining the tie of blood-relationship and passionate friendship, built on shared memories and the unique understanding between two sisters, close in age and with the same interests; the only human relationship which extends, unbroken, from the nursery to the grave.

When they were apart, Maggie not only missed her, but said so. "A balloon attached to this sheet by a strong magnetic current running straight through this steel pen into your heart, is the only simile that can describe my state..." They used to count the days until they could be together again and "go into training with our books" and "have our long walks and *silences* together".[10] It was an affectionate joke between them that if they were both left on the shelf they would set up house together with their books and painting. "I have just finished Balzac's *Vieille Fille*, such an absurdly melancholy book that I really require you to console me with a more hopeful idea of one's future state. It won't be quite so bad in company, you know."

It was typical of Beatrice's self-torturing puritanism that she forced herself to forgo her third Season with Maggie to go on a tour of Germany, with her elder sister Mary and Mary's dull husband. "It is better for health... and morale," she told herself severely. "My life is wanting in aim... perhaps the German lessons will become an aim... If I choose to be self denying I can make it well worth my while to have missed one short season." But as she sat in the dull *pension* selected by Mary and Arthur, every English boat-train whistling into the station gave her a pang of home-sickness and she found herself positively disliking Mary, who was such a poor substitute for Maggie, that best of comrades and most stimulating companion. "We have really led such different lives, have lived in such completely different atmospheres that it is impossible for us to talk on any serious subject," reflected the cosmopolitan, intellectual twenty-year-old, contemplating her smug, provincial sister. "She has a grudge against 'intellectual people' and learning because she feels inferior." Considering the Potter inability to conceal feelings, on both sides, it was not surprising that presently there was a full-scale Potter scene, in which it was put on record that neither Arthur nor Mary would tolerate Beatrice's contemptuous attitude any longer. One of Beatrice's most disarming characteristics was her readiness to admit herself in the wrong; usually followed by a private agony of self-reproach and unhopeful resolutions to do better. "Mary is right. . . . if I cannot exert myself sufficiently to make friends . . . I can at least be scrupulously polite and considerate."

The party proceeded, scrupulously polite and considerate, to Nuremberg, where they examined the torture-chamber, and to Vienna, where they agreed that the Viennese habit of drinking in cafés to be sociable was preferable to the English one of drinking in pubs to become beasts. Mary and Arthur were too "deficient in historical and artistic cultivation" for proper sight-seeing, but Beatrice kept this fact to herself and they trudged unprofitably about the streets until Arthur could take no more. ("Poor fellow, he is in rather a weak state of health," Beatrice commented kindly.) It gave her the chance to go off alone to St. Stephen's Church and to sit there, dreaming, looking down the dusky nave at the blaze of light on the altar, drawn, as always, by the outward and visible signs of a faith she could not share. Beautiful churches, the obedient pupil of Herbert Spencer reminded herself, are after all nothing but living pictures of one passing phase of evolution of the human mind and the spirit that created them was now (post-Darwin) dead. But watching the Austrian men and women at their untroubled devotions had the irrational effect of raising her spirits and putting her in a happier frame of mind. At Budapest, she discovered a kind of "sweet beauty" in the gay colours and slovenly dirt, and Prague intrigued her because of the "lordly arrogance" of the statues of strong men looking scornfully down over handsome doorways. At Dresden ("the picture-gallery most delightful") they met a Prussian officer who impressed her with his description of the high moral tone of army life. But Beatrice's patience was wearing thin, and by the time they got to Berlin she decided crossly that the buildings were hideous and the statues coarse and that a little of the "discipline of misfortune" would do the Berliners' characters all the good in the world. But her own stretch of self-imposed discipline was over and at last she was able to record in her diary, with relief, "Arthur and Mary left this morning," and to draw up a report on her own behaviour over the last five months.

She had made a real effort to adapt herself to Mary's level. "In order to get on with her you must be content to talk about nothing but personalities," but "on the whole this trip to Germany was a mistake... Poor Arthur has been miserable and Mary has not enjoyed herself... How she can be happy with such an inferior man I can't understand." On the credit side, Beatrice's German had improved, but the other "aim in life" which she had set herself for the tour—to improve her health by a strict diet ("putting an X to all meals I can say I have eaten according to my conscience") had not. "It seems strange that when one knows that health will make all the difference... of being able to give pleasure and make oneself and other people happy, one should so... lack the self-denial to get and keep healthy." But now Maggie had written begging her to join them at Rusland (although Laurencina expected her to stay by herself and finish up a course of German lessons), and had added that she needed Beatrice's companionship because every discussion with Laurencina ended up with "a fundamental difference of opinion, which in Mamma is of a proselytising nature, so we must often agree to differ".

At Rusland, during the next few weeks, Beatrice and Maggie had "a perfect communion of pursuits and ideas. We had a delightful little trip among our sublime little hills; and read through the first two volumes of Ruskin's *Modern Painters* together; and this experience has inspired us with a wish to go sketching and reading tours together, should we remain lonely spinsters". She added in her diary, "I do believe I have started on a brighter path of existence... with a spirt of love instead of with a spirit of jealous ambition."

When they actually got permission to go on a tour, they prepared for it with as much excitement as though they had been children going for a half-holiday picnic. They packed up provisions from the Rusland larder—"home-made potted-meat, a pound of tea . . . and a large pot of sugarless gooseberry compote which, with some lemons, was to serve us as anti-fat or anti-scorbutic," Maggie recorded in her diary of the trip.[11] They were about to add a leg of mutton, when Laurencina caught them, and there ensued one of those angry scenes which so often—and so strangely—used to take place in this household of a railway magnate, reputed to be almost a millionaire. To Laurencina, it was the sacred duty of the god-fearing rich to be thrifty, and she found this combination of wastefulness and physical greed "highly dishonourable", particularly since their over-indulgent father had already given them £6 to spend, not to mention that Maggie was insisting (unnecessarily in her mother's view) on taking her entire dress allowance (£3) with them as well.

When Laurencina (who could steer the most unpromising argument into theological channels) added that this kind of thing was typical of her daughters' lax religious views, Beatrice—constitutionally unable to leave well alone—flared up and asked what her mother meant by "religious"? Did she mean conventional churchgoing? She herself preferred Herbert Spencer's kind of religion to that of Laurencina. And in addition, she added, reverting, inevitably, to her own private King Charles' Head, she had had a miserable childhood, owing to Laurencina's unfairness to her. At that Laurencina retired to her room again, leaving her daughters, as Maggie observed sardonically, "well pleased with the force and clearness of our own minds, to prepare for our expedition".

If it was typical of Laurencina to give permission for the jaunt and then to cloud it by sending them off on the crest of a quarrel, it was equally characteristic of Richard to make it up to them, as far as he could, by driving them down to the station, buying their tickets, and saying goodbye to them, commented Maggie, "with a beaming face at the thought of our lark. Dear, good Papa, who is always happy when we are, and wretched when we are, who works and contrives and manages to get richer in order that we may have larger fortunes, never caring to spend anything on himself and content to put up with all our criticism".

They steamed up Windermere "on a sweet blue-green day" and installed themselves in a cottage overlooking Rydal—the one in which De Quincey had drugged himself and dreamed—unpacked their stores and got out their books and sketching materials.

Everything was amusing because they were together and free. They agreed that Maggie's sketches were "a libel on nature or rather a slander, since libels may have some truth in them", and that her only hope was to beg Ruskin to take her on as a pupil. When the landlady offered to introduce them to some Oxford undergraduates on a reading-party, they decided it was a cunning plot to find out whether they were respectable girls, probably put up by her suspicious sister next door. When they went up over the pass to Ullswater, Beatrice struck up a friendship with a travelling Scotsman and shared his milk-and-whisky so coolly that he gave her the whole bottle and Maggie hoped she felt properly ashamed of herself. When a thunder-storm sent them running for shelter to a little book-shop with a parlour behind it, these two prospective heiresses of one of the great Victorian fortunes were enchanted to get "a most gorgeous tea—such bread and butter, jam and apple pies!"—for sixpence each. And all the while they talked, about George Eliot and Goethe and John Stuart Mill, and Auguste Comte's "three stages in the development of the human intellect", striking sparks from each other's imagination, agreeing and disagreeing violently, taking the universe to pieces and re-building it on an improved plan, perhaps the most enjoyable of all the amusements of intellectually curious youth.

This escape into the mountains with Maggie was the most joyful episode of Beatrice's girlhood, perhaps even of her whole life, in which full happiness came so rarely. With Maggie she was a different person from the one the rest of the world knew. Only Maggie among her family realised that Beatrice's passion for study was not simply to "make a show before old and young philosophers" (as Georgina suggested), but the result of an overpowering need within herself. Like George Eliot's "Dorothea", Beatrice "yearned for something by which her life might be filled with action at once rational and ardent; and since the time was gone by for guiding visions and spiritual directors, since prayer heightened yearning but not instruction, what lamp was there but knowledge?"[12]

But this long-planned walking-tour was the end of their exclusive relationship. After it, Maggie went on a six-months' tour of Egypt with Kate and the Barnetts and Herbert Spencer. Beatrice wrote sorrowfully in her diary, "Maggie left this morning. I feel her loss terribly. We are perfectly intimate and at one with each other, and when I am with her I want no other society. We have had a very happy time here together—have read, walked, slept and talked together and now she has gone it is a dreary blank." She knew that sooner or later Maggie would have to accept one of the suitable proposals she received regularly, and wrote anxiously to Egypt to ask if Maggie was perhaps contemplating "any change in life?" Maggie wrote back reassuringly that she would probably not do so until she was nearer thirty, and "until then we will be together." But the relief was short-lived. Maggie came back to Standish at Easter still heart-whole, but early in the Season Kate brought a young barrister, Henry Hobhouse, to a dance in Prince's Gardens; he and Maggie took a "sudden fancy" to each other and by the end of the month they were engaged.

Beatrice wrote politely to Henry that "Maggie's perfect happiness quite consoles me for her temporary loss—for I have full intentions of regaining her when you and she are one". She listened patiently to Maggie's raptures, but—as Maggie gaily confided to Henry— "the cynic-philosopher shakes her head sagely and ventures to doubt whether what she calls my idealism on the subject of marriage can ever be realised." In the autumn, they held their wedding at Rusland. "And what a quaint one!" wrote Kate. "All wedding-dresses prohibited and we all come out in old finery. Maggie in short white dress and large white hat—very funny little bride."[13] The honeymoon was spent in wandering around the Lake District, where Maggie and Beatrice had wandered just one year before.

Beatrice, alone again, agreed to go on a trip to Italy with a trio of elderly strangers. In Rome, purposeless and desolate, she took to drifting into St Peter's, looking, unhopefully, for that road-to-Damascus conversion to Roman Catholicism which might satisfy all her hungers at once. "I cannot write down what I felt on this Sunday morning—watching the silent Mass in St Peter's," she wrote in her diary. "Perhaps there was a good deal of mere emotion in it —but it made me look back, with regret, on those days when I could pray, in all sincerity of spirit, to my Father in Heaven."[14] She tried to work out a scheme by which she might keep her intellectual integrity and still get all the benefits of a religious faith. Protestants, she reflected, insisted on having a religion which they could defend by rational argument, and when someone like Herbert Spencer proved conclusively that the Bible was wrong, they had to admit that their faith was founded on a falsehood. But Roman Catholicism appealed to a different faculty, "the emotional—which is the dominant spirit in all my better and nobler moments." She could, perhaps, admit the Church's authority on the one subject, while retaining her own on every other. It seemed a good idea, for a time. But she decided that it would be wrong for her to be tempted, by the alluring Catholic ritual, to commit "intellectual (and perhaps moral) suicide".

Theresa joined her, "intoxicated with delight" at being in Italy, and Henry and Maggie, on a second honeymoon, came to stay. Maggie was pregnant—"seedy and miserable, the natural result of the condition of married existence," Beatrice reported bitterly. "Painful to me to see her so poorly and now, since her marriage, it is painful to me to be with her. She was a complete companion to me and is not to be replaced." She decided that she would never be really friends with Henry. "He has no gift of drawing out what is best in you, nor does he understand anyone's thoughts but his own. Acting like a wet-blanket on Maggie's intellect." When Henry and Maggie, "silently happy" together, had gone, Beatrice collapsed altogether. For a fortnight she lay, sick and broken-spirited, in her dark little pension room, and Theresa was obliged to tear herself away from the riches of the picture-galleries to nurse her. Theresa was sweetly uncomplaining. "Poor girl, how irritating to have her whole visit spoilt by an incapable sister," Beatrice noted perfunctorily. "But it will soon be over, this long stay in this most *ennuyant* of places." She was unable to be fair to Theresa, because Theresa was not Maggie. She was "a sweet girl, full of bright sympathy, but lacking in judgment". But when the two joined their parents and Rosy in San Remo, and Beatrice saw how shocked and anxious her father was at finding her in such a state, she had the grace to be sorry for causing him so much anxiety. "Dearest old Father, it adds to one's self-disgust, the thought that some day one will bitterly regret having added to his worries." She added to them a little more by falling out bitterly with her mother before they returned dispiritedly to Standish.

That summer, Theresa surprised them all by deciding to marry Alfred Cripps after all. ("It is sad, this last final break . . . though our intimacy has never been so unclouded as between Maggie and me.") Theresa seemed to be destined, by her undemanding gentleness, to be overshadowed by her more domineering sisters. (When Maggie got engaged, Laurencina had observed that she wished it had been Theresa instead, so that she need not part with her favourite daughter.) Theresa's bridegroom, Alfred Cripps, was the younger brother of Blanche's husband, Willie, and the wedding took place in the same church in which Maggie had been married the previous year. Theresa was quietly happy in her marriage, bore five children in seven years and died when the youngest of them, Stafford Cripps, was four years old.

Now Beatrice was left alone with Laurencina, apart from Rosy, who was still in the schoolroom and whom Beatrice referred to, irritably, as "my problematical younger sister". After the excitement of the wedding, life was suddenly quiet. "All my relationships, with men and with things, seem to be passing dreams... How curious that feeling is, that one's lifetime is a dream, all outward existence a dream." Most dream-like of all, a new relationship was growing up, imperceptibly, between Beatrice and her mother. Laurencina had become strangely gentle and humble and unlike her old self. She no longer cared about imposing her will on the household, and she turned, so late in life, to the daughter whom she had always belittled, perhaps because, of all the family, Beatrice most nearly mirrored her own frustrations and dissatisfaction with her own achievement.

With the barrier down, Beatrice found herself talking to Laurencina as she never had before, finding in her mother an exact reflection of her own problem of mental energy running to waste and a blind, hopeless longing to do something with her own life. As they paced up and down the gravel walk together, and talked of Laurencina's studies and of Beatrice's ambitions, Laurencina suggested that Beatrice might perhaps succeed where she had failed and become a distinguished writer of books. Incredulously, Beatrice realised that she was now, at last, on the verge of love and complete intimacy with her mother.

Her father and mother went to the Argoed, the house which they meant to use when Richard retired, to superintend the necessary alterations. Beatrice was left alone at Standish. One afternoon, as she came in from a solitary walk, she saw that the carriage had driven up, and her mother was being helped out of it by her father and Kate, and that she was in obvious pain. They got her to bed and Beatrice slept with her. Next morning, Laurencina told Beatrice that she thought she was mortally ill. Her other daughters were sent for and came hurriedly: Mary, Georgina, Theresa, Lallie, Blanche, and little Rosy, already in tears. Beatrice wore herself out with nursing until her father insisted on getting in some outside help before she herself collapsed. But when the doctors gave them no more hope, and it was only a matter of hours, Maggie came, and it was Maggie whom Laurencina wanted, and on-one else. Beatrice had to stay with the other seven sisters, waiting in the next room, Laurencina's boudoir, full of her books, and there they sat, looking silently at each other, while Maggie sat by her mother's side and talked to her and comforted her and held her hand, until she died.

Dutiful Daughter
1882—1890

RICHARD POTTER COULD SCARCELY BELIEVE that his wife was dead. "I must show this to Laurencina," he said, when he opened his letters at breakfast next day, and then, realising it, burst into tears. After the funeral his daughters composed themselves sufficiently to discuss the "equable division", as Rosy described it later, of their mother's jewels and wardrobe. "Of the former she had some valuable specimens, the most valuable being a diamond star. I suppose all this was inevitable, but it did not create a very favourable impression."[1]

A few months later Beatrice wrote remorsefully, in her diary:

> I never knew how much she had done for me, how many of my best habits I had taken from her, how strong would be the influence of her personality when pressure had gone.... When I work with many odds against me, for a far distant and perhaps unattainable end, I think of her and her intellectual strivings which we were too ready to call useless, and which yet will be the originating impulse of all my ambition, urging me onward towards something better in action and thought.

Once, she dreamed that her mother held out her hand and kissed her, while she herself begged forgiveness for her lack of tenderness and sobbed, "It was my nature, Mother, I could not help it."

But now, as the eldest unmarried daughter—since Kate had recently become engaged to Leonard Courtney—she felt she should try to fill her mother's place. Her duty as she saw it was to foster her little sister Rosy, now on the verge of womanhood, and heartbroken at her mother's death; to cherish and advise her bereft father, and to maintain Standish as a home for the family, whose tribal instinct impelled them to gather together under the parental roof at frequent intervals, in order to renew the ties of kinship.

Beatrice was not in the least dismayed by the prospect of stepping into her mother's shoes. The idea of leaving home, to lead a dedicated, independent life, as Kate did, had not yet entered her head. Describing Beatrice, Rosy wrote (in the diary of which like all the Potter girls she was an addict), "By theory she is an ascetic and lives up to her ideas, but she loves comfort and even luxury."[2]

Before settling down to her new position, Beatrice decided it would do the three of them good to go abroad for a change, and the sorrowing father set off with his two daughters on what was to be his last foreign trip, murmuring confusedly as they departed, "Lost for ever." But, once on the move, he began to recover his spirits, and by the time the mourning party had reached The Hague he was making jokes about Beatrice's despotism. Here Herbert Spencer joined them, and over supper Richard listened, uncomprehending but affectionately amused, to the lofty conversation between his daughter and the philosopher.

The two fell at once into their customary comradeship of perpetual discussion. The eccentric, elegant philosopher and the bright-eyed girl at his side made an odd pair as they prowled through museums and galleries, talking all the time. They cared little for Dutch pictures; but neither of them had any criticism to make of the beautiful cathedral in Cologne. Beatrice and Rosy and her father were soothed and delighted by the lovely vesper chanting, but Herbert Spencer grumbled in a whisper about "excessive monotony" and "superstitious awe", until Beatrice whispered back, "I like it," and moved her seat to be nearer the music. They were still arguing as they came out of the church behind Rosy and her father who were consolingly arm-in-arm. In the evening the philosopher led his favourite disciple through the moonlit streets, back to the cathedral and in a "softened questioning voice" murmured, "It is curious, is it not, that I should be leading you into a place of worship?"—to which Beatrice sharply retorted, "Yes—especially as you led me out of it." Later, on the way back to their hotel, she tried desparately to explain to the relentless atheist her need for spiritual comfort. After Cologne, they parted company and the Potters went up into the Alps, where a young professor fell in love with Beatrice. As she walked and talked among the crags in the mountain air, she succumbed to the charms of a platonic idyll ("after four months of loneliness it was delightful to have the companionship of a refined mind"). She added guiltily, "Alas! Father and Rosy neglected."

They returned to England refreshed; and for the next few months Beatrice was busy establishing herself as mistress. She paid a round of family visits. At Maggie's house, she had some "delightfully doleful talks, reminding me of old times (only three years ago) when we wandered over moor and moss, gossiped cynically and talked tragically and enjoyed and suffered 'weltschmerz' ", but it was not the same, and never would be again. Maggie was kind and considerate in her own circle, but never looked beyond it. "There is no sacrifice she would not make for husband and children. It is natural she should feel wholly uninterested in all which does not affect this holy of holies." She stayed with the Alfred Crippses during Theresa's dangerous confinement and reflected on "the immense sacrifice a woman makes in consenting to become a mother". When she got back to Standish ("this old—I cannot say dear old—place where I have droned out so many years of existence—twenty-five"), it seemed empty and lonely and she had a fit of depression. One evening, as she was walking alone through the fields at sunset, she felt mysteriously aware of "an outward presence . . . a sense of downcoming help", and the words "thy servant" came into her mind and she bowed her head. Afterwards, peaceful and exalted, she marvelled that what she felt was an idea "from outside and yet not from man" should break in and govern her. She was more than ever convinced that she was moving towards some definite objective, which was still not in sight.

In the spring, she installed her household in the Prince's Gardens house and decided to cultivate society, partly because—she told herself wryly—it offered immediate and easily obtained gratification for her craving for vulgar and obvious praise, partly because the family so bitterly disapproved her trying to concentrate on her studies. Mary reprimanded her for "trying to be a blue-stocking when you were meant to be a pretty woman", and Georgina contemptuously referred to "Beatrice's intellect—or what she calls her intellect—what's the use of it?" But this new position of a certain authority inside the family suited Beatrice's temperament. From a seedy girl often nervously exhausted or ill, she blossomed into a beautiful young woman. Rosy recalled her appearance at this time as "strikingly handsome, her features lit by her keen intelligence. Above the broad, intellectual forehead and dark, glowing eyes her brown hair grew in profusion."[3] Beatrice had many admirers, but she responded to their wooing only with the cool abstractions of intellectual love. She firmly believed that emotion, together with sensuality and appetite, dragged a woman down, and her passion remained unawakened.

She was a devoted daughter without effort, and was determined to school herself into being a dutiful sister as well. Richard Potter was tolerant and easy-going, glad to have someone to run his various establishments and to be a companion to him, even if he sensed that he had only exchanged one female tyrant for another. Beatrice took an active part in his affairs, and used to insinuate the word "we" into business transactions when she could. He called her his "little busy Bee" and offered to make her a partner in his business if she did not care to marry. She made a point of protecting him from women friends whom she considered undesirable. Once, when she realised that he was going over Carlyle's house with a neighbour of theirs—Mrs Eustace Smith who figured in the Dilke scandal—she firmly went along with him, and noted enigmatically in her diary, "Quaint association, Mrs Eustace Smith revelling in every gratification human nature could desire. The other one denied all."

But Beatrice's other charge, Rosy, was not so easy to manage. Rosy was a child of nature, longing to be loved, and with a capacity for affection which she had always lavished, not only on those around her but on her white mice, her fat pony at Standish, her emerald toad, "Magic", the "water-boatmen" on the pond, and the mysterious grass-snakes she found coiled up and which her father cultivated in the garden as pets. (Once, many years later, an adder bit her on the neck as she lay on a mountain-side. She said only, "Don't kill the poor little creature—it meant no harm.") But this sweetness of character and Rosy's essential humility and lack of self-assertion (attributes so rare among the Potters) had no appeal for Beatrice.

Beatrice had been jealous of Rosy, from the moment Laurencina's tenth baby had been born. All their childhood Rosy had been indulged by Laurencina and spoiled by everyone around her. Laurencina had always insisted—in face of all evidence to the contrary—that this cherished baby of the family was going to turn out to be the intellectual one. One of the many pin-pricks which Beatrice had had to endure was the suggestion that Rosy would outstrip her on her own ground. A highly qualified governess from Newnham had been engaged to coach Rosy, so that she could have a chance to go to one of the new women's colleges—an opportunity which had never been offered to Beatrice. Rosy herself found the prospect supremely uninteresting.

Now Beatrice was in the position of mother to her little sister. At first she tried to love her. She wrote affectionately to their father:

> I wish Rosy were here. Someday she must come with me, and while she attempts to imitate some of the perfect little pictures of vegetation and rocks and waters I will sit by and envy the power of expression and the pleasure it adds to all experience of beauty, and if the darling old father is not here, with silk pocket-handkerchief round his head looking beamingly at his daughters, then I will scribble all my little sensations and thoughts to him."[4]

But there were many things about Rosy which irritated her. Rosy wished to be cleverer than she was. "At present she has no intellectual interests of her own, but she knows it and acknowledges she affects them in order to impress others. With Father, this desire is prompted by love and a wish to be a comfort to him." Nevertheless, "at present she is a bore. The mind that seeks perpetually the 'why and wherefore' of all things is tedious and tiresome." It annoyed Beatrice that Rosy had absolutely no ambition, perhaps because Rosy's lack of it underlined her own ambition and vanity which she was always striving to overcome. Even Rosy's efforts to be more like her elder sister were tiresome. "Great difficulty not to be too intimate with her lest she should adopt me as a model. At present it is sufficient for me to say anything, for her to immediately copy it with ridiculous results. She is not intelligent enough to see this." When Rosy, unable to get over the morbid despair into which she had fallen since her mother's death, turned to Beatrice for love, Beatrice could not give it. Instead, she replaced it by duty, and did only what that could do.

Rejected, Rosy turned to her father and her affection for him grew in intensity until it became an exacting tyranny. Richard loved her dearly, but as a child to be petted. He called Rosy his "little maiden", but it was Beatrice on whom he relied for help and judgment. Rosy knew it and resented it bitterly. Her jealousy of Beatrice created such a strain in the household that Beatrice decided it was her duty to send Rosy away. She was installed in a finishing-school at Fontainebleau, where she learned to speak French, but little else. She was miserably homesick—though her father wrote to her every day—and tormented herself with the thought of Beatrice spending the summer with him in London. At the end of a year, she rejoined them, but the situation was exactly the same. Rosy and her father seemed to be fonder of each other than ever; she rebelled against Beatrice's discipline and was even more depressed. Beatrice continually reproached herself for not being able to make Rosy's life more beautiful, but she could not love her or alter their relationship.

She did not allow the disagreeable situation between herself and her sister to spoil the rest of her life; the round of dinners and balls; the daily party which was held at the Potter home—as in other rich men's houses—for an hour or two before luncheon and again before dinner. No invitations were sent for these, but few came who would not in any case have been invited. Much as Beatrice disapproved, in theory, of what seemed to her the idle and useless life of "Society", she loved impressing people and talking and smoking with clever men, though she reminded herself that this was indulging her vanity. Smoking was her only indulgence and she boasted about it in an absurd way which was somehow endearing. "Did we smoke? Let men beware of the smoking woman," she wrote, as though she were a Delilah blowing smoke into Samson's eyes.

The pretty dress and the sweet smelling cigarette with its outward token of woman's sympathy and man's ease. Defenders of man's supremacy should fight female use of tobacco with more vigour than is displayed in the female use of the vote. It is far more fatal to power. It is the wand with which possible women of the future will open the hidden stores of knowledge of men and things and learn to govern them.

Beatrice chiefly smoked and talked with politicians, scientists and intellectuals. She did not meet the racing set and moved only on the fringe of aristocratic circles. She attended the main functions of the season where she saw—and sometimes met—the great figures of the age. On Sundays she went with her sister and father to hear the great preachers of the day or—with equal enthusiasm—to hear Frederic Harrison lecture on Comte's "Religion of Humanity". This had always been a favourite subject of discussion between Maggie and Beatrice, during the years of their close intimacy. Maggie was inclined to dismiss it as "underbred theology with no bishops to bless it". But now Beatrice had taken up the works of Auguste Comte again, partly because Frederic Harrison and his wife were frequent guests at her dinner-parties. They were a brilliant young couple; he, in Beatrice's description, "an insistent lecturer, a most versatile and sympathetic conversationalist ... an original thinker and a public-spirited citizen, always eager to appreciate new ideas"; and his wife, "with her luminous dark eyes and consummate coils of hair, her statuesque figure and graceful garments was a befitting mate ... a 'St Clothide' to her Auguste". But although the Harrisons had a great influence on her and became her loyal friends, she never joined their "Church of Humanity", but finally decided that it was "a valiant effort to make a religion out of nothing; a pitiful attempt by poor humanity to turn its head round and worship its tail".[5] Even Spencer's "Unknowable" was closer to the unattainable God, for whom she was always looking.

Any energy left over from what Beatrice called her "practical life" she felt entitled to use as she wished, and her happiest hours were those she spent privately in her bedroom pursuing her studies, hoping one day to realise her secret ambition and win recognition through intellectual distinction. From her window she could see in the evenings

the sun slowly setting behind the Museum building and gardens ... undisturbed by the rushing life of the great city; only the brisk trotting and even rollings of the well-fed horses and cushioned carriages. Altogether we are in the land of luxury ... living in an atmosphere of ease, satiety and boredom. ...
I feel like a caged animal bound up by the luxury and comfort and respectability of my position. I can't get a training without neglecting my duty.[6]

Beatrice struggled over the next few months to find some kind of career for herself. Mathematics, according to Comte, was the most important of the abstract sciences, and it seemed to Beatrice that it was her duty to understand this. During the autumn when she and her father and Mary were staying at Rusland, she discovered that the local parson had been a Cambridge wrangler and engaged him as a tutor. But the struggle to force her brain into unfamiliar and uncongenial channels, combined with the eternal conflict between what she longed to do and what she must, almost resulted in a nervous breakdown. One morning Mary burst in on her and found her sitting by "an open window in an untidy dressing-gown, with dishevelled hair and pale and spotty complexion, straining hand and brain to copy out and solve some elementary algebraic problem". Mary scolded her and warned her that her mania for study would prevent her from ever getting married. "This is *my* room and *my* time—go away," said Beatrice angrily. Halfway through the morning's still unsolved algebra, she looked up and saw Mary come silently into the room again, wearing a white flannel wrap with dark-blue spots (the same she had worn the last time she had upbraided Beatrice for her intellectual pretensions). Beatrice screamed at her to leave the room and she vanished silently. It struck Beatrice suddenly that it was odd that Mary should be wearing this old wrap and she hurried downstairs where the butler informed her that Mary had gone out with her father wearing her usual clothes some time before. Beatrice sat in the hall for the next hour in a panic of guilt, superstition and brain-fag, until at last Mary and her father came in from their walk, relieved that Beatrice had recovered her temper, and a little surprised at the warmth of her welcome. After that, Beatrice gave up mathematics.

She next applied herself to the study of physiology. She found a woman teacher and went to her for regular lessons, and she worked for her brother-in-law, Willie Cripps, who was a cancer specialist. She struggled to master his book, *Adenoid Diseases of the Rectum*, but found that helping him to prepare specimens for his microscopic work was more comprehensible and more rewarding. ("One leaves behind all personalities, and strives hard to ascertain the constitution of things . . .")

But at this point she discovered her vocation. In her thirst for education, she had been methodically studying Herbert Spencer's *Social Statistics*, a work of three stout volumes, 900 pages long. His concept of the "social organism" convinced her that social evils could be not only diagnosed by scientific examination, but also eradicated, and society thus made perfect. The fact that this implied the sacrifice of the individual to the social good—when there was any conflict of interest—greatly appealed to Beatrice, though it was ignored by the great philosopher of individualism. Her own puritanical inclinations were always prompting her to extinguish her individuality and she longed to discover an object for this "higher sacrifice". Now she decided that the scientific investigation of social institutions was to be her "worth-while" purpose in life. "From the flight of emotion away from the service of God to the service of man, and from the current faith in the scientific method, I drew the inference that the most hopeful form of social service was the craft of a social investigator." This conclusion started her, at the age of twenty-five, on the path which eventually led her beyond the wildest dreams of her ambition, to be the star of the coming age of Socialism and one of the founders of the Welfare State. During the next four years she often hesitated, was sometimes side-tracked, and once almost took another road altogether, but in the end went back to her original purpose.

In 1883, however, she was far from being a Socialist and strongly objected to "gigantic state experiments . . . state-education and state-intervention in other matters which are now being inaugurated and which flavour of inadequately thought out theories—the most dangerous of all social poisons". On one occasion she met the daughter of Karl Marx, in the refreshment-room of the British Museum—a dark-eyed, picturesque, slovenly girl, connected, Beatrice remembered, with "the Bradlaugh set", and "a Socialist writer". Said Miss Marx, no doubt echoing her famous father, "Last century free thought was the privilege of the upper classes—now it is the privilege of the working classes. We want them to disregard the mythical next world and live for this world and insist on having what will make it pleasant for them." Beatrice departed, thoughtful but unconvinced. She dwelt rather on the socialist girl's peculiar views on love, guessing that her relations with men were "somewhat natural", and did not give much for her chances of "remaining long within the pale of respectable society".[7]

Two years after Laurencina's death the Potters gave up Standish, their family home, and Prince's Gate, and moved to York House, a former Royal residence in Kensington Palace Gardens. It stood in a large garden of its own, with two lawn tennis courts, wide gravel paths, beautiful herbaceous borders, vegetables, a paddock, and a rookery, the whole surrounded by a red brick wall. It is curious that Beatrice, with her avowed contempt for society, and her newly formed resolve to become a social investigator, should have chosen to take this expensive house in one of the most fashionable districts in London, especially as Standish was more suitable for family gatherings, and all her sisters, except Mary, had London homes. But it is reasonable to suppose that now that Richard Potter was no longer subject to the rigid economies of his wife's régime, and Beatrice was inspired with ambition to shine in society, they decided to move to a better address where they could entertain in a style appropriate to their considerable income. York House suited this purpose admirably.

Beatrice's activities had become so complicated that she began to lead a double life. The active and social side of her life (which she thought superficial and often called the "whirlpool"), had grown shadowy and she moved among society men and women as in a dream, talking and listening only with the fringe of her mind. The rest of it, withdrawn and veiled, was absorbed in what she thought of as her real life, her thoughts and problems and ambitions, so real at times that she often longed to tear away the veil and face the world as she really was.

This duality was part of Beatrice's nature. A revealing entry in her diary describes her dilemma. "I have in me a nether being," a despondent, gloomy, religious phantom, "dominated by superstition", affecting asceticism and doomed to failure, "whose natural vocation and destiny is the convent." The other Beatrice was lighthearted, patient and truthful—a realist, a rationalist and a sceptic, a being whose "origins lie in my sensual nature". Thus, in this conflict between the spirit and the flesh, she took the unusual view that the things of the spirit were evil and those of the flesh good. If she were a man, "this creature would be free, though not dissolute in his morals, a lover of women". But being a woman, "these feelings, unless fulfilled by marriage, must remain unsatisfied", and find "their only vent in the phantom companion of the nethermost personality—religious exaltation". She looked for faith and found reason, she prayed for humility and remained proud; an enthusiast for truth, she told lies; found peace in solitude and yet was stimulated by society; and, yearning for love, pursued power.

Her family, however, and her old friend Herbert Spencer, were outside the sphere of this conflict. To them she remained a devoted daughter, a dutiful sister and an affectionate disciple. Her friendship for the philosopher never cooled. She cheered his loneliness, and when he was sunk in misery and boredom, her bright companionship revived his spirits. He encouraged her work and persuaded her to publish what she had written. At Christmas with the family, he retaliated to her mischievous kiss under the mistletoe by chasing her round the billiard table, calling for a forfeit. They were so often together that rumours began to get around that an engagement was imminent. These were quickly denied. The two often visited the Royal Academy, where they indulged "the pleasurable gratification of the artistic sense"—as she called it, parodying his style—and joined the Society parade. Once, on her way there, Beatrice, with great coolness, stopped a runaway horse and cart in Hyde Park. A policeman had refused to leave his beat to do so. "Want of public spirit in passers-by not stopping it before," growled the philosopher, adding inconsequentially, "Another instance of my first principle of government. Directly you get state intervention, you cease to have public-spirited individuals." Perhaps his prophetic old eye had already detected the seeds of deviation in his beloved disciple.

The family was rapidly increasing in prosperity and numbers. Hardly a month passed without a birth, or one of the sisterhood lying seemingly lifeless on her bed having a miscarriage. Richard Potter had enlarged his fortune by the clever manipulation of his capital. He was not interested in possessions, but liked to spend his money on show. This had always been a source of disagreement between himself and his wife. Now, he took pleasure in watching Beatrice's determined onslaught on society, which involved garden parties, receptions, banquets and the squandering of a great deal of money. He enjoyed it all, from the morning ride with Beatrice and Rosy in Rotten Row, to making generous gifts to the family in general. On one occasion Beatrice wrote: "I am so glad you have sent the married sisters £500 each. But... Rosy... and I have no right to it and I should not think of accepting." (One cannot help wondering whether Rosy was consulted)... "We both enjoy handsome allowances. Rosy has her horse and I give from out of your pocket to my charities."[8] (One such gift was the considerable sum of £4000.) He loved his grandchildren and his excitable daughters, with their emotional upsets, their affectionate reunions and their disputes over money, such as the one described in a letter of Beatrice's from York House. "... there is an awful row going on with Cripps (Theresa's husband) about settlements... Poor dear Lallie, what a firebrand she is. I always remain perfectly silent through her tirades."[9] With his family around him, Richard was a happy man.

In the autumn of 1885 he took his "little maiden", who was in her usual emotional frame of mind, on a visit to their relations in Tadcaster. Beatrice was against it; but Rosy pleaded with her father, who could never deny her anything, and the two went off together. They returned a month later looking, as Beatrice put it, "very ill, but apparently enamoured of each other". The next day was Election Day, and as he walked to the polling booth he said to Rosy, "You generally take my arm, little maiden, but today I will take yours." When they got home he sent out for sixty pairs of slippers and dictated an "extraordinary letter" (whose contents remain a mystery) to Rosy. Beatrice, alarmed, sent for the doctor. He diagnosed a paralytic stroke and feared softening of the brain.

It was a blow for Beatrice. Her first thought was for Rosy, who was convinced that she was to blame for her father's illness and was beside herself with remorse. Beatrice also blamed herself for neglect, but she thought Rosy not far wrong. Once again her answer was to send Rosy abroad. But Rosy was no longer a child, she was a young woman in her twentieth year, and it was only after formidable pressure from Beatrice and all her sisters (with the exception of Theresa, who took her part) that Rosy, for her father's sake, set sorrowfully out once again, in the company of her maid and the family doctor and his wife, whom she did not like.

With Rosy out of the way Beatrice took stock of the new situation. Although dismayed by the prospect of, as she put it, "companionising a failing mind", it never occurred to her to abandon her trust. She made her father's comfort and happiness her first consideration, caring for him with noble devotion.

Sea air was recommended, so she took him and his nurse to Bournemouth and settled into comfortable lodgings in Kildare House. The pine-wooded town with its memories of her youthful search for religion revived a flicker of faith which helped to resign her to the monotony of life with an invalid. Herbert Spencer joined them. He was in low spirits and stuffed with laudanum. "Poor Herbert Spencer," she wrote, "his life entirely given up to philosophy with no near friends." Indeed, the only one was herself. Spencer had just finished his autobiography and wanted her to be his executor. She thought it was the least she could do in return for the encouragement and help he had always given her. Her disinterested and tender compassion for the querulous old philosopher made their relationship one of the most delightful of Beatrice's life. He took rooms below them and begged Beatrice to spare him a few moments of the day. She sat in his room. "Are you suffering?" she would ask him. "No," he would reply, "only why suffer more todays?" and she would chaff him out of his gloom with her lively anecdotes.

It was not long before her father had a relapse and they were hurrying back to London. Here Beatrice had to face a new crisis. After his recent speculations, Richard Potter's immense fortune had diminished alarmingly. On several occasions Beatrice had intervened by refusing to post letters to his stockbrokers, or by "checkmating his efforts in speculation by writing to his brokers to discourage it". He complained mildly, "I know she does it for my own good. But it is rather hard." Whether or not the losses were due to his speculation or Beatrice's interference is not certain, but Daniel Meinertzhagen (her banker brother-in-law) thought that but for Beatrice Richard Potter would have left a much larger fortune than in fact he did. But in any case it was now necessary to make considerable and immediate reductions in their expenditure. Beatrice therefore got rid of York House and turned her back on "society".

Rosy returned in a state of collapse from her enforced travels on the continent. After visiting Corsica, where—enchanted by the beauty of the island—she almost forgot her unhappiness and resentment, she went to Rome where she had been struck down with Roman fever. Beatrice was shocked. Unable to face life in London with two invalids on her hands and the unnecessary extravagance this involved, she decided to move back to the Argoed. Often during the past months she had prayed for her father's death in order that she might be free to die herself; but now, in their old home with the "old face happy and thoughtless", and the "young face withered and lined", mysteriously she felt happy. In the beautiful countryside, free from the strain of society life in London, she devoted her early morning hours to reading and the evenings to thought and prayer, and felt more serene than she had done for a long time.

Beatrice's sisters, although they felt little sympathy for what seemed to them her foolish ambitions, now offered to look after their father and relieve her of her responsibility for four months of the year. During the rest of it, she devoted any time she could spare, from being her father's companion and her sister's guardian, to study. She read the works of Karl Marx and made her first serious attempt at writing, an article on "The Rise and Growth of English Economics". She sent this "little thing of my own out into the world", but it was not published. Alfred Cripps said he had "never read a stiffer article", and her friends advised her to put it away for six months. But success was soon to follow with the recognition she had always wanted.

Though at times she longed for her father's death, because of the release it would bring, at other times, when she was chatting and reading to him, the thought that she was making his last years happy overwhelmed her and she felt "softened and humanised by her relation to him". When Lallie was taking her turn at looking after him, he wrote to Beatrice affectionately,

> My dearest little Busy Bee,
> I found Laurence the cobbler (a relation) very jolly and gave him five pounds. We are enveloped in fog, but I have a certain respect for my very old friend the Manchester fog. I was born in fog... am reading *Emma*. What an artist Jane Austen is![10]

But a subtle change began to creep into her attitude towards him. She began to question whether it was justifiable that their ten able-bodied servants should minister to the comfort of the now useless life of the failing old man. "It's wrong—wrong—wrong!" she wrote, indicating that even at this time she was beginning to question seriously the privileges of wealth.

It was perhaps in the hope of checking a drift towards socialism (or what he called the "coming slavery") that Herbert Spencer introduced Beatrice to his other disciple, Auberon Herbert. She was familiar with his writing and at one time had intended to write a criticism of his articles on Individualism. She had also read his satirical dialogue, "A Politician in Trouble About His Soul", which it first appeared in the *Fortnightly Review*, and which, she observed patronisingly, seemed to be "written with the purpose of disproving the usefulness of the politician".

Auberon Herbert was the third son of Lord Carnarvon. He was an individualist, a lover of freedom and a convinced disciple of Herbert Spencer. He resigned his seat as a Liberal Member of Parliament because he thought the reforms he advocated would be more effectively implemented by lecturing and writing. Beatrice described him as a chivalrous crusader for good causes, a widower of fifty years, tall, stooping, frail and grey-haired, with truthful grey eyes. He lived as far removed from his fellow men and women as possible, in the depths of the New Forest. Here, with his children, their tutor, five servants, half a dozen ponies, two dogs and a few mangy cats, they led the simple life. He was as enthusiastic about anti-vivisection, virgin forests, fresh air and silence as he was about freedom and individualism.

Their first meeting was over lunch with Herbert Spencer, and they were sufficiently impressed with each other to arrange a second. In 1887, Beatrice visited the eccentric recluse in his remote woodland retreat, Old House, a collection of cottages all painted red. She arrived tired after a fourteen-mile pony-ride from the station, but, lighting up the inevitable cigarette, she plunged straight into talk—"religiously-minded individualism, disputing with scientific fact finding". Disagreement stimulated rather than stifled their discourse, and a romantic though short-lived friendship kindled between the two. Beatrice was charmed by the simple house, its rough walls adorned with eastern hangings, bare floors covered with bright rugs, its soft couches and lavishly burning peat fires. There were separate quarters for the servants and stalls for the cattle. It had the air of a brigand's lair hidden away in the forest, and contrasted oddly with her gentle, delicate-voiced host. On a second visit a month later, the two rode together through the overgrown forest and talked far into the night. To Beatrice, Auberon Herbert seemed "a Don Quixote of the nineteenth century, who had left the real battle of life to fight a strange ogre of his own imagination—an *always immoral State interference* (her italics); a creature, the uncouthness of whose name was a sufficient guarantee for its non-existence". Auberon Herbert playfully told Beatrice that she was "a woman without a soul". But these differences did not spoil the delight they found in each other's company. Beatrice went to see him again a year later, after she had been attending a Trades Union Congress at Dundee, when he had moved to Larich Bay on the banks of Loch Awe. Between them the two, who had turned their backs on society, started a novel, *Looking Forward*. Beatrice supplied the characters and he worked out the plot on individualist lines. The result of this co-operation between the investigator of facts and the imaginative idealist might have been interesting. But the project faded with the moonlight on the lake. Instead, he told her the story of his life and discussed marriage. Beatrice "suddenly perceived that he was considering possibilities", but she added, "He will doubt too much to make the offer. So friendship is preserved. As we pushed

off to join the steamer I watched the expression of inhuman senti-
mentality on the face of the old Don Quixote of modern
society. Did I laugh or did I shudder?" The figure of her unsub-
stantial friend disappeared into the Highland mist and an irrelevant
interlude was behind her.

6

Joseph Chamberlain
1883—1887

IT WAS INEVITABLE that sooner or later Beatrice should meet the Right Honourable Joseph Chamberlain, M.P., the famous monocled, orchid-wearing ex-mayor of Birmingham. He was a colleague of her brother-in-law Leonard Courtney, and her neighbour in Prince's Gardens. He also frequented the Society jungle through which Beatrice was at that time prowling and was often an eminent guest at the dinner-parties and receptions she went to during the London Season.

He was forty-seven years old, while she was only twenty-five. But she was used to the company of older men. Herbert Spencer was twice her age. Chamberlain, like Spencer, was a Liberal, but otherwise the two men were fundamentally out of sympathy. Chamberlain was a reformer who had been drawn into politics, he said, by his wish to improve conditions for the majority, whereas Spencer, believing that society would be perfected by the survival of the fittest, was suspicious of reformers.

There is a notion, always more or less prevalent and just now vociferously expressed that all social suffering is removable and that it is the duty of somebody or other to remove it. Both these beliefs are false. To separate pain from ill-doing is to fight against the constitution of things and will be followed by far more pain.[1]

he wrote, and remarked of Chamberlain that he was "a man who may mean well, but who does and will do an incalculable amount of mischief". Chamberlain said witheringly of Spencer, "Happily for the majority of the world, his writing is unintelligible, otherwise his life would have been spent in doing harm." Beatrice had long realised that Spencer, in spite of his influence on current thought, was never going to be more than a popular philosopher, whereas Chamberlain, with his purpose and passion, was already a leader of men and the most dazzling political figure among his contemporaries.

Her first meeting with the glamorous popular demagogue, as Beatrice noted in her diary, was on a Saturday afternoon in June 1883, on the occasion of Herbert Spencer's annual picnic at St George's Hill. Beatrice was in one of her "sinking-into-a-do-nothing —Ah me!" moods and found the company dull. It consisted of numerous Potters, some "elderly persons", a Mr Mitford ("a diplomatist with a divine French accent"), and the Chamberlains, Joseph and his daughter Beatrice. She spent the afternoon with Miss Chamberlain, whom she found likeable but provincial, and it was not until the evening that she held some interesting conversation with Mr Chamberlain. "I do and don't like him," she confided to her diary afterwards.

As soon as decorum permitted the great man was invited to dine with the Potters. Beatrice sat between him and a "Whig peer" (whose name seems to have escaped her), and who "talked of his possessions" while Chamberlain talked "*passionately* of getting hold of other people's for the masses". He was also entertaining about American society and told her that although it was often regarded as vulgar by cultivated minds, it was infinitely preferable to any other for the working-class man. He spoke of his own career and how his "interest in the social question, and his desire to promote the welfare of the majority", and the fact of two million extra working-class votes, had inspired his "Unauthorised Programme", which he had launched in a series of articles in the *Fortnightly Review* and in speeches throughout the country. Its irreducible propositions were the compulsory purchase of land for artisans' dwellings; compulsory free and undenominational education; graduated taxation; disendowment and disenfranchisement of the church; local government reform and the appropriation of unearned income for the purpose of betterment. "Hitherto the well-to-do have governed the country," he told Beatrice, "It is my aim to make life pleasanter for this great majority."

These socialistic ideas had caught the imagination of the public. He had become Birmingham's most popular citizen and was hailed by sympathisers as the only politician who was "feeling his way towards the light". The majority accepted him as their champion and affectionately dubbed him "our Joe" and "a bonny fighter". His opponents called him a "red revolutionary". Lady Randolph Churchill rebuked her father-in-law for asking to her table "a man who was a Socialist . . . reputed to have refused to drink the

Queen's health when Mayor of Birmingham", and Lord Salisbury denounced him as "the Cockney". His revolutionary tendencies estranged his own party, but he stoutly proclaimed that he was not a communist, although if anyone cared to call him a socialist he would not complain. But he turned the tables on those who insisted he was a raw demagogue with his hand raised against religion, property and monarchy when he entertained the Prince and Princess of Wales, who were visiting Birmingham and, as *Punch* described it, "Put his red cap in his pocket and sat on his *Fortnightly* article, and of red republic claws and teeth displayed not so much as a particle."

Even *The Times* reported the "courteous homage, manly independence and gentlemanly feeling" of his speech. (Chamberlain always resented the idea of his being "ungentlemanly".) In the House of Commons, to the surprise of members, this stormy petrel of the Liberal Party turned out to be "an urbane, elegantly-dressed figure . . . an accomplished debater and one of the best speakers in the House".

Beatrice, whose avowed faith at the time was "political agnosticism tempered by individualist economics", was not converted to socialism by this champion of the working-classes sitting at her side, but she was deeply interested in the man. What motive was concealed behind the impudent eyeglass and the flashy orchid? Was it ambition? And what passion would move that handsome, expressionless face—love of power or compassion for his fellow men? She decided that in any case she would like to know more of him.

The opportunity soon came. Joseph Chamberlain had twice been left a widower. His first wife, a Birmingham girl named Harriet Kenrick, the mother of his son Austen, had died in 1863. His second—her cousin, and the mother of his son Neville and his daughter Beatrice—had died eight years before he met Beatrice. Now he was looking for a third wife.

The brilliant and beautiful Miss Potter, who was making something of a name for herself by writing in distinguished monthlies, was entirely suitable. Chamberlain's sister, Clara, who kept house for him and was looking for someone else to take over the responsibility, favoured the idea. Accordingly, Beatrice was invited to stay at their London home. In her world, such visits were the normal preliminary to matrimonial negotiations.

During the week she spent with them, she learned a good deal more about her host, through conversations with Clara, and from her own observations of him. His enthusiasm, his ambition, his impetuous arrogance and even his air of unscrupulousness struck an echoing chord in Beatrice and kindled in her something more than curiosity. When she returned home her father sensed what was in the air, and became disturbed and unhappy, because he objected to Chamberlain's views and disliked him personally. Herbert Spencer, too, was put out; went off his food, took his pulse more often than usual and muttered about "the pernicious tendency of political activity" and the monotony of married life. Beatrice herself was greatly agitated.

"After six weeks of feverish indecision", as she described it, Chamberlain made his expected return visit. He turned up at the Argoed early in the new year, when there had been three days of dancing and games, during which Beatrice had felt herself "floating towards a precipice". The party, which already included two of Chamberlain's children, Beatrice and Austen, were seated round the tea-table when the great man was announced. No-one except Richard Potter and Beatrice knew exactly why he had come. In her excitement Beatrice almost pressed six pounds, which she was holding, into his hand, while her father, not troubling to hide his displeasure, scarcely looked up from his Patience. It was an unusual welcome for the great man accustomed to the enthusiastic acclaim of crowds and the adulation of the fashionable world.

That evening he and Beatrice were on "susceptible terms". It was not until the next day, wandering about the garden paths (Chamberlain elegantly turned out, and Beatrice hatless with her hair blowing in the wind, from time to time walking backwards facing him) that the two laid down their cards. He told her what he expected of women. He must have complete authority. If she believed in Herbert Spencer she could not believe in him. It pained him, he told her, to hear his views contradicted, and what he required from women was "intelligent sympathy". She replied, wishing to be candid, that to her this was nothing more than servility, and that she could never agree to it. They returned to the house exhausted, Beatrice, at any rate, feeling that all was over between them. Two tyrants had met, and this was the first skirmish in a struggle for power which lasted (at least for one of them) for four years.

A week or so later, Beatrice received a pressing invitation to visit the Chamberlains at Highbury, his house in Birmingham. She was surprised because she had been certain that, as she put it, "negotiations were off". But she accepted eagerly, intrigued by the idea of seeing the great politician in the town of his adoption. She was also curious to see the red-brick mansion with its many bow windows, which Kate had described as "rather gorgeous, over-coloured though, and certainly over-heated and rather a gloomy atmosphere about the inmates", and the famous long glass orchid houses. Chamberlain was very rich. As a young man he had come to Birmingham from London, to join Nettlefolds, a firm which manufactured wooden screws. He had profited by his knowledge of French and his genius for mathematics, and had increased trade in France considerably by using the decimal system to describe the screws and also by making them up in packets rolled in the blue paper familar to French workmen. Very soon he had amassed a fortune by resorting—according to the *Daily News*—to "the most questionable dodges"—an accusation which was withdrawn and replaced by the less objectionable statement that "other firms had suffered indirectly through Nettlefolds' success".

Beatrice paid her visit on the occasion of a political demonstration. John Bright, Muntz and Joseph Chamberlain, the three members for Birmingham, were to speak. The family were assembled to meet her in a drawing-room sumptuous with satin-covered walls and carved marble arches and "not even an antimacassar to relieve the oppressive wealth". The sad splendour of the apartment cast a gloom over everyone. The two Miss Chamberlains were ill at ease and dowdily dressed (though Beatrice liked their honesty and devotion and later they became close friends). Her host emerged from his orchid house and greeted her sombrely. "Miss Potter," he said gravely, "I shall reserve the orchid house for tomorrow and then I shall do the honours myself. I don't want my sister to take you there." Beatrice wondered as she sank into a "perfectly constructed chair" whether they were about to take part in a funeral, and John Bright, who had joined the company, did not strike a happy note by recalling her mother's grace and beauty (an observation recorded on different occasions by at least two of the Potter sisters with some irritation). All the speakers were nervous. At last the moment came when the party, escorted by Austen Chamberlain, made their way to the packed Town Hall. Beatrice scarcely heard what the first two speakers—John Bright and the long-winded Muntz—had to say. She watched Joseph Chamberlain, the demagogue, the popular hero, pale and impassive, high above the excited throng, as though she had been mesmerised. "Then," she recorded, "he rose slowly, and stood silently before his people, his whole face and form transformed.... There was one loud uproar.... Perfectly still stood the people's tribune. At the first sound of his voice ... they became as one man.... It might have been a woman listening to the words of her lover! Perfect response and unquestioning receptivity." Beatrice fell passionately in love. Next morning she wandered with him among his orchids, forgetting for the sweet moment her wish to dispute his authority, glad just to be near him, to watch him. He showed her his exotic blooms, eager for her approval and impatient of any difference of opinion. When she told him that she only loved wild flowers, he seemed "curiously piqued". Beatrice felt "susceptibility" increasing. "It did not show itself in any desire to please me, but in an intense desire that I should think and feel like him ..... by a jealousy of other influences, especially that of the old philosopher, Herbert Spencer."

Beatrice had never fallen in love before. In the past, in spite of many flirtations and a good deal of admiration, men had left her cold. But Joseph Chamberlain's "gloom and sensuousness", his absence of gallantry, his assumption of superiority and complete domination over her was the kind of "courtship" she found irresistible. She had never before met anyone who assumed superiority over her or demanded "perfect response and unquestioning receptivity". She had not expected ever to feel like this about anyone and she went home wondering how it would all end, knowing that whichever way it did, it could not be for her own happiness.

During the following spring and summer her thoughts were absorbed by him, her mind torn between ambition for the position in the world she would have as the wife of a great man, a longing to bear his children, and her ambition to make her own name famous; between her longing for love and submission and her fierce determination to subordinate others to her will. "Marry so as to satisfy *first* your ambition and secondly your affections," advised her cousin Maggie Harkness, "for so I read your necessity! "[2]

Her confused state of mind did not prevent her from seeing a great deal of Chamberlain. He was a constant visitor to York House. The two would pace round and round the garden paths, occasionally bumping into Rosy coming in the opposite direction with an admirer, which was disconcerting. Engrossed in each other, Chamberlain and Beatrice tried to settle their differences. He repeated that he desired a woman to acknowledge his absolute authority, to sympathise and encourage him, to admire him without reservation and to devote herself entirely to his aims. She objected that his aims were not hers, and that she could not subordinate her views.

In many ways their two characters were alike. Both were inordinately ambitious, inclined to fanaticism, and neither of them had ever before encountered an opposing will. Beatrice was eccentric and careless about her appearance, while Chamberlain was conventional and impeccable about his. But in spite of the obstacles of temperament Beatrice's passion increased and it cannot be supposed that Chamberlain remained indifferent. On one occasion, according to family legend, Chamberlain was seen hurrying away from York House, pale-faced and distraught, while Beatrice was discovered weeping indoors. "I've just refused him," she sobbed. Whatever the truth, Beatrice had met her match. Chamberlain was not the man to submit to anyone, and certainly not to a woman. At length, unable to come to terms, they agreed to part in friendship, but such encounters are not easily ended. Chamberlain, who had grown accustomed to their friendship, was a lonely man and Beatrice was a good companion. He made every effort, in spite of her reluctance, to see her as often as possible. Beatrice remained passionately in love and their paths continued to cross.

She pursued her philosophical interests and cut herself off from the fashionable world. But when she opened a book, thoughts of a crowded hall raced through her mind, and when she turned to duty for consolation, the voice of the "people's tribune" beat upon her brain. At one moment she was desperate enough to make an informal will, leaving her diamond brooch to Maggie "who should really have had it", and advising her father—"if he lives"—to get the Courtneys to look after him. "If Rosy is wise she should press for this," she went on. "The position of an unmarried daughter at home is unhappy for a strong woman. . . . and impossible for a weak one." Fortunately there was never any need to follow this advice, and whether Maggie ever got the diamond brooch after all remains a matter of speculation.

When Beatrice went to London she was constantly reminded of Chamberlain. His portrait, among those of other distinguished men of the age, on Dolly Tennant's mantelpiece, gave her a jealous pang. It reminded Beatrice of the proud moment one evening in that very house when he, the lion, had sought her out from all the glittering company. Dolly Tennant, whose position in society Beatrice perhaps envied ("a magnificent perfect creature—but for a squint"), was, she decided, "really an adorer of power". When she dined at Kate's, Beatrice painfully remembered a gay evening there, when Chamberlain and the well-bred Balfour had delighted her with their cynicism and wit. Now Balfour's clever remarks merely sounded to her forced and insincere. On one painful occasion, at Clara Ryland's, Beatrice sobbed bitterly when she heard Clara talking to her husband "in a low voice below—and at the time I little doubted that he was told all. I don't think I resented it—what is pride beside true, deep feeling? True deep feeling, that never leaves one's mind in placid rest, but keeps the depths stirred and tinges all one's thoughts with deep emotion. Will the pain of it ever cease?" Then a ridiculous misunderstanding occurred which exasperated her. Unable to face meeting Chamberlain at a dinner-party, she pleaded a headache and sent Rosy to take her place. Rosy was delighted. She was taken down to dinner by the great man himself, and although he talked to the lady on his other side throughout the meal, the young man on Rosy's right, Dyson Williams, was delightfully attentive. The evening had two unforeseen consequences. Rosy eventually became engaged to Dyson, but—which exasperated Beatrice far more—it was reported that Rosy was engaged to Joseph Chamberlain. This report was promptly followed by an invitation to Rosy from the Chamberlains to attend the coming-of-age celebrations of Austen at Highbury. The sisters agreed that it must have been sent so that Rosy's name might be associated with Austen's and the false rumour thus contradicted. "Of course you must go, and take all your best clothes—I will order a new ball dress for you," said Beatrice. The episode, although Rosy enjoyed it, rankled with Beatrice as everything connected with Rosy always had done—and as everything connected with Chamberlain now did.

Rosy was a changed human being. The only trace of her former black mood was a wild look at the back of her hazel eyes, reminding one of a pony about to bolt. She had grown pretty enough, with a mass of auburn hair, to attract many admirers. When her engagement to Dyson Williams was announced, Beatrice commented, "Poor fellow, I pity him ... Not up to my other brothers-in-law ... In short a nonentity, but then Rosy is the least gifted mentally and physically of all the sisterhood." Rosy, intimidated by her sister's tyranny, was in a state of hopeless indecision about her marriage ."Shall I ever care for him? Shall we ever get on?"[3] "If you think of yourself you'll never be happy," retorted Beatrice. "You have to learn to be a companion." In spite of Rosy's misgivings the wedding took place at the Argoed, with the parishioners and tenants giving the blushing bride an ovation. Beatrice was remorseful over her failure to love Rosy, but she remained grudging. "Rosy now has love which she never had before except for poor Mother's jealous preference... poor little weak-hearted, weak-minded thing. To me an unmitigated discomfort," she wrote after the wedding. Rosy did not in the least mind whether or not Dyson was a nonentity. All she wanted was to love and be loved.

At one time Beatrice decided never to see Chamberlain again, even as a friend. It was when Leonard Courtney's career was in jeopardy owing to his support of Proportional Representation, which Chamberlain considered ridiculous. He had also voted against the Medical Bill,[4] which had made Chamberlain angry. "Your brother-in-law is an ass," he told Beatrice at dinner. "P.R. lost him his chance of distinction in politics. This has lost him his seat." Hoping to mend matters, Kate arranged an elaborate picnic to which she invited Chamberlain and Beatrice. Beatrice accepted in spite of her resolve. They went to Burnham Beeches by train and sat under the spring foliage, but the expedition was a failure. The "people's tribune" was not at his best. He forced Beatrice (who was not accustomed to being forced to do anything) to tell him his fortune. Afterwards he behaved with "marked rudeness and indifference", and hinted darkly at the poor prospects of Leonard's political future. On the return journey, when he was given an impressive reception by railway officials at the station, he arrogantly left Beatrice and the Courtneys to trail behind him "like so many little dogs". Railway officials! It was too much for the daughters of a Chairman of the Great Western. On reaching home the Courtneys were further outraged. The dark hints were only too well explained when they opened a package from Leonard's agent in Cornwall enclosing a local paper containing an abusive letter urging constituents to vote against Courtney, the "renegade Liberal". The author was Chamberlain's "henchman", Jesse Collins.

But Beatrice remained under the spell of her "evil genius". She listened from Kate's seat in the gallery to the debate on Home

Rule in April 1886 when Chamberlain, after resigning office, rose to speak, pale and excited and cheered by the Opposition. His boyish enthusiasm, his low clear voice and his stinging oratory all thrilled her. Only when she saw him "talk to that beast Sir Charles Dilke", she shuddered and felt sad.

For his part, Chamberlain saw no reason for breaking off their friendly relations. While he was President of the Local Government Board, he had read Beatrice's leter in the *Pall Mall Gazette*, "A Lady's View of the Unemployed", and begged her to meet him and talk about the distress in the East End. Beatrice answered protesting that her knowledge of the East End was "superficial", and deploring the Mansion House fund. She suggested that there should be "some systematic investigation of unemployment on the one hand, and of labour on the other".[5] Chamberlain answered her letter:

> Pray do not think that I can have too much information on the subject on which I consulted you. I know that you have much experience, and that you are not "crochety", and you will find me ready to profit by your suggestions. . . . I cannot think that any registration of labour would be more than a trifling convenience. Whenever there is work wanted, workers will find it out very quickly for themselves. If the distress becomes greater, something *must* be done to make work. The rich must pay to keep the poor alive. . . . . for the workman who has been in ordinary constant employment and who . . . finds himself on the verge of starvation, it will be necessary . . . to find some poorly remunerated employment which *a*) will not tempt him in any way to remain in it longer than is absolutely necessary, *b*) will not be degrading in its character, *c*) will not enter into competition with workers at present in employment, and *d*) is of such a kind that every workman . . . can turn his hand to it. There is only one kind of work which answers these conditions, and that is spade labour . . . works of sewage, extra street cleaning, laying out recreation grounds etc . . . I wish you would tell me when you have time what you think of these rather crude suggestions.[6]

Beatrice could not agree to this admission of state responsibility. She replied to Chamberlain on 4th March, 1886:

> You take me out of my depth. . . . As I read your letter a suspicion flashed across me that you wished for some further

proof of the incapacity of a woman's intellect to deal with such large matters. I agree that "the rich *must* keep the poor alive"; always supposing that the continued existence of that section of the poor with liberty to increase is *not* injurious to the community at large. . . . . I fail to grasp the principle "something must be done". It is terribly sad that 100 men should die in semi-starvation . . . but . . . if by relieving these 100 men you practically create 500 more, surely the unsatisfactory nature of these men's lives outweighs in misery the death of the smaller number? . . . .

I have no proposal to make, except sternness from the state, and love and self-devotion from individuals. . . . . But is it not rather unkind of you to ask me to tell you what I think? I have tried to be perfectly truthful. Still, it is a ludicrous idea that an ordinary woman should be called upon to review the suggestion of Her Majesty's ablest minister, especially when I know that he has a slight opinion of even a superior woman's intelligence in these matters. . . . and . . . a dislike of any independence of thought . . .[7]

Chamberlain, perhaps more hurt by his unsuccessful wooing than he cared to admit, and piqued by the reminder of their differences, replied on 5th March, 1886:

I thought we understood each other pretty well. I fear I was mistaken. In the hurry of this life it is not easy to get a clear conception of any other person's principles and opinions. But you are quite wrong in supposing that I under-value the opinions of an intelligent woman. There are many questions on which I would follow it blindly, although I dislike the flippant self-sufficiency of some female politicians.
Neither do I dislike independence of thought. On the contrary, the only men with whom I have cordially worked are men of striking originality of ideas—a very rare but a most reliable quality in man or woman.
Of course eccentricity is not true originality, and fertility of resource is a very different quality to the ignorant self-confidence which assumes that virtue.
I hardly know why I defend myself, for I admit that it does not matter what I think or feel on those subjects.
On the main question, your letter is discouraging, but I fear it

is true. I shall go on, however, as if it were not true, for if we once admit the impossibility of remedying the evils of society, we shall all sink below the level of brutes. . . . .

I do not think your practical objections to public work . . . are conclusive . . . If men will starve rather than dig for 2s. od. a day, I cannot help them, and I cannot greatly pity them.

It will remove one great danger, *viz*, that public sentiment should go wholly over to the unemployed, and render impossible that state sternness to which you and I equally attach importance. . . . .

I thank you for writing so fully, and do not expect any further answer.[8]

The correspondence between these two passionate lovers of reform ended with a note of anguish from Beatrice:

Now I see I was right not to deceive you. I could not lie to the man I loved. But why have you worded it so cruelly, why give unnecessary pain? Surely we suffer sufficiently. Thank God! —that when our own happiness is destroyed, there are others to live for. Do not think that I do not consider your decision as *final*, and destroy this.[9]

But it was not yet the end of the affair. Beatrice dragged herself up to Birmingham once more to hear Chamberlain speak, in June 1887. There was none of the intoxication of her first visit. Chamberlain was now no longer a demagogue, but a statesman. All the same, his voice and manner had not lost their charm, and as Beatrice sat within a few steps of him, their eyes met, as they had so often done before. Afterwards, at his brother's house, where she was staying, she talked to him and his daughter. She described his manner towards her, indignantly, as that of "the triumphant lover —a man who is sure of his conquest". Nevertheless, she was "weak and romantic" enough for the result of the encounter to be— "Invited him to come and see Father and enjoy bracing air and beautiful scenery."

It was during this last visit of Chamberlain to the Argoed that Beatrice burst out with the passionate declaration of love which she repented so much afterwards. She wrote to him saying that having declared it, further meetings would humiliate her and she would rather not see him again. His reply was guarded and friendly, and perhaps indicated that if Beatrice had not been so clearly pursuing power she could even now have satisfied her social ambition and her desire for him:

> I cannot help feeling depressed and discouraged at times. I value greatly the sympathy you have shown me. The concluding part of your letter has given me much pain. Did I indeed do wrong in accepting your invitation? If so forgive me.... As to the future. Why are we never to see each other again? I like you very much—I respect and esteem you—I enjoy your conversation and society and have often wished that fate had thrown us more together. If you share this feeling—why should we surrender a friendship which ought to be good for both of us? I have so much confidence in your generosity as well as in your good sense, that I am encouraged to make this appeal to you in what I feel to be a very delicate matter. My past life has made me solitary and reserved, but it is hard that I should lose one of the few friends whose just opinions I value and the sense of whose regard and sympathy would be a strength and support to me. I cannot say more. You must decide, and if it is for your own happiness that we should henceforth be strangers, I will make no complaint. I return your letter as you wish it, but there is surely no reason why you should be ashamed of feelings which are purely womanly and for which I have nothing but gratitude and respect.[10]

It was more like a letter from a Prime Minister accepting the resignation of one of his favourite ministers than one in reply to a declaration of love from a young woman whose hand in marriage he had so recently sought, and Beatrice was hurt and indignant. "This letter, after I had, in another moment of suicidal misery, told him I cared for him passionately!" she complained. She tried to console herself with the thought that at least she had not dissembled, but had shown her true self to the man she loved. "Ah," she wrote sadly, "but how much sweeter than truth is love."

Her friends were consoling and relieved that the unhappy association was over at last. Mary Booth wrote, "I can't tell you the feeling of relief your letter has given me... I rejoice that the answer is no... You would never be happy... with that man.[11] Kate wrote:

[99]

It seems to me there was no trace of any feeling other than intense personal ambition and desire to dominate, at whatever cost to other people's rights. I do not even see any room in his nature for such an affection as would satisfy one of us. It would be a tragedy—a murder of your independent nature.[12]

But Beatrice would not be comforted. At the Argoed, she wandered over the countryside, accompanied only by her St Bernard dog, Don, her constant companion, "an animal idealisation of strength, gentleness and perfect obedience to the beloved will"— perhaps a significant description. Now she could not account for "this desperate clutch at power, power to impress and lead" which had brought her only this impotent despair.

Soon after Beatrice had broken off her relations with Chamberlain, he announced his engagement to the daughter of the American War Minister, Endicott. "I have only just seen the news about Mr Chamberlain," Kate wrote to Beatrice. "How did he manage to leave Liverpool in a Cunard without being recognised? He must have been disguised with a beard... Leonard thinks that Miss Endncott runs a great risk."[13] (His apprehensions were needless. The marriage turned out very happily.) Beatrice's other sisters lost no time in reporting news about the bride to her. Lallie thought her charming with lovely skin and a pleasant smile. ("Not much behind it," commented Beatrice.) From Maggie came the information that she had frank blue eyes and a charming retroussé nose. (Beatrice's was distinctly aquiline.) Said Kate: "If she were not Mrs Chamberlain she would be a pleasant nobody." Everyone asked Beatrice if she had seen the bride. She had not, she would reply—but had heard that she was charming.

"The black cloud has rolled away in a terrific peal of thunder. Every romance has a conclusion," she wrote in her diary. The black cloud was the passion for Chamberlain, which had hung over her for years, and the peal of thunder the wedding bells. But a ray of love was left behind. "If he could only feel my sympathy and understand it. God bless him."

It was all over. She had lost her chance of making a brilliant match and fulfilling herself as a woman. But now that she had renounced passion and desire she felt full of new strength. "I once longed for power. I have it now," she wrote. "Shall I sink under the very vastness of my opportunities or rise to fulfill them?"

7

The Investigator
1882–1890

SOCIAL WORK, in the eighteen-eighties, was the conventional spare-time occupation for an unmarried daughter of the leisured classes, though *Punch*—with the brutality about "the spinster" which was characteristic of the time—ridiculed her for trying to "solace herself for her failure to attract men", "fluttering about the bye-ways of charitable effort, establishing herself as a visitor, a distributor of tracts and blankets and an instructor of factory girls". Kate Potter had taken up charitable work because she was a literal Christian. She used to warn her younger sister to "avoid discussions on religious topics" with that irreverent old freethinker, Grandpapa Heyworth, because "I think it is very dangerous to treat the Bible as a matter of argument and curiosity and not as the practical guide for our lives for which it was given us."[1] But, unlike Kate, Beatrice said flatly that she was "not led into the homes of the poor by the spirit of charity", but by what she called the "time-spirit",—that is the stage which mid-Victorian thought had reached in grappling with the problem of poverty in the midst of riches.

It was the combination of the two which prevented them from taking "the poor" for granted as their predecessors had. The whole splendid business of Victorian prosperity, with its steam-power and factories and new fortunes and widening markets, was marred by the fact that it had failed to provide so much as a decent livelihood for millions living in the mean streets into which they had been swept by the Industrial Revolution. "The association of poverty with progress is the great enigma of our time," said the American Henry George, who advocated land-tax and made a Socialist of Bernard Shaw. Or, as Vaughan Moody put it,

Who hath given to me this sweet,
And given my brother dust to eat?

The contrast hung over the comfortably-off all the time. Their writers would not allow them to forget it. Engels warned them of the growing bitterness between classes; Dickens described the horrors of the slums; Mayhew assured them that these were fact and Carlyle and Ruskin thundered against the moral values which allowed it all to go on. In the seventies and eighties, you could hardly pick up a periodical without finding something in it about the problem of poverty, and in Beatrice's circle it was a constant topic of discussion. It created what she called "the mid-Victorian consciousness of sin"—"the starting-point of progress,"[2] said the Christian Socialist, Canon Barnett, hopefully—coupled with uneasy fear about what the under-privileged might do if the privileged did not find the answer first.

"You should prevail on our future masters to learn their letters," advised Robert Lowe, when the Reform Bill of 1867 was passed, and Richard Potter shocked his Conservative friends and infuriated his Radical acquaintances equally by maintaining that "If necessary, we must send our daughters to educate the masses", though—perhaps fortunately for his peace of mind—he did not live to see what happened when one of them did.

The traditional remedy against a bad conscience about the poor was to buy it off by giving them money, and charitable societies grew up like mushrooms. Between 1880 and 1890 alone one hundred and thirty-six new ones were founded. Even an old-fashioned Christian like Kate believed that it was not merely useless, but wrong to give to all who asked—a cheap way of making yourself feel virtuous which actually injured the community and the recipient himself. "The poor starve because of the alms they receive," said Canon Barnett, who was Kate's colleague and friend in Whitechapel during the worst of the hard times. But it was agony to him to refuse them.

On a freezing night, with the wind tearing down Commercial Street, human brothers and, worse still, human sisters slept on the clean hearth-stoned Vicarage steps, and one dared not give them 4d for the doss-house bunk, or even the 2d for the rope lean-to . . . a rope stretched across a room and men paid twopence a night to lean against it.[3]

When Beatrice first decided to investigate the causes of poverty, she joined the Charity Organisation Society, whose original title was "The Society for Organising Charitable Relief and Repressing Mendacity", and which aimed at rationalising the many other charitable societies and making sure that all proceeds were distributed only among the deserving.

Beatrice's job was to examine applicants in their homes in Soho. What worried her far more than having to ferret out the pitiful deceptions of the society's clients was that, even when she had got these collected, they threw no light on the basic problem. She had joined the C.O.S. because she thought it "an honest though short-circuited attempt to apply the scientific method of observation and experiment, reasoning and verification to the task of delivering the poor from their miseries".[4] But the facts collected by all the Society's workers, "small groups of heroic men and women, struggling day in and day out ... with crowds of destitute persons clamouring for alms, were too doubtful and restricted to lead to any proven conclusion as to the meaning of poverty in the midst of riches".[5] They did not measure the extent of destitution, nor classify it, nor find out whether it could really be explained by the popular theory of "delinquency, drunkenness, unwillingness to work or a lack of practicable thrift". All her research had done was to uncover the social workers' fundamental ignorance, her own included. She realised that she had not even got a standard by which to measure the lives of the down-and-outs, because normal working-class life, "that is of four-fifths of my countrymen", was a closed book to her. And whereas a "lady" doing charitable work had a vested right to walk into a slum tenement and cross-question its occupant about his most private concerns, members of the respectable working-class which ran its own "network of Nonconformist chapels, the far-flung friendly societies, the much-abused Trade Unions and that queer type of shop, the Co-operative store",[6] were unlikely to be so poor-spirited. It was, after all, the class from which Beatrice's own independently-minded grandfathers had sprung.

The fact that she was only two generations away from it gave her the idea of crossing the barrier by visiting her own "kin". Martha, the beloved "Dada" of her childhood, came from the home-town of Beatrice's Grandpapa Heyworth, Bacup, in Lancashire, and agreed to take Beatrice with her on her next visit. (On this visit Beatrice learned for the first time that Martha was also one of her kin.) At first Martha demurred that their prospective hosts, unaccustomed to "grand folk", would be "flayed" to have one of the Miss Potters visiting them. Beatrice, "jumping up with the delightful consciousness of an original idea", suggested that she should pretend to be a simple Welsh farmer's daughter, "Miss Jones", which would add a romantic note to the whole scheme. (Heroines of Victorian fiction were much given to disguising themselves as humble nobodies when they were really great ladies.)

Bacup had a sentimental appeal for her in any case because it had always been the background of stories of the old days of the family, told by Martha to the Potter children. Their mother had been taken there, as the little lady, the first daughter of the Heyworth new fortune, to visit her humble (but alarmingly authoritative) grandmother, and, awe-struck, had watched the old woman "sitting bolt upright in her wooden stays in her straight-backed chair, giving sage advice to her four sons; or kneeling by her bed in the midnight hours praying to her God . . . in the dim light of the moon or coming dawn".

But none of the grand Miss Potters, born into comfortable wealth, had ever gone back to look at that other world, with its background of mills and chapels and weavers' cottages and dirty lanes, from which the foundation of their maternal grandfather's fortune had come, until Beatrice went in search of "my first chance of personal intimacy, on terms of social equality, with a wage-earning family".[7]

"It was a wet November evening 1883 when Mrs Mills and Miss Jones picked their way along the irregularly paved and badly lighted back-streets of Bacup," she wrote, dramatically. "The place seemed deserted. There was that curious stillness in the air which overtakes a purely manufacturing town when the mills with their noise and their lights are closed—the mill-hands with their free loud voices are 'cleaning up' or enjoying 'Biffin' by their own fireside . . . the small river Irwell splashed as merrily as it could, considering its free mountain descent, over bits of broken crockery, old boots and pieces of worn-out machinery." Martha's and Beatrice's hosts—"a regular old Puritan and his daughter a mill-hand"—welcomed them warmly and impressed Beatrice by immediately offering up prayers for their safety and spiritual well-being while under his roof. Everything was delightful, "the delicious tea and home-made bread and butter", and the friendly natives who dropped in afterwards and who "all showed themselves anxious to lighten my ignorance on things material and spiritual".[8] It was entirely characteristic of Beatrice that after seeing the most splendid and the most picturesque cities of Europe and America without being moved by them personally she should lose her heart to this drab industrial small-town, set in an uninteresting part of the manufacturing north of England. To her, places only mattered as a background for people, and were remembered by her for the subjective experiences she had in them. Here, she found herself welcomed and admired, as she had been below-stairs when she was a forlorn child growing up at Standish. To the "company" who came in to meet "Miss Jones", the wit which had earned her the reputation of being alarmingly satirical in London society was merely the acceptable tartness of a smart young woman who was "interesting-like to talk wi' ",—as she wrote happily to her father. The old men, she told him, admired her "white teeth and glistening 'air", and said that if all Welsh lasses were as good-looking they would visit Wales themselves, and the old women, who "took a bit of backy", teased her about her cigarettes. "It is curious how completely at home I feel with these people," she mused, and added smugly, "It would be as well if politicians would live amongst the various classes they legislate for and find out what are their wishes and ideas."[9]

She liked the kindliness of their home life. Unlike her own family circle, with its upper-class habit of brutal frankness, these people were soothingly considerate, sparing each other's weaknesses and leaving unkind truths unspoken. She was impressed by "the depth and realism of their religious faith" and by the fact that the chapels were self-governing communities, regulating not only chapel matters but the private lives of their members. She began to comprehend that "these dissenting organisations" were in process of educating the rising working-class in democratic self-government and that she was seeing a new political movement in embryo. "That part of the Englishman's nature which has found gratification in religion is now drifting into political life." But she was still too embedded in the convictions of her own class to acknowledge that the Nonconformist conscience was moving, inevitably, towards Socialism. Instead, she speculated hopefully as to whether the entrance of the "earnest, successful working man" into local government might perhaps be "one of the best preventives against the socialistic tendency of the coming democracy".[10]

Beatrice took home with her from this expedition some new pieces of knowledge which influenced the whole course of her subsequent life. She had visited the cotton-mills with her newly-found relatives and acquired a new respect for the Factory Acts, which led her to the inevitable conclusion that "*laissez-faire* breaks down when one watches these things from inside", and thus to throwing over Herbert Spencer's most cherished belief in the wickedness of government interference, once and for all. She had discovered the reason and nature of the "Co-op shop" by coaxing the local manager into explaining the system to her and letting her see the books. ("I told him I had been sent by my father to inquire into the management of the Co-ops as you wanted to start one," she wrote gaily to Richard Potter.) Above all, she had been touched and warmed by finding that she was accepted, both by her poor relations (to whom she eventually disclosed her real identity) and by the community as a whole, not because she was "one of the fashionable Miss Potters who live in grand houses and marry enormously wealthy men", but for herself, as "a right useful sort of body as would be a comfort to my father", and "the sort of woman they can talk straight away with". Whenever she spoke about them afterwards, she referred to the Bacup people as "my dear old friends with their kindly simplicity", "my gentle cousins", "higher working-class life —with all its charm of direct thinking, honest work and warm feeling".

In later life, Beatrice chose to claim that her "socialist evolution" had been a series of entirely rational stages, from one reasoned conviction about politics to another. In fact, like anyone else, she first chose which side she would belong to on a personal and emotional basis and the reasons came later. She had no burning sense of injustice (at least not about other people) and she was unsentimental about the poor to the point of callousness. But she did respect solid working-class people and minded a great deal that they found her likeable. Among them she had a unique position, accepted as an equal and yet with special privileges. It suited her to be a welcomed alien—a kind of naturalised citizen—in their circles and a nonconformer in her own, and to the end of her life she enjoyed the piquant contrast between her upper-class background and her working-class affiliations; the grand Miss Potter assuming the identity of Miss Jones in order to cross the barrier between Disraeli's "two nations".

When Kate married, Beatrice switched her charitable efforts to Octavia Hill's housing reform project, which was to buy up what would now be called Rachmanite property and improve and repair it on condition that the tenants also mended their ways and became thrifty and law-abiding. Whitechapel at that time was a centre of enlightened upper-middle-class effort to improve the lives of its slum-dwellers. Canon Barnett reported that Kate had brought in her wake "hosts of friends ... not the 'goody' sort but people holding the world's plums of wealth, high social position and posts of national responsibility". Kate also brought her sister, "Miss Beatrice, so strong in mind, graceful in limb and noble in feature, yet fearlessly, in her search for facts, working in sweating-shops and living as a lone girl in block dwellings".[11] Kate was married, to Leonard Courtney, at the Canon's church and had a wedding-breakfast at which "the coster sat side by side with the member of Parliament and the overworked mother ... talked and listened to 'the quality' who had handed her to her seat", and Beatrice took over Kate's job as rent-collector.

The rent-collector was an important part of Octavia Hill's scheme. Canon Barnett summed up her work among the tenants as "not only a rent-collector but a friend to help by wise counsel before the time of need and with sympathy for them as creatures capable of the fullest life", which was his own view of his unhopeful parishioners. Octavia Hill used to lament that she could not get the kind of authoritative young woman she needed ("I do not yet see in most of our courts ... a powerful rule and will at work among them"), so it must have seemed a direct answer to prayer when she was joined by the Potter sisters. Beatrice, soon after her arrival, was assigned to look after a new block, Katharine Buildings, near the docks. It had been designed by Octavia in firmly utilitarian mood—five tiers of apartments, with open galleries, each gallery with a set of water-closets (sluiced every three hours) and the whole distempered in dull red—"unpleasantly reminiscent of a butcher's shop," commented Beatrice distastefully. All social life, including courting operations, centred round the lavatories, and the tenants were selected from the residue of a slum-clearance site in the neighbourhood. Her first duty was to select them; and after that to see that they behaved themselves and paid their rent regularly and to evict them otherwise.

At first she found it so exhausting that when she got back to Kensington in the evening, she had to go straight to bed. At times the "collective brutality, heaped up together in infectious contact; adding to each other's dirt, physical and moral", depressed her unbearably. Physically, she was absolutely fearless, indifferent to the danger of footpads, wandering drunks, and threats of violence from the Irish navvies and part-time criminals among her tenants, whom she had to keep in order. In fact, after a stormy scene, she would reproach herself for being too domineering and resolve to cultivate "more patient gentleness in manner".

After the first few months of dogged endurance, her natural vitality began to revive. Her first-hand experience of real life in the slums gave her a new status at fashionable dinner-tables. She had an ironical turn of phrase; she was amusing about it all. A "dancing idiot" offered to come down to Whitechapel and help with the boys' club there, and a dashing major of the Black Watch, quartered at the barracks next door to York House, tried vainly to grasp the whole incomprehensible business of up-to-date philanthropy because he was so impressed by Beatrice's conversation. His idea of sending a group of kilted Highlanders to march round the York House garden playing their bagpipes, to divert a party of East End children whom Beatrice was entertaining was an unqualified success. But his insistence on "being initiated into the mysteries of rent-collecting" was over-ambitious. He went down to Katharine Buildings and observed that the tenants' problem was that they were apt to owe more back-rent than they had any hope of repaying, before meeting the current demand. The practical soldier instantly found a solution, by offering to pay their arrears out of his own pocket. The incident amused Beatrice, but scandalised the tenants who knew by now that indiscriminate charity was the worst thing in the world for their moral welfare.

The long-term result of Beatrice's experience as a social worker was to drive her, inevitably, in the direction of socialism, because none of the charitable projects touched the real problem of more progress bringing more poverty. In working for the Charity Organisation Society, she learned that whatever the answer might be, it was not to be found in urging the poor to pull themselves up by their own bootstraps. And from her job as a rent-collector she learned that it was not enough to gather together the flotsam and jetsam of slum-clearance and house them in sanitary surroundings in the hope of transforming them into god-fearing and thrifty workers, because in order to be that you first needed a job which would bring in a living wage. Most of her tenants failed to qualify for this condition, and even those who were usually in work were beginning to be affected by the growing shadow of unemployment in the docks, which was to culminate in the great dock strike of 1889. Canon Barnett and his wife agreed with her that begging the poor to reform was not enough, but they believed that the transformation could only come from within, and put great faith in "raising the desires of men and women—to cultivate their higher tastes; to give the poor the luxuries and not the necessaries of life".[12] Beatrice enjoyed the discussions in the Barnetts' self-consciously artistic drawing-room (because "Whitechapel needs lovely colours"), and Henrietta Barnett restored her morale, at a time when she was trying to resign herself to permanent spinsterhood, by declaring roundly that the common opinion that a woman was a nonentity unless joined to a man was "blasphemy". Beatrice added approvingly, in her diary, "It will be needful for women with strong natures to remain celibate, so that the special force of womanhood —motherly feeling—may be forced into public work." She began to build castles-in-the-air about a new "ruling caste" of single women in public life, those "to whom a matrimonial career is shut and who seek a masculine reward for masculine qualities" and who would "give up their lives to the management of men". She found another potential recruit to this female Samurai in Emma Cons, who was, like herself, an apostate from the Charity Organisation Society and had turned a down-at-heel music-hall on the wrong side of the Thames into a cheerful, orderly place of jolly entertainment for the poor (which subsequently became famous as the "Old Vic" and is now the National Theatre). But all the same, Beatrice gradually became convinced that all the efforts of enlightened philanthropists, including Octavia Hill and the Barnetts, could do no more than scratch the surface of the fundamental obstacle, which was that "it is the poverty of the poor that, in a quite literal sense, is their destruction".

The Barnetts themselves came round to that point of view in time and "sent a thrill through the philanthropic world of London" by breaking away from the Charity Organisation Society, whose theories they had once supported. They still believed that indiscriminate charity was wrong, but their alternative scheme—of municipal welfare on a scale never visualised before—was startling.

I do not want much, (said Canon Barnett). I should like the best things made free ... baths and wash-houses, specially swimming-baths ... books and pictures should be freely shown so that every man may have a public library or a picture-gallery as his drawing-room ... more open spaces.... Poverty cannot pay for the pleasure which satisfies and yet, without the pleasure the people perish.[13]

When he went so far as to suggest old age pensions for all, the secretary of the Charity Organisation Society, horrified, accused him of "favouring outdoor relief in a new guise and depreciating thrift".

When Beatrice had to absent herself from Whitechapel in order to look after her sick father, she was flicked into irritable interest by reading in the papers that some misguided philanthropists proposed to start some relief work in the district around St Katharine's Dock. She knew by now that announcing a hand-out for the unemployed, in a single district, simply resulted in a flood of other unemployed making a bee-line for it, and she wrote a letter to that effect to the *Pall Mall Gazette*, which was a platform at that time for the discussion of social problems. On St Valentine's Day she was enchanted to get a letter—"not a love-letter, dear reader", she wrote jubilantly in her diary, but a prosaic communication from the editor saying he would like to print it with her signature above it. This article, "A Lady's View of the Unemployed", not only impressed Joseph Chamberlain, but led to her association with Charles Booth in his great inquiry into "The Life and Labour of the People of London".

She knew about the project, because Charles Booth was her cousin-by-marriage and she had known him and his wife since they came to stay at Standish long ago. Charles, whom she later described as "The most perfect embodiment of ... the mid-Victorian time-spirit", was a Liverpool ship-owner, caught up in the intellectual ferment of his day. Like Richard Potter, his first loyalty was to business, but, unlike Richard, he was tormented by the mid-Victorian sense of guilt about the poverty of the poor and the hypocrisy of the rich who countenanced it. He broke away from his Unitarian upbringing and became a Positivist because this seemed to him the only religion offering a morality which dove-tailed with the discoveries of science. He believed that the social system could only be reformed by applying "the scientific method", and was angrily impatient of "the patronising philanthropy of Lady Christian Charity and the Reverend Ebenezer Fanatic".

Booth's great London inquiry was first sparked off by his reading a piece of Socialist propaganda on the same subject. There was a vogue at this time for writing pamphlets about the state of the poor, such as *The Bitter Cry of Outcast London, Squalid Liverpool* and *The Maiden Tribute of Modern Babylon*. They tended to have a regular formula, to be the account of what a middle-class explorer had seen for himself by going to live in the urban working-class jungle, disguised, so to speak, as a native. (Booth himself had made a foray of this kind.) In deference to "the scientific method", it was fashionable to sprinkle in a few figures about the extent of poverty or vice or whatever it was. The Social Democratic Federation, under Hyndman, got out a pamphlet of their own with the (perhaps rather loaded) object of discovering "how large a proportion of wage-earners were receiving payment insufficient to keep themselves in proper physical health for the work they had to do". According to Hyndman's calculations it was 25 per cent. To Booth, who was anti-Socialist, this seemed to be "sensationalism of the cheapest and most reprehensible order on the part of the Socialist movement", and he called on Hyndman to say so. He offered to disprove the figure at his own expense, launched on a survey of the London poor and invited his cousin Beatrice to help him.

The lives of the poor, Charles Booth explained to her, "lay hidden behind a curtain on which were painted terrible pictures; starving children, suffering women, overworked men; horrors of drunkenness and vice, monsters and demons of inhumanity; giants of disease and despair."[14] His plan for drawing back the curtain was to classify a given section of London into groups: Misery, Poverty, Decent Comfort, and Luxury. A team of interviewers were to go round collecting descriptive information. This classification of a mass of material was his great contribution to social research, and all the Gallup polls and market surveys of today are a direct inheritance from it. He sifted and cross-verified the evidence as it came in, to make a sample of the whole, and eventually, to Beatrice's awed admiration, drew the whole thing up in map form so that you could see at a glance the exact location of misery, poverty, comfort and luxury distributed over the metropolis.

(The Inquiry's original aim, of refuting Hyndman's overstatement was not an unqualified success. It turned out that his estimate of 25 per cent living below the poverty-line was too modest. 30 per cent was the correct figure. Shelley's description of Hell as "a city much like London" was, as the Fabian William Clarke said, unfair to hell.)

Beatrice found that her habit of including descriptions of people and scenes in her private diary was now beginning to bear fruit. Her thumbnail descriptions of dockers and their daily life were exactly the kind of thing Cousin Charlie wanted. She and Charlie became very fond of each other through the work, but it was, she added hastily, "a close intimate relationship between a man and a woman without sentiment (perhaps not without sentiment but without passion or the dawning of passion)."

The next time she had to give up her own work to look after her father, she filled in the months in the country by writing an article on "Dock Life in the East End of London", which was published in the distinguished monthly, *Nineteenth Century*. When she went back to London she was asked to attend a meeting of dock labourers. She found that her appearance had been advertised before-hand, and "as I made my way up to the platform enjoyed my first experience of being cheered as a public character". She was escorted home by the chief speaker, a newly-rich, left-wing philanthropist, who asked her to have supper with him and also to be his mistress, both of which she declined.

"Settled with Charlie on the autumn's work," noted Beatrice briskly. "The Sweating System is to be the subject of my next paper. I have it in mind to make it more of a picture than the article on Dock Labour, to dramatise it." She thought this plan over. "I cannot get this picture without living among the actual workers. This I think I can do."[15]

Now it was her turn for the fashionable Haroun Al Raschid game, to move, in disguise, among the natives of sub-civilised London. "If you want to conceal yourself, you must be yourself," was Booth's theory, but Beatrice, after her success as "Miss Jones" at Bacup, scorned such poor-spirited advice. She put on a short, bedraggled skirt, boots with buttons missing, an ill-fitting coat and a tumbled black bonnet over artistically untidy hair. Thus dressed for the part of a typical trouser-hand, she took a tram down the Mile End Road in search of a typical "sweat-shop".[16]

"Sweating" really meant sub-contracting in the manufacture of cheap goods. A middleman used to distribute work to women in their homes, or employ them to do it in his own, without reference to the regulations of the Factory Acts. Beatrice, after one or two false starts, descended into a basement containing a "lowgrade Jewish shop", and asked (in a stage Cockney accent) for a job "finishing" trousers.

In later years she must have described this adventure to Bernard Shaw, since a scene in his play *The Millionairess* is clearly taken from Beatrice's own exact account of the dialogue she had with her "employers". The "millionairess"—like many of Shaw's heroines—has Beatrice's habit of reducing a man to meek submission by her brisk third-degree methods. ("Let me see what you make here. Tell me how you dispose of it.") Beatrice herself wrote a bowdlerised account of her experience—"sufficiently expurgated to be suited for a female pen". (Since much of the work-girls' conversation consisted of teasing each other about having babies by their own fathers and brothers, this was not unduly prudish of her, in 1888.)

By now, Booth's survey was attracting public attention, and when a Lords' committee was appointed to inquire into "sweated industries", Beatrice was called upon to give evidence. She was riding high by this time and not only gave the Lords a graphic account of her experiences, but the benefit of her views about sweating in general. She had begun to realise that it was not a question of a few grasping employers—the "bloated middleman" of Parliamentary speeches and *Punch* cartoons—but due to the capitalist system allowing uncontrolled free competition, and that "sweating" existed in any industry which could escape the regulations of the Factory Act and the Trade Unions. She had a tremendous public success. The papers found it piquant that this good-looking young woman of a wealthy Society family should have boldly masqueraded as a work-girl and should now be listened to, with respectful attention, by a national committee. She became a "lion", much in demand in fashionable drawing-rooms, and her self-confidence blossomed to the point where she could afford to be blasé about it all.

"Society, even now that it is gracious and flattering has no charm for me." "Disagreeable consequences of appearing in public. Descriptions of my appearance and offensive remarks by the *Pall Mall Gazette*. The economic side of the question is an unattractive one and attracts abuse of all kinds from the least scrupulous class of men."

One writer accused her of deliberately "misleading" the Committee about her sweat-shop experience. Unfortunately, Beatrice did have something to hide. "In my hasty answers to the Lords' cross-examination I had exaggerated the number of weeks during which I had thus 'worked' and it was this exaggeration that got widely reported." All her childhood guilt about telling lies came back to her and she had a traumatic sense of waiting for certain exposure. When the proof copy of her evidence arrived for her to sign, she altered the account of what she had said, to cover up the exaggeration. Once she had posted the altered document she was overcome with remorse. "This double sin of saying what was not true and then altering it in what seemed a sly way caused me many sleepless nights."

The *Nineteenth Century* had accepted her article, "Pages from a Work-girl's Diary", but now she began to dread its publication because it would expose "my false step and the inaccuracy of my evidence before the Lords. The fear that this may be dwelt on by my enemies in the Press haunts me." She was staying at the Argoed, with nothing to distract her, and she thought about it night and day, "One of those horrible nights of self-torture". "Tossed about during night, if I sank into a doze woke up in a cold perspiration." "The clouds look as if they were gathering. God help me!" Once she even thought of suicide. "A prey to Mania. The laudanum bottle loomed large as the dominant figure." One afternoon, she went out into the mountains and "prayed for strength to cleave to the Truth, to walk through the valley of humiliation in sight of all men, rather than descend to mean subterfuge to conceal my error", and then wrote to the editor of the *Nineteenth Century* telling him, with scrupulous honesty, that the press reports of her having worked for three weeks during her personal experience of workshops were not true. But she never posted the letter.

And after all, nothing happened, just as nothing had happened when she once lied to Martha and Martha unaccountably let her get away with it. Her "Pages of a Work-girl's Diary" article was published and was an immense success. At parties, people asked to be introduced to her. No-one even mentioned the Lords' committee. At the end of the year she told herself gaily, in her diary:

Well! my dear, if notoriety be desirable as a preliminary step in a literary career, you have achieved it! Enough and to spare of you in the daily papers—why, even a bogus interview with you telegraphed to the United States and to Australia. But how much of that is frothy foam raised by your plunge into an

original adventure? How much the result of the piquant co-
incidence of "a pair of black eyes and a supple figure" with a
turn for laborious statistical research?

"Charlie wants me to do 'Women's Work in the East End' and
have it ready by March," Beatrice reflected shortly after the
"Work-Girl" success. By now she was becoming something of an
authority about women in industry, in her own right, since she had
also written a more serious summary of the tailoring trade. But she
was reluctant to go on in the same channel, because now that she
had tried out her own wings, she did not want to be tied to Charles'
survey indefinitely; and also because she was now at the third stage
of what she afterwards called her evolution as a socialist. Her
stretch in the East End had convinced her first that it was necessary
to control the landlord and the capitalist, in the interests of the
community; and second that it was necessary to ensure a "national
minimum of civilised existence" for every citizen. Now she was
beginning to think that industry would have to be governed, not,
as it always had been, by "the class that gives orders", but by "the
community of consumers, for their common benefit as consumers"
and the best example of that, so far as she could judge, was the
Co-operative movement, which she had seen in action at Bacup.
What she really wanted to do, now, was to make a study of that.

She asked a friend, the distinguished economist Professor Alfred
Marshall, if he thought she was equal to it, but he was severely
discouraging, and irritated her by telling her to stick to subjects
suitable to the female intellect. "The woman must not develop her
faculties in a way unpleasant to the man . . . If you compete with us,
we shan't marry you." This unconscious echo of Chamberlain, coming at this exact moment, stung Beatrice into writing crossly in her
diary, "Still, with the disagreeable masculine characteristic of
persistent and well-defined purpose I shall stick to my own way of
climbing my own little tree. Female labour I may take up some day
or other, but the Co-operative movement comes first."

For the next few months she wandered through the country
getting material for her study, attending Co-operative conferences
and meetings and interviewing individual co-operators. She enjoyed
the hard-headed masculine discussions and being the only woman
present at lunches and dinners. "A higgledy-piggledy dinner; good
material served up coarsely and shovelled down by the partakers

in a way that is not appetising ... but I get a lot of stray information, mostly through chaff and rapid discussion. ... After dinner
... we smoke cigarettes and our conversation becomes more that
of business camaraderie." At first, "to one who had been bred in a
stronghold of capitalism, the Consumers' Co-Operative Movement
seemed a unique romance in the industrial history of the world."
The Christian Socialists believed that it could substitute the spirit of
fellowship for that of competitive selfishness; dreamers like William Morris saw it as a resurrection of the idyllic days of the crafts-
man; even Conservatives thought it promised stability; to the
workman it suggested being his own master, and it had all been
started by eight-and-twenty flannel weavers planning to set up a
self-governing workshop. But as Beatrice studied the current development of the movement she came to the conclusion that self-
governing workshops were impracticable and that although
"democracies of consumers" could be an alternative to profit-
making, the actual workers in a "Co-op" were no better off than
they were anywhere else. This led her eventually to the final stage of
her "evolution as a Socialist". She decided they needed "democracies of workers by hand and brain" to protect them; that is,
Trade Unions.

Meanwhile, although she often argued and disagreed with the
co-operators, she found herself, among them, in a unique position,
an upper-class intellectual in a working-class setting, a still attractive
young woman in a world of tough and hard-headed men. ("Here
is Miss Potter, who is going to study the question and show us the
way out of our difficulty. Come, Miss Potter, leave Mitchell to his
tea, and come and help me to make Dent understand our view of
the question.")

As her self-confidence increased, she decided that she must learn
to speak in public, though it meant conquering her natural nervous-
ness. She went to hear the famous Annie Besant, who had left her
curate husband and her church, fought through the courts for the
custody of her children, been involved in a birth-control scandal with
the atheist Bradlaugh, and become a revolutionary socialist, all in a
blaze of nation-wide publicity. Annie was so romantic that Shaw
later immortalised her in *Arms and the Man*, and so moving an
orator that St John Ervine said that the flaming fire of her eloquence
"must consume every man and woman who listened to her". But it
did not strike so much as a spark off Beatrice. "That woman with

her blighted wifehood and motherhood and her thirst for power and defiance of the world," she wrote severely. "To *see* her speaking made me shudder. It is not womanly to thrust yourself before the world." In the same way Beatrice saw clearly that although it was right for her to have a "masculine intellect", it was definitely wrong for other women to try to "ape men and take up men's pursuits". When she was approached by the best-selling novelist, Mrs Humphrey Ward, and asked to add her signature to an anti-women's suffrage manifesto, Beatrice agreed and excused herself afterwards by saying that it was a reaction against her father's over-valuation of the female sex, and also because suffragists were so narrow in outlook. (To prove it, she complained that an American one who asked her to lunch had not even offered her a cigarette.)

Years later, Beatrice publicly recanted her anti-suffrage statement and admitted candidly that she had been anti-feminist simply because the fewer women there were in her field, the higher her rarity value. But with the Potter lack of perception about other people's feelings, she did not realise, at this time, that other women would resent her assumption that what was good enough for them was not good enough for her. At the Co-operative Annual Congress, one of the men co-operators asked bluntly why Miss Potter had lent her influence to the anti-suffragists and answered his own question, "I believe it is just this; she is satisfied with her own position because she is rich and strong; she does not see that other women need the power to help themselves which would be given by the vote." Beatrice made a clumsy effort to laugh it off by saying that she herself was "a woman who is the personification of emancipation in all ways; who clings to her cigarette if she does not clutch at her vote". But the men's smiles were reluctant and she knew she had not impressed them. She spent the rest of the evening in the smoking-room, joining in the "chaff" and offering to tell their fortunes from their hands, in an effort to recover her position. But she noticed that the other "exceptional women" who were also attending the congress, "glorified spinsters like myself", were deliberately cold-shouldering her. Wonderingly, she discovered that she minded about this a great deal—"even in a company of men".

Sidney
1889–1892

"WE CANNOT KINDLE when we will the fire that in our hearts resides." This quotation from her childhood hero Matthew Arnold was the only entry in Beatrice's diary for January 1, 1889. She gave no indication whether it was a lament for what was past or an intuitive hope for what might come. She was thirty-one, still beautiful, wealthy and now a celebrity. Her knowledge of the rich, her recent study of the poor, her disappointment in love and her failure to find God had combined to increase her desire to reform the world.

She had moved with her father, who was now bedridden, to Box House, close to Arthur and Mary Playne in Gloucestershire. There she was—characteristically—employing her spare moments in mastering the technical and commercial details of the Longfords cloth mills. She was growing weary of being tied to an invalid and had come to a standstill in her writing. She felt cut off from the outside world and longed to be in London where "strikes were the order of the day", with her cousin Maggie Harkness and Tom Mann, Tillett and Burns, the strikers' leaders, who were in the thick of it all.

She was halfway through writing a paper on the Lords' Report and unable to get any further when a slim volume with a disarming green cover, called *Fabian Essays*, came to her notice. The contributors were a group of young men of whom she had scarcely heard: Bernard Shaw—the editor—, Sydney Olivier, Graham Wallas, William Clarke, Hubert Bland, one woman—Annie Besant—, and Sidney Webb. "By far the most interesting essay is that by Sidney Webb: he has the historic sense," Beatrice wrote to a friend. Curiously enough, Sidney Webb himself, a month or two earlier in a review of the first volume of Charles Booth's *Life and Labour in London*, had written, "The only contributor with any literary talent is Miss Beatrice Potter." The group of able young men were "aspiring towards a socialist community in which there will be individual freedom and public property, instead of class slavery and private possession of the means of subsistence". They were "leading Socialism" and "manipulating the radicals". This was where Beatrice felt she belonged, among young leaders and manipulators of society; and socialism was the kind of creed she was looking for. Despite her recent experience she was also looking for a husband. She lost no time in making their acquaintance and invited the young Fabians in turn to visit her at Box House, receiving the following reply from one of them:—

My dear Miss Potter,

This is the most unreasonable thing I ever heard.... You may reduce the rest of the Fabians to slavery—but if I am to go through my amusing conversational performances for you, *you* must come up to town; this lion is untameable.... To think that I should have lived to be so misled—to be inspected by daylight by a fastidious young lady in search of an eligible socialist society to join!....

Yours sincerely, G.B. Shaw.[1]

In February, a few months after the great London dock strike, there occurred the first meeting between the future authors of the *History of Trade Unionism*. They were introduced by Maggie Harkness in her rooms near the British Museum. Beatrice invited Mr Webb to dine and meet her close friends the Booths. There is no record of the conversation during dinner, nor what, at the time, the Booths thought of him, but Beatrice was not impressed by the appearance of her future husband. He was twenty-eight. His huge head was covered with black hair. He had a large nose, protruding lips, and eyes bulging behind thick-lensed pince-nez. He wore a goatee beard. His clothes were not very clean, his manner inelegant and he dropped his aitches, and his complacency and conceit were "at once repulsive and ludicrous". He struck Beatrice as something between a German professor and a London "card". "His tiny tadpole body," she goes on, "unhealthy skin, lack of manner, cockney pronunciation and poverty were all against him." Yet there was a warmth and directness about the man which she liked.

A less brutal contemporary account of the young socialist by another woman can be found in *Transition*[2], a novel written by the author of *"A superfluous woman"*, herself a member of the Fabian committee. In it Sidney Webb figures as the hero, Paul Sheridan. Paul is against revolution because it defeats its own ends, and believes that the real enemy of Socialism is an anarchist.

> His bearing was ... quiet, modest and retiring. Shyness as an accompaniment of ability and force of character has a charm ... it rather set off than obliterated the strong lines of his head and jaw ... He had a smile of inimitable sweetness ... He had passed every examination and competed for and won whatever prizes were open to general competition .... No one ever had his nose less in the air.... A fact was his delight... "Your truest poetry is found in statistics", he insisted. "I am simply engrossed in working out that matter of gas and water."

A beautiful schoolmistress, Honoria, condescendingly argues, " 'If everything were equally divided today, tomorrow there would be rich and poor again.' The grave timidity of the eyes looking into her own changed instantly to amusement: 'It would be rather difficult to divide some things equally wouldn't it? Main drains for instance,' " the hero replies.

From now on Beatrice thought and talked of nothing but socialism, defiantly telling her friends the Booths that what she meant by it was not merely making conditions better for the majority, but what Sidney Webb and Karl Marx meant by socialism—the transference to the state of the means of subsistence. Sidney became a frequent visitor to Box House. He and Beatrice took long walks in the Longfords' beechwoods, talking as they went, and she began to perceive that a companion had materialised in her life who could show her how the conflicting needs of her nature could be satisfied by socialism and its dream of a kingdom of Heaven on earth. Now, she could claim, "At last I am a socialist."

There is little information from which to reconstruct Sidney Webb's early life. He was always extremely reticent about himself ("No personalities please," he told his biographer, Mary Agnes Hamilton), and the nearest he ever came to describing his youth was in a letter to his fellow-Fabian, Sydney Olivier, when on a walking tour in 1885. "I don't think I ever told you about my boyhood," he wrote. "But we were always in the thick of the fight, and I feel now that the great influence I have missed is this peace which I have never known."[3]

From the reminiscences he and Beatrice wrote in *St Martin's Review* in 1929, we learn that he and his brother and sister were brought up in the heart of London, in Cranbourn Street off Leicester Square; that his mother told him on the steps of St Martin's that he might one day aspire to be Lord Mayor of London; that he and his brothers were sent to Germany to be educated by a Lutheran pastor until the age of sixteen, when it became necessary (for unspecified reasons) for him to come home and earn a living; and that, as a boy, he found Kelly's Directory more fascinating than any other book, and the press notices so absorbing that it took him an hour to walk the length of Fleet Street. His father was a disciple of Mill and a hairdresser. (Beatrice described him as a shop-keeper and Shaw said he was a tax-collector.) Later he turned to accountancy, but whether this odd change in his profession can be explained by his connection with the turf—his nephew was twice the winner of the Derby—is not known. He died leaving £5,000 and a pleasant house in Park Village East in which Sidney was living, with his mother and sister and a German woman who helped in the house, when Beatrice first met him.

Sidney is said to have been able to read and memorise accurately a whole page at a glance. With his interest in miscellaneous information and ability to keep everything in his head, he was a champion examinee, and passed easily into the first division of the civil service where he worked as a clerk in the Colonial Office. But he had other aspirations. "Don't be like me," he wrote to Graham Wallas, "wanting at each step to see my whole life in advance. This has landed me in the *Impasse du Bureau des Colonies* instead of on the *Avenue direct à mon désire*."[4] He was, like his father, a disciple of Mill—Shaw called him a "ready-made socialist"—and had reached the conclusion before ever having read Karl Marx that his "*désire*" was State enterprise and ownership (a very good alternative to capitalism he considered), and that his private interests, therefore, conflicted with those of a civil servant. He joined the Fabian Society in 1885, and earned a little extra money as a journalist on the *Star*, but it was ten years before he was able to leave the service and devote his entire energies to Socialism.

His two great friends were Graham Wallas, a master at Highgate Grammar School whom Beatrice already knew, and Bernard Shaw. The three of them were known as the three musketeers of the Fabian Society. He had met Shaw at a debating society which both

of them had joined in order to practise public speaking. Sidney had
very quickly become a brilliant speaker drawing on his vast store of
information with precision and effect. Shaw, in the belief that Sidney
Webb knew everything and was the ablest man in England, made a
point of getting to know him straight away, and Sidney tried to
teach him German in order that they might read together *Das
Kapital* in the original, but the enterprise was a failure because
Shaw got no further than the German for "and" and "the only"
But they remained good friends and spent their holidays together on
walking tours of which Sidney was especially fond. He was chiefly
interested in recording the exact distance between one point and
another. They bicycled and fell in love indiscriminately on the
continent and in England. Sidney was particularly "susceptible"
and came out in spots, as Shaw observed, whenever he was smitten.
He had considered matrimony at least twice before he met Beatrice.
One of the young ladies married another. The second, Ilse, who
lived in Brussels, was as Sidney explained in a letter to Graham
Wallas,—"apart from this inexplicable emotion which bloweth
where it listeth beyond ken or reason", not reasonable enough . . .
"It is interesting to note how man is still an irrational animal,"
Sidney added. "How little influence the intellect has compared with
that exercised by the emotions!"[5] Even after he had met Beatrice,
he reported from Rochdale to his friend. "Beatrice spoke excellently
well last night. Mrs Carr is here, by the way, looking ethereally
pretty—Carr is absent."[6] On one occasion he wrote a sonnet:

Our years are beads blown by uncertain fate
At birth strung on the narrow film of time:
Unhappy good despair and evil crime;
Love, passion, grief, unfathomable hate:
Each bead is coloured by the chequered state
As youth's gay show or sunset's winter time,
Till death with pallid smile and calm sublime,
Does burst the film alike for small and great.
O happy they who tell their beadlets right,
Dropping like gold into the silent sea,
Fate's colours change beneath the burning glow,
Transfused, what e'er their hue in that bright light,
Which spreads from lives of those who ever know
Their deeds live on in all eternity.[7]

This romanticism had little chance of flourishing in what he described to Graham Wallas as "the self-devouring activity which consumes my life." When he told Beatrice his life-story he said he had done everything he set out to do. "Take care Mr Webb," Beatrice warned him. "Don't be too complacent about small successes." She wrote in her diary that he was "a monstrosity to be justified only by success, and above all a loop-hole into the Socialist party. One of the small body of men with whom I may sooner or later throw in my lot."

Once again Sidney had fallen in love. "Too beautiful, too rich and too clever," he said despairingly to a friend. It is not to be supposed that the proud and celebrated Beatrice Potter made it easy for her little suitor to woo her, for all his prodigious ability. Often she reduced him to a "pulp" (his own word) and then, before he had time to recover his wits, imposed on him her own opinions, or made him feel horribly insignificant by her arrogance. Sidney patiently persevered with his courtship. In May, when Beatrice attended a Trade Union Congress in Glasgow, Sidney was at her side, much to the surprise of the Trade Union Leaders, who were at her feet. Walking through the streets of Glasgow in the setting sun, the two Socialists shook hands over a pact to work together for the cause of humanity, Beatrice insisting on a clause that Sidney should promise not to dwell on the "purely personal" side of their friendship.

After this, Beatrice left Sidney to carry out his part of the agreement and went off on one last trip to the continent before settling down to fulfil her own. She stopped at Cologne Cathedral, where she prayed to overcome her vanity and selfishness, and to be made pure enough for the "man's soul now in her keeping", and to be worthy of the worship he was giving, through her, to womanhood. Then she proceeded with her friend to Oberammergau to see the Passion Play. On their way the young women invited a "blue-eyed" and then a "brown-eyed" fellow traveller to join them. They stayed with them at "wayside inns, paddled in streams, slept in the shade and laughed in the sun". Her comment on the Passion Play shows the influence of her new creed: "A great original conception. The revolt of the workers... against the aristocratic class.... Ends by a socialist sacrificing his life to the interest of the community."

While Beatrice was abroad, Sidney was working for the Cause by urging the kind of municipal reforms in London that had already been carried out in several towns in England—and which were associated with Birmingham and the name of Joseph Chamberlain. His booklet, *The London Programme*, bore such a strong resemblance to Chamberlain's *Unauthorised Programme* that W. E. Stead in the *Pall Mall Gazette* hailed Sidney as the "Chamberlain of Socialism", a fact noted by Beatrice with a good deal of interest. Although the immediate objectives of the two were similar, Chamberlain was a Liberal and Sidney a Socialist and they were working for fundamentally different ends. But there were similarities. Sidney followed his rival in politics as he had done in love. He too became Minister to the Board of Trade and the head of the Colonial Office.

When Beatrice's frivolous interlude abroad was over, she returned to Sidney and to work on her new book, the *Co-operative Movement*. She and Sidney went everywhere together. They spent one July afternoon in Epping Forest, discussing religious socialism, and Sidney read the poems of Keats and Rossetti as they lay under the trees. Afterwards, Beatrice relaxed the rules of their pact and permitted him to "think of her personally" when (and only when) he had not enough energy to think of work. They travelled north together when Sidney was invited to address the British Association in Leeds, and back again, with a tipsy variety artiste who gave them a lively account of her life in tights, and offered to engage Sidney as a performer in her troupe. There was a good deal of laughter, but on their next journey they travelled first class and Sidney read "John Ball's Dream" to Beatrice.

Sidney was finding it increasingly difficult not to infringe the terms of their pact, and began to assume the privileges of a lover. This, coupled with the fact that the Booths had practically dropped her on account of the friendship with Sidney, made Beatrice decide to break it up. Sidney took it well, though he insisted that they could never now be strangers, and sent despondent letters to Box House, where she was working on her book and receiving a procession of "interesting men", journalists and socialists. Among them was Graham Wallas, "one of the knot of Fabians who would run the world", and also Sidney's great friend, which made Sidney angry and jealous.

Haldane, now an M.P., was another constant visitor, and one Sunday in December he came down with two particular objectives. One was a proposal for a Radical-Socialist alliance. The other was an *"arrière-pensée* of a suitable wife". Haldane, Beatrice and

Wallas discussed the possibility of a radical-socialist programe for seven hours, and Beatrice and Haldane devoted three to that of possible matrimony. Beatrice refused him, adding that she looked upon marriage as an alternative to suicide and that she "could not contemplate an act of *felo de se* for a speculation in personal happiness". She assured Haldane that she was not capable of love, and that such passion as she had in her was for another man who was now married. (Why else—she wondered—had she "watched for hours at the entrance of the South Kensington Museum, for two days," unless in the hope of seeing him?)

Beatrice was now surrounded by men who, if they were not all in love with her, certainly found her distinctly attractive, and with all of whom she had long and intimate talks. At the same time she was receiving anguished letters from her pining Fabian and she was also making successful progress with her first book. It all combined to provoke in her a boisterous vanity (her self-confessed besetting sin) which would have been inexcusable if it had not been ridiculous. "Men may come and men may go but I go on for ever," she wrote on her thirty-third birthday.

For six months, Sidney went on sending her his miserable jealous letters and Beatrice continued to keep him at arm's length, and it was not until the summer of 1891 that they met again. In June, on the eve of the publication of her first book, Sidney's patience was at last rewarded, and they set off on a cruise of the Norwegian Fjords together with Graham Wallas and a young lady named Clara Bigden. Sidney, by this time in a weakened and subdued state, was eager to submit, like Beatrice's dog Don, "in perfect obedience to the beloved will". In the dispassionate light of the arctic summer, their two minds mingled and became as it were eleven, according to the calculation which Sidney had worked out when urging his suit —"one and one make not two but eleven," he had explained, which was the first specious argument on which was built the edifice of their subsequent life and work together. Hand in hand over the tundra went the two socialists, drawn to one another by their common wish to serve the weal of all, plighting their troth in what must be one of the oddest love scenes ever enacted. Beatrice records the following dialogue. "I think it is time that you deliberately planned what you intend to be." Sidney replied passionately that his heart's desire was to play a part in the government of the country after replacing capitalism by a socialist administration of his own devising.

"Quite so," answered Beatrice. "That is exactly my view of what you want to be. In order to become a first-rate administrator you want more education in the technique of administration, and in order to think over social problems you want technical knowledge of those very problems. The London County Council will help you to the one—helping me will help you to the other." The doubting Fabian hesitated. "But what I am undecided about is whether you are not. . . . too ambitious for me, whether you are not expecting too much of me?" "No," Beatrice assured him, "I don't expect anything . . . from you. I don't know . . . whether the opportunity will offer itself for you to become a really big man . . . but it is clear your abilities are sufficiently good to enable you to do first rate work on the London County Council." Thus Sidney and Beatrice became engaged to one another.

Beatrice was not in love, and even, to begin with, had misgivings about the wisdom of giving up her dazzling position in order to marry a man with so little to recommend him. "On the face of it," it seemed to her, "an extraordinary end for the once brilliant Miss Potter. . . . to marry an ugly little man with no social position and less means . . . and I am not in love with him, not as I was." Moreover, Sidney was not at all the kind of son-in-law her father had had in mind for his "little Bee", when he had murmured, "I want one more son-in-law. A woman is happier married. I should like to see my little Bee married to a good strong fellow." But she was drawn into the engagement by their common wish to serve the masses and in gratitude for Sidney's persevering worship. They did not tell her father, to whom the news would have been a death-blow, about their engagement. In order to keep their secret, there was always a more acceptably eligible bachelor, in the form of either Haldane or Graham Wallas, invited to Box House with Sidney. Under their cover he courted Beatrice. But in London or elsewhere they ignored convention and stayed quite openly together in hotels, making no attempt to hide their relationship from their friends.

Soon after their return from Norway, Beatrice established herself in Herbert Spencer's house, in the leafy suburb of St John's Wood. Here, night after night, she entertained Sidney and their Trade Union friends, filling the absent bachelor's room with tobacco smoke and whisky fumes, both of which he particularly disliked. When Sidney and Beatrice were alone, they planned for the coming socialism—with "intervals for human nature"—under the portrait of its most bitter opponent and her oldest friend. Each day, the association into which she had entered so dispassionately became a source of deeper happiness. They settled how they were going to help each other. Sidney—with his computer-like ability to reduce vast quantities of information to a clear, precise statement of facts— would help her with her writing, and she, with her money and influence, would enable him to leave the civil service and realise his political ambition. His first assignment would be to assist with the Trade Union book she intended to write next, and to relieve her of the mental drudgery she had found so tedious over the Co-operative one. She pointed out that in any case the enquiry into Trades Unionism would be invaluable to Sidney, from the point of view of his future political career. It would not only give him an insight into industry and an understanding of economics otherwise un-available to a London civil servant, but would also help him to make useful personal acquaintances among working-class leaders. "So that in helping me he does not feel, nor am I conscious, that this work is my particular concern . . ." Beatrice explained to herself in her diary. It was, indeed, an idyllic arrangement.

Their engagement, though secret, did not, of course, escape the notice of Beatrice's friends. Most of them, glad to see her happy at last, remained on good terms. Auberon Herbert told them a little reproachfully, "You'll do a great deal of harm and be very happy doing it." But the Booths, her closest friends, refused to meet either Sidney or herself. Beatrice was deeply hurt, and an extra twist to her pain was added when Mary completely ignored her book on the Co-operatives which everyone else had received so enthusiastically. However, she took comfort in the hope that perhaps, when she and Sidney were respectably married, the two Booths would again become her friends.

She had left Sidney for a fortnight's research on documents in Durham when she received the news which was to release them from their furtive engagement and enable them to marry. By a strange chance of fate, she had travelled that day by the same train as had Joseph Chamberlain, who was on his way to speak at Sunderland. Unseen, she watched him walk up the platform with his prettily-dressed wife. As she imagined the life she had missed Beatrice blessed him "for his clear understanding of my deficiencies for the role of 'walking gentlewoman' to the play of 'Chamber-lain' ". When she reached Durham she was called back to Box

House where her father's end was fast approaching. On January 1st, 1892, he passed peacefully away. Immediately Sidney telegraphed that their engagement had been published in the papers.

Her sisters received the news politely—they were getting used to Beatrice's bohemian ways. A family dinner was held in London so that they might meet Sidney; after which they were more distant. Kate wrote: "It would not be sincere to say that we rejoice over it (the engagement) for as Mr S. Webb is unknown to us and as we have different impressions of him, it is impossible not to feel some anxiety that a brilliant young woman and dear sister should be going to link her life entirely to his..."8 From Mary she received the following: "I wish you every happiness with the husband of your choice.... If he thoroughly despises the class to which we belong and the traditions we think have a real value, it is not likely there will be much sympathy between us..."9 Maggie merely disapproved silently, though it is only fair to add that much later, when Sidney had become famous, she was heard to remark, "If I had known what could be made out of Sidney Webb, my attitude would have been different." (One wonders how much of all this disapproval was on account of Sidney's socialism and how much due to his poverty and accent.) Rosy's attitude towards Beatrice's marriage was entirely approving, and she and her husband, who was now tragically dying, were the only ones, Beatrice thought, with whom she and Sidney might become friends.

Before Sidney made an honest socialist of Beatrice one other tie with her past was broken. Herbert Spencer no longer wished her to be his literary executor—a position which she had valued. They met at his club, the Albemarle. "I cannot congratulate you, that would be insincere," he announced. She protested that there was nothing against Mr Webb, and that even her family had come round to him, adding defiantly, "You see he has succeeded in marrying me, Mr Spencer. That shows he has a will." The philosopher was cordial, even affectionate, but firm. He was in a fix, he told her. He could not, for the sake of his reputation, be openly connected with a socialist. What was he to do? Beatrice suggested an alternative executor. The philosopher objected. "He has not the gift like you of making his subject interesting." Beatrice generously put her old friend's mind at rest, by promising to help with the arrangement of the material and to add her own reminiscences. She left Spencer at ease about his reputation and returned to her Fabian; but it was a blow to her pride.

In July, 1892, Beatrice and Sidney were married. "Exit Beatrice Potter—enter Beatrice Webb, or rather Mrs Sidney Webb, for alas I lose both names," Beatrice marked up their wedding in her diary. The Holts, who approved, came down from Liverpool. They dined Sidney and Beatrice at the Euston Hotel where Beatrice was staying the night with them. The next day, Saturday the 23rd, Robert recorded in his Diary:

> About noon a considerable detachment of the family assembled at the St Pancras Vestry to witness the marriage of Beatrice Potter to Sidney James Webb—the ceremony is not impressive but legally it is as binding as if performed (sic) by all the clergy. It was over in ten minutes and we returned to a light lunch at the Euston Hotel under our presidency. The party consisted of our two selves, the bride and bridegroom, best man Graham Wallas—Miss Webb—Mr and Mrs Webb (brother) 2 Courtneys, 2 Alfred Cripps, 2 Chas Booth, Blanche Cripps, Maggie Hobhouse, 2 Dyson Williams (he looking awfully seedy) making 18 of a party.
>
> We had a perfectly cheerful time though there were many criticisms in confidence—the "happy pair" left by 2 o'clock train for Chester and then our party broke up. Beatrice looked remarkably well being for once tidily dressed.[10]

After a "bewildering time at pretty little Chester", they entrained for Glasgow where they delved in municipal cellars for sociological facts, starting out straight away, like Maeterlinck's Mytil and Tytil, with their scientific sociological cage, to capture the bluebird of collective happiness.

9

Young Fabians
1893–1898

"THERE IS NOTHING to tell nowadays. No interesting gloom and light, no piquant relationship. . . . all warm flat midday sunlight— little excitement, no discomfiture," Beatrice wrote, when the honeymoon was over and they had settled down in a furnished flat in Hampstead. "So far as I can tell, our life will be—or rather my life will be—that of a recluse, with Sidney as an opened window into the world. . . . The distance from London and our pre-occupation in work, and strange opinions will combine to isolate us from our class." Sometimes she teased Sidney by telling him that "I miss the exciting relationships with marriageable or marrying men, that I feel 'hemmed in' by matrimony." But "truly am too happy to seek excitement and too satisfied to look for friendship. . . . I doubt more than ever whether I would have been long satisfied with a life in which intellectual effort was not the main . . . part." In the mornings they worked at their book; in the afternoons, Sidney would go to the L.C.C.; and in the evenings they would discuss research with each other—perhaps indulge in a little "browsing over periodicals or light literature", or some of the Fabians might come in to plan the next piece of propaganda.

Beatrice, who had seen Sidney as a man without intimate relationships in his life, had perhaps not realised what a close and dedicated circle the Fabians were. They thought nothing of walking the seven miles to Hampstead and back since neither the old horse-trams nor the new electric ones ran beyond the working-class district of Gospel Oak. She was not herself actually a member of the Fabian Society. Shaw said that "she began with an intense contempt for it as a rabble of silly suburban faddists."

Sidney had already belonged for seven years and the society was two years old when he joined. It had been conceived in 1883, the same year that Karl Marx died with *Das Kapital* still unfinished and not yet translated into English, although its ideas had been summarised by Hyndman of the Social Democratic Federation (without sufficient acknowledgment, which threw Marx into a black gloom of resentment). Six months after Marx's death, an earnest young city clerk, Edward Pease, lent his room for the first meeting of a society which aimed at promoting "The New Life", which was to consist of self-supporting communities of superior persons indifferent to material possessions. It was a time when "everybody was very much in earnest about something", and London was peppered with little clubs of the kind, each sure that it alone had the key that would reform the whole social system, and the only remarkable thing about this club, in shabby lodgings behind Great Portland Street, was that eventually it did just that.

A few weeks later its members had second thoughts—not about the practicability of reforming society, but about doing it at once—and before the grass was green on Marx's grave they had settled on the Fabian philosophy of Socialism through slow and bloodless reform. They christened themselves after the Roman general Fabius: "For the right moment you must wait, as Fabius did most patiently when warring against Hannibal, though many censured his delays; but when the time comes you must strike hard as Fabius did or your waiting will be vain and fruitless." At this point some of the original members, disillusioned, withdrew from the club and formed their communities of superior persons, though in Croydon and Bloomsbury instead of Brazil, as originally planned. At one time they had as their honorary secretary an earnest young Scot, recently come south, named James Ramsay MacDonald.

By the time Beatrice was drawn into the group, the Fabians had already started on their tract-producing. Their first one, "Why Are the Many Poor?" had attracted Shaw into the society and he got Sidney to write "Facts for Socialists", because he himself had been reading Marx (in French) in the British Museum library and had come to the conclusion that it was the damning facts and figures which Marx had assembled and not his "Jeremiad against the bourgeoisie" which made the impact. Sidney's tract (which cost a penny when it was first printed and was still selling, at two shillings, half a century later) established the Fabian philosophy that no reasonable person who has the facts explained to him could fail to deduce that Socialism is the only solution. Sidney lectured the Fabians, personally, against talking and thinking of an "insurrectionist" kind and advised them to give up the idea that Socialism stood for either "insurrectionism on the one hand or Utopianism on the other".

Before the Fabians, aspiring Socialists of their kind had been limited to exactly this choice. William Morris's Socialist League favoured a neo-mediaeval Utopia in which London should be "small and white and clean"; the Guild of St Matthew believed that Socialism was Christianity translated into politics; and the Social Democratic Federation could only carry on, as Hyndman explained, by "expecting the Revolution at ten o'clock next Monday morning". He was a revolutionary aristocrat, William Morris an aesthete, the Guild was run by progressive parsons and the Fabian Society by middle-class intellegentsia. For those who wanted straight working-class socialism the prospect was unpromising. Keir Hardie did not found the Independent Labour Party until 1893 and the Trade Union movement counted for so little, at this time, that none of the seven Fabian essayists had thought it worth discussing as a political force. But there was a certain amount of coming and going between the four organisations, and the Fabians included varying shades of opinion, from the seven essayists in the centre to cranks and simple-lifers, anarchists and nihilists on the outskirts. Edith Nesbit (the author of children's books which are still read today) was one of the earliest members, with her husband, Hubert Bland. She wrote to a friend in Australia:

> I should like to try and tell you a little about the Fabian Society. Its aim is to improve the social system—or rather to spread its news as to the possible improvement of the said S.S. . . . There are two distinct elements in the F.S., the practical and the visionary—the first being much the strongest —but a perpetual warfare goes on between the parties which gives to the Fabian an excitement which it might otherwise lack. We belong—needless to say—to the practical party and so do most of our intimate friends.[1]

The Blands were dedicated socialists, continually attending lectures and debates and having Fabian gatherings in their house. Edith even christened her son "Fabian" in honour of the society.

At other times, the Fabians would gather at the home of Charlotte Wilson, an ex-Girton Socialist, anarchist and suffragist. She invented the cult of the idealised country cottage (still fashionable today). "They have 2 rooms, study and kitchen," wrote Edith

Nesbit. "The kitchen is an *idealised* farm kitchen, where of course no cooking is done—but with a cushioned settee—open hearth, polished dresser and benches, and all the household glass and crockery displayed mixed up with aesthetic pots, pans, curtains, chairs and tables—a delightfully incongrous but altogether agreeable effect."[2] Another Fabian, Harold Cox, established himself in a "co-operative farm" in Surrey, but according to Shaw his only successful crop was radishes, from which he made jam. Henry Salt—founder of the Humanitarian League—lived with his wife Kate in a labourer's cottage near by. Once, when the Webbs went to visit them, the local innkeeper was reluctant to serve them because Beatrice looked so like a gipsy, with her dark hair dishevelled, and carrying a huge bunch of wild flowers she had picked on the way. (Beatrice always loved to pick flowers, but Shaw's mother took a permanent dislike to her because she would crush one as she talked.)

At the time when Beatrice married, the Fabian society was run by a "junta", consisting of Sydney Webb, Sydney Olivier, Shaw and Graham Wallas. Later, when Olivier went abroad, Beatrice stepped into his shoes in this unofficial hierarchy. But at first she was doubtful about becoming too much involved, in case Fabianism should hamper the objectivity of her own research work. She said, "It seemed to my cautious temperament that any pronounced views about social changes to be aimed at . . . might bias my own selection of facts and hypotheses . . . the way of discovery might be blocked by those who held contrary opinions." At the time, it even seemed possible that the Fabians might form a definite political party of their own, instead of sticking to propaganda and "permeation". ("We want the things done and we don't much care which persons or which party gets the credit.") They claimed that permeation had helped to get the County Council Act of 1888 passed by Lord Salisbury's government, giving new weapons to those working for municipal socialism, and had also got the Liberal Party to include a great slice of Fabian doctrine in its election programme in 1891. But after they had won the election, the Liberals recanted, and the Fabians retorted by threatening to form a working-class party. Subsequently, however, they went back to their original tactics, though they sent a delegate to the Labour Representation Committee, which eventually became the Labour Party, and succeeded in getting twenty-nine candidates into Parliament in 1906, of whom four were Fabians.

Sidney was fond of pointing out that the work of the society was the sum of the work of individual Fabians, and they were expected to spend their free time on what Shaw described as "squalid little committees and ridiculous delegations to conferences of the three tailors of Tooley Street, with perhaps a deputation to the Mayor thrown in".[3] The "junta" lived in each other's pockets, and when Sidney married, the others assumed that they would go on just the same but that the party would now include Beatrice. "The Fabian old gang can only afford a country house for a holiday because one of us has a wife with a thousand a year,"[4] Shaw summed up matter-of-factly. When Sidney and Beatrice went down to the Argoed to work, Shaw and Wallas joined them, and made themselves useful. The Webb book had run into a bad patch. Graham Wallas criticised the work and gave it back to Beatrice to rewrite, while Shaw praised it and then spent several days polishing and improving it, sacrificing his own work to do so. "Sidney certainly has devoted friends," Beatrice wrote gratefully. "But then it is a common understanding with all these men that they use each other up when necessary. That is the basis of the influence of the Fabian society on contemporary thought; the little group of leaders are practical communists in all the fruits of their labours."

The Webbs' plan for their married life was that they should give unpaid service to society in return for their unearned income. "Our income sufficed for our needs and we felt none of the usual temptations to increase our joint little fortune and ... thus become entangled in the trammels and trappings of wealth," Beatrice wrote piously, adding, in a characteristic relapse into realism, that it was easy to be financially "disinterested" since their marriage was childless, and that in any case they made some money from lectures and articles and from their "solid but unreadable books". They decided to divide the year between London when the L.C.C. was in session and the provinces, researching, or the country, writing the rest of the time. Soon after the wedding they gave up the Hampstead flat and took a long lease on the house in Grosvenor Road, which became the chief home of their married life. The rent was the correct ten per cent of income favoured by sound Victorian householders, but Beatrice bought furniture with all Laurencina's guilt about being lavish with money. "I have deliberately spent money on it because I do not wish it to be thought that simplicity of daily life means ugliness and lack of order and charm," she argued with her officious conscience.

The ideal to be aimed at is strict economy in weekly expenditure —no self-indulgence and show, but beautiful surroundings.... efficiency demands plenty of nourishing food, well-ordered drains and a certain freedom from petty care.... It is somewhat softening to contend that you *need* beautiful things to work with ... I have deliberately spent ... this extra £100 in buying prettier, better-made things than were absolutely necessary, yet I am not altogether at rest about it. At any rate, as Sidney says, we must work in order to deserve it.

In the summer, they launched on what became a regular habit of taking a country house for three months or so—a farm in Surrey, a rectory in Suffolk, or the Argoed until it was sold, and the rest of the "junta" came to stay with them. These working holidays developed into one of the established Fabian traditions— the "summer school" of later years. "Four hours writing in the morning, four hours bicycling in the afternoon.... I have to spend a lot of time mending punctures in female bicycle tyres," [5] Shaw wrote to Ellen Terry. "I wonder what you would think of our life, our eternal political shop; our mornings of dogged writing, all in our separate rooms; our ravenous plain meals; our bicycling, the Webbs' incorrigible spooning over their industrial and political science." The Fabians graduated from tricycles to bicycles during the great cycling craze of the nineties. They did it, as they did everything else, with dedicated enthusiasm tempered by what Shaw called "the invaluable habit of laughing freely at ourselves which has always distinguished us ..." They learned to ride the dangerous machines (rather strangely) on Beachy Head, glorying, like school-boys, in the various injuries they suffered. Now everyone had his own bicycle-crash story. Shaw's was intensely dramatic. "The hills and clouds and farmhouses began to tumble about drunkenly ... Webb told me afterwards that my lips were violet ... nobody but a teetotaller would have faced a bicycle again for six months." [6] Bracingly encouraged by Beatrice, he rode forty miles by her side the next day. Beatrice's favourite story was about Sidney's agonised reaction when she came home with blood all over her blouse. Like most upper-class Victorian daughters who learned to face up to pony-riding at a tender age, she was tough about physical injury, and earned Shaw's awed admiration, when she fell into a wasps' nest, by the coolness with which she stripped and cured herself with a bottle of whisky. But she was terrified of Sidney hurting himself, and once when she was laughing appreciatively at Shaw's tumbles, as he tried to ride an old penny-farthing he had found in the stable of their current country-house, she became suddenly serious when Sidney wanted to have a turn, and utterly forbade him to do anything so dangerous.

The bicycles were, as she said, their most absorbing new toys, but they also had a moral value. They provided daily outdoor exercise, without wasteful expense. (Shaw was almost as obsessed about his health as Beatrice was about hers and Sidney's.) They also provided what she called "our only vision of the beautiful", since, in deference to Sidney's tastes, she had turned her back on music and drama, art and literature. With bicycles, they could at least wander "by river and forest path, over plain and mountain, in mist, cloud and sunshine".[7]

But the most rewarding part of these working holidays in the country, shared with Shaw and Wallas, was in the mental exercise they gave each other. Their evening discussions would rise to such a pitch that visitors to the house would go to bed expecting breakfast to be an agony of embarrassment, with no-one on speaking terms with anyone else, and would come down to find them all as amiable and friendly as possible.

Beatrice regarded Graham Wallas as "a loveable man" and if Sidney had to be in London, she was quite content to go for long walks in the summer twilight with Wallas and listen to his troubles. But his King Charles's head about the wickedness of organised religion bored even her, though in the ordinary way she was a glutton for agnostic debate. "He is lonely and overworked and wants a little mental coddling," she wrote kindly. "We are inclined to douche him with cold water! ... I must see whether I cannot show more tact. I am terribly narrow and limited and Sidney and I are obviously self-complacent in our perfectly happy married life. I must rouse myself to show more sympathy." She was at ease with him because he was "an English gentleman in his relations with women, to whom a flirtation, let alone an intrigue would seem underbred as well as unkind and dishonourable." Unfortunately, the same could not be said about Shaw. As Beatrice confided later to one of her nephews, "The first time we were alone together Shaw simply flung himself on me."

Shaw flirted elaborately and openly with his friends' wives. He established himself as the "Sunday husband" of Kate Salt (who was herself an "urning" or homosexual) and based his heroine "Candida" on her. (Of all Shaw's play-heroines, Beatrice disliked Candida the most.) The Sunday husband was one of Shaw's schemes for improving the institution of marriage by allowing the wife an intellectual-romantic relationship with another man. (The Webbs used to say that they wished they had a Sunday baby, which would provide them with the satisfaction of parenthood without the bother.) Besides these triangular relationships, Shaw had a series of intense romances with various unattached Fabian women; but it was only the small change of love-making and the image of himself as a heart-breaker which mattered to him. If he was not actually impotent, the temperature of his physical desire was at least uncommonly low, which probably explains why none of his reputed mistresses, when taxed, admitted to it, and why there was never any whisper of his having fathered any illegitimate children. When Sidney, whom he valued above all his other friends, male and female, married Beatrice, Shaw set out to establish his standard ironically sentimental relationship with her and came up against a stone wall. "Silly, these philanderings of Shaw's," Beatrice wrote crossly in her diary. "He imagines he gets to know women by making them in love with him. Just the contrary. His stupid gallantries bar him out from the friendship of women who are either too sensible, too puritanical or too much otherwise engaged to care to bandy personal flatteries with him." "Beatrice thoroughly disliked me and it is enormously to her credit that she forced herself to have me in the house because I was Sidney's loyallest and best friend," said Shaw. On the surface, it was a tug-of-war over their rights in Sidney. "I think Shaw regards me as a very useful wife for you," said Beatrice to Sidney, in Shaw's presence, and Shaw, thinking it over afterwards (as he was doubtless intended to), decided that she meant that "I see a certain distance between herself and Webb and that I stand closer to him myself and therefore am an influence tending to make him conscious of the distance and thrust them asunder." Like Beatrice, Shaw felt that he had a deep need of Sidney and Sidney's abilities, in order to fulfil himself. He said that as soon as he met him he realised that Sidney was "at all points the very collaborator I needed and I just grabbed him. . . . I at once recognised in him all the qualities in which I was myself pitiably deficient." [8] Beatrice, who had also seized on the same talents for the same reason, had too possessive a nature to share Sidney without a struggle, particularly now that her new happiness in the marriage was teaching her to love him personally more than she had ever thought possible. Shaw's disturbing presence made her uneasy for another reason. She was settling herself to accept Sidney's standards and limitations, and making a virtue of doing so. It was now a moral issue that she should stifle her literary imagination and get down to "this horrid grind, this analysis—one sentence exactly like another, the same words, the same construction—no relief in narrative." She told an enquiring acquaintance that the secret of a happy marriage was "unity on the one vital issue—self-expression or self-control". Sidney, she wrote, describing their partnership, had her "on the lead" and when she strayed into "morbid" ways, gently but firmly pulled her back. Sidney was allergic to temperamental women. He disliked philosophical speculation, introspection, and also all the arts, so Beatrice dutifully put them out of her life. The very limitations which Sidney imposed on her authorship began to stand for intellectual chastity. Shaw and Beatrice had the same kind of reverence for Sidney's trained, analytic mind that an artist has for an accomplished technician. "I was an incorrigible histrionic and mountebank and Webb was the simplest of geniuses," [9] said Shaw. "He is stronger-brained than I am and can carry more things in his mind at once," said Beatrice humbly, after they had got into "such a hopeless state of continuous argument" that she had to let Sidney go on with their chapter alone and write it according to his judgement. She assured herself—perhaps rather often—that Sidney's achievements were worth all Shaw's brilliance. "Sidney insinuates ideas, arguments, programmes and organises the organisers. Bernard Shaw leads off the men of straw, men with light heads—the would-be revolutionaries who are attracted by his wit, his daring onslaughts and amusing paradoxes." She granted his physical attraction—"six feet in height with a lithe broad-chested figure and laughing blue eyes", and admitted that he was "a brilliant talker and therefore a delightful companion", always producing "epigrams, sparkling generalisations or witty personalities". Only she never managed to get any of them down on paper. No-one could guess, from her diary, that for six years she was the close companion of one of the most brilliant conversationalists of the day. She herself had an ironical turn of phrase, could record her own dry repartees or sum up a new acquaintance in a neat thumbnail-sketch. But when Shaw turned ideas upside down, or mocked at values to which she subscribed or relapsed into the crazy logic of his Irish background, she was not only irritated, but alarmed, as though he was a will-o'-the-wisp beckoning her onto dangerous ground, away from the safe highway where she and Sidney plodded with their cut-and-dried conclusions. "Shaw is gambling with ideas and emotions in a way that distresses slow-minded prigs like Sidney and me and hurts those with any fastidiousness," she wrote, after seeing *Major Barbara*. Shaw stood for things she had resolved to give up: speculation and creative art and "the smart world".

"I—G.B.S., have actually suffered from something which in anyone else I should call unhappiness," [10] wrote Shaw, sitting up at night, when he was staying with the Webbs at the Argoed, pouring out his troubles in a letter to his romantic affinity, the actress Janet Achurch.

I would give anything for a moment of really sacred solitude and perhaps twice as much for a moment of really sacred intimacy. The frightful sensation of being always on guard with another man's wife ... seems to develop itself here to a perfectly devilish intensity. Beatrice's nature is so hostile to mine that in spite of all the admiration, esteem, kindly feeling and other dry goods that abound between us, it is only by holding my edge steadily at the most delicately felt angle to her grindstone that I can ever avoid becoming hateful to her ... Even she, though it is I who do the holding and though she can always relieve the strain by bathing her heart in Webb's endearments, has to admit that we embarrass each other frightfully when we are alone together, without some subject of keen and immediate interest to discuss. ... Of course I could put forth my subtleties and bring her to a point of view where we could really understand each other if only she were a perfectly free woman; but that would involve an intimacy with her even closer than Webb's (you will understand that I am not here dealing with any sexual or physical intimacy) because there are no such obstacles of temperament between her and Webb as there are between her and me and he can therefore never be forced to get down and back into the very foundation of her mind as I should have to do. If I did this, she would no longer be in any really special personal sense Webb's wife; the marriage, spiritually, would dissolve and vanish. The knowledge (conscious or unconscious) of this would prevent her from allowing me to take the first steps and equally prevent me from taking them because we are not in love with one another and nothing short of that could nerve us to such an enterprise. . . .[11]

If Beatrice herself was conscious that she and Shaw might have had an "intimacy" deeper and more demanding than the partnership she had chosen, she rationalised it by nagging disapproval of Shaw's romanticism, on the grounds that it compromised his intellectual integrity. "His incompleteness as a thinker, his shallow and vulgar view of many human relationships; all these defects come largely from the flippant and worthless self-complacency brought about by the worship of rather second-rate women." She had to prove to Shaw that the relationship between Sidney and herself included all the comforts of everyday marriage, as well as unique mental affinity, and considering her otherwise puritanical habits, it was astonishing how much freedom she allowed herself about "spooning" with Sidney in front of Shaw. According to Shaw's description, she used to put down her pen and "hurl herself on her husband in a shower of caresses which lasted until the passion for work resumed its sway; then they wrote and read authorities for their footnotes until it was time for another refresher,"[12] while Shaw went on placidly writing and dreaming of a future in which the pleasure taken in brain-work would surpass that induced by sex.

Sometimes, when both Sidney and Shaw were away and she was alone, she found herself thinking about other things she had put aside, in settling for this marriage, such as "the holiness of motherhood—its infinite superiority over any other occupation that a woman may take to". She would wish any woman she loved, she confided to her diary, to be a mother.

The other alternative, so often chosen nowadays by intellectual women—of deliberately forgoing motherhood seems to me to thwart all the purposes of their nature. I myself—or rather we —chose this course in our marriage—but then I had passed the age when it is easy and natural for a woman to become a child-bearer—my physical nature to some extent dried up at 35 after ten years' stress and strain of a purely brain-working and sexless life. If I were a young woman and had the choice between brain-working profession and motherhood, I would not hesitate which life to choose (as it is I sometimes wonder whether I had better not have risked it and taken my chance).

It seemed to her that if she could get Shaw's disturbing presence out of her life, by settling him into a carbon copy of her own marriage, everything would be easier. When she first met Charlotte Payne-Townshend, who was Socialist, rich and unattached after an unhappy love-affair, Beatrice thought she would do for Wallas. But Wallas with his morality and his learning bored Charlotte, whereas Shaw clearly enthralled her. As soon as Beatrice realised this, she helpfully arranged opportunities for Shaw to see more of Charlotte and a rumour to that effect went round among Shaw's second-rate women.

Beatrice, calling on the artist and Fabian, Bertha Newcombe, to return one of Shaw's books, found herself involved in an immensely dramatic scene which she wrote up afterwards in her diary:

Bertha broke down and told the story of her five years' devoted love for Shaw and his cold philandering. . . . and now her feeling of resentment and misery against me when she discovered I was encouraging him to marry Miss Townshend. 'You are well out of it, Miss Newcombe', I said gently. 'If you had married Shaw he would not have been faithful to you . . . there are few men for whom I have so warm a liking—but in his relations with women he is vulgar, if not worse . . . it is vulgarity that includes cruelty and springs from vanity.' As I uttered these words, my eye caught her portrait of Shaw, full length, with his red-gold hair and laughing blue eyes and his mouth slightly open as if scoffing at us both. I kissed her on the forehead and escaped down the stairs . . . And then I thought of that other woman with her loving easy-going nature and anarchic luxurious way, her well-bred manners and well-made clothes—her leisure, wealth and knowledge of the world . . . Would she succeed in taming the Philanderer?

She did not. But Beatrice might have done, since Shaw came to respect, like and admire her more than any other woman he knew, not excepting his wife, and their friendship was deep and lifelong. (If his story of having deliberately given up the chance of marrying Beatrice because he did not want to cut Sidney out was true, that was Shaw's loss.) There is only one portrait of Charlotte in the whole of Shaw's plays (in *The Apple-Cart*) but the well-informed, strong-minded, bossy but likeable woman, who turns up regularly, over and over again, and who is one of his favourite female characters, constantly echoes Beatrice. Tanner (a self-portrait of Shaw) in *Man and Superman*, who is nagged by the domineering Ann for being a shocking flirt, says about her ruefully, "Ann will do just exactly what she likes. And what's more, she'll force us to advise her to do it; and she'll put the blame on us if it turns out badly." Lavinia, the fearless free-thinking Christian martyr in *Androcles*, echoes Beatrice in believing in a God even when she finds she cannot believe in "all the stories and dreams" of religion. Beatrice liked *Man and Superman* because it dealt seriously with "the most important of all questions, this breeding of the right sort of man". (Sidney thought it was silly.) She disliked *John Bull's Other Island* because it was "derision unaccompanied by any positive faith or hope", and *Misalliance* because it harped on "the mere physical attraction of men to women, coupled with the insignificance of the female for any other purpose but sex attraction". She preferred Shaw when he wrote straight-forward Socialist tracts in dramatic form, and admired his first one, *Widowers' Houses*, whole-heartedly, which was not surprising, since its subject was slum-landlordism and its moral irreproachably Fabian. But she suggested that another time he should "put on the stage a real modern young lady of the governing class—not the sort of thing that theatrical and critical authorities imagine such a lady to be". Shaw took her point and "Vivie Warren" was the result. (When *Mrs Warren's Profession* was finished, Shaw sent it to Beatrice and she took it away into the woods to read by herself. She told Balfour, long afterwards, that he ought to study it particularly because it was Shaw's "most serious play".) Vivie, who is "attractive . . . sensible, able . . . strong, confident, self-possessed", is the moving spirit of the play, because it is her determination to know the real facts which exposes the whole social problem of prostitution. Vivie is only happy when she is at her desk, drudging at dull brainwork; cannot bear to waste time from work on cultural entertainments, smokes heavily, and—also like Beatrice—calls her lover "my boy" as a term of endearment, in one of the most embarrassingly sentimental love-dialogues Shaw ever wrote. But he had plenty of chances to observe and learn.

10

Wily Webb
1895–1903

AT THE EXACT TIME when the Webbs were writing, in their history of Trades Unionism, "Thus we find through the whole Trade Union world an almost unanimous desire to make the working-class organisations in some way effective for political purposes,"[1] the unions were just beginning to wake up to the fact that political power was within their grasp. In fact, the stage was all set for the Webbs to be the midwives at the birth of a political party founded on the unions. It did not work out because they were more perceptive about social institutions than about the individuals who make up the institution. Beatrice's surgeon brother-in-law, Willie Cripps, once told her that he would believe in the existence of the soul when he found one in the course of dissecting a human body. The Webbs, laying bare the anatomy of the trade union, discovered everything except its heart. They could not understand what made the trade union leaders tick. Long afterwards, Lord Attlee said of Beatrice, "She underestimated or did not appreciate the extent to which a movement such as that of the British Labour Party is influenced by sentiment. I think her judgment of people was often faulty for this reason."

She could not endure Keir Hardie, who for most British socialists will always be the Theseus of the dawn of the Labour party—a heroic, larger-than-life figure round whom folk-legends gather. When Hardie was first elected he went to the House in a brake—"the kind of thing you saw going to Epping Forest," said his rival and enemy, John Burns, contemptuously. "And dressed in an old deer-stalker cap and knickers of check, you could have played draughts on them." To Beatrice, Keir Hardie's costume was merely part of a "pose".

Keir Hardie believed passionately that "Socialism, I say again, is not a system of economics. It is life for the dying people,"—an attitude which Beatrice found not merely embarrassingly emotional, but definitely wrong, just as she believed that working among the poor because their wretchedness broke your own heart was wrong. Hardie could not see that the long-sighted (that is, the Webb) view of supporting Liberals when they were in socialistic mood was a necessary compromise towards socialism. "Keir Hardie," wrote Beatrice irritably, "who impresses me very unfavourably, deliberately chooses this policy as the only one he can boss. His only chance of leadership lies in the creation of an organisation 'agin the Government'; he knows little and cares less for any constructive thought or action."

The kind of trade-unionist whom she liked and understood was Broadhurst, the stone-mason who was a "Liberal-Labour" MP, and secretary of the T.U.C. for fifteen years. She accepted that Broadhurst was "a commonplace person", with a limited vision "appealing to the practical shrewdness and . . . mediocre sentiments of the comfortably-off working-man", and that he was "somewhat gluttonous" and coarse-grained. (She rather liked a flavour of coarseness in a powerful working man.) But she appreciated his down-to-earth shrewdness, and the way he used the Webbs for his own advantage. "He realises that without some middle-class help he can do nothing—so finding no one he can trust more than us he unreservedly places himself in our hands." When he learned that Beatrice was "an anti-suffrage woman, he immediately thought me sensible and sound". But among the "new unionists" of the nineties, Broadhurst was regarded as a reactionary. It was the dynamic, militant ones who were riding high, since the successful strikes of the last few years—that of the match-girls, and of the gas-workers and of the dockers (for a "tanner" instead of fourpence an hour). It was the heroes of the strikes who were in the ascendant, men such as Tillet, and John Burns—the "man with the red flag" and Tom Mann, whom the Webbs thought they had converted to their own brand of socialism at the time of the Royal Commission on Labour.

The government, aware of the thunder-cloud coming up on the left, appointed this commission as a homely remedy which at any rate could not possibly do any harm. "Royal Commission on Labour a gigantic fraud," Beatrice wrote crossly, when she learned who had been appointed to it. (She had secretly hoped to be an assistant commissioner, at least, herself.) "Made up of a little knot of dialecticians plus a carefully picked parcel of variegated Labour men and the rest landlords, pure and simple." Among the dialecticians were Professor Alfred Marshall, who had snubbed her so severely about her Co-operative book, and her brother-in-law Leonard Courtney, who had been so patronising over her marriage to Sidney. At first, they made rings round the workmen witnesses they examined, like matadors around a slow-witted bull and Beatrice waited impatiently for Sidney's turn to give evidence and to meet them on their own ground. When the day came, Kate Courtney and Charles Booth and his wife also turned up to listen. Sidney, perhaps determined not to be brow-beaten by any ancient-university dons or his wife's upper-class connections, was rude and aggressive and there was a distinct drawing-aside of skirts by the well-bred party. But if they thought they could score off the Webbs, on a socialist issue, they learned better.

The next day, presumably after a lecture from his wife, "the dear boy made a pretty apology and bore the examination with perfect good-humour", and peace was restored. Leonard even confided to the Webbs ("with pompous superiority", said Beatrice) that the commissioners were all agreed on their report and that there was no prospect of any minority one. But months before, Tom Mann, who was one of the variegated Labour men on the commission, and unhappy about the way it was shaping, had privately asked Sidney to draft him one. It included such startling proposals as an eight-hour day, improvement in working conditions of the employed and, for the unemployed, the acquisition of agricultural land which they could till, and a regret that it was not possible to nationalise land forthwith.

Mann brought some of the other variety of Labour commissioners (including Mawdsley, the right-wing leader of the immensely powerful "cotton" union) along to Grosvenor Road with him in the hope that Sidney could somehow talk them round into supporting it as well. This was an assignment after Sidney's own heart. He offered to read them the "gist" of the draft and took up a position with his back to the fire (by-passing any over-the-shoulder reading on their part). He skilfully edited it as he went along, to spare the feelings of the more reactionary. Mann threw in some well-timed objections that it was too mild, which Mawdsley, supported by Sidney, turned down, and by the end of the afternoon Mawdsley had a dazed impression that he had invented the whole report himself.

It was flung (like a bomb exploding, said the *Manchester*

Guardian) into the proceedings of the commission just as the majority report was ready. The chairman sneered that the signatories had obviously not written it themselves. Mawdsley answered sharply, "Certainly not, nor has the Duke or any of you written the majority report. The only difference between us is that you have paid your man, and we have been sharp enough to get it done without payment and better done too." This was the Webbs' first discovery of the possibilities of using a minority report as a propaganda weapon, which they took to using whenever they could. Broadhurst got Sidney to draft one for him, to present to the Royal Commission on the Aged Poor. The Webbs began to be accepted as "clerks to the Labour movement", but what they really wanted was to get all the various organisations under one (Fabian) umbrella. After the rapprochement with Mann, they assumed that he would stay permanently in their orbit and were perplexed and disappointed when he would not.

Ramsay MacDonald, Hardie's most important disciple, also was a member of both the Fabian society and the I.L.P. (Shaw once told MacDonald that the Fabians thought he was an I.L.P. spy, and the I.L.P. thought he was a Fabian one). MacDonald suggested that the I.L.P. and the Fabians ought to come to an understanding, and Sidney and Beatrice accordingly arranged a little dinner for their respective representatives at Grosvenor Road. At this dinner, as Beatrice reported distastefully, Tom Mann "gushed out his soul." He could not bring himself to fall in with the Fabian practice of supporting what he called "mere Liberals" if it seemed to be advisable. "It was melancholy to see Tom Mann reverting to the old views of the Social Democratic Federation and what is worse to their narrow sectarian policy," Beatrice wrote, when the unsuccessful evening was over. "He is possessed with the idea of a 'church'—of a body of men all professing the same creed and all working in exact uniformity to exactly the same end. No idea which is not absolute . . . has the slightest attraction to him." She granted Mann's "high character and personal purity" (though she thought he drank too much whisky) but it was a perpetual irritation to her that he could not be talked into more flexibility.

She was so certain that her own guiding principle—the best action is that which procures the greatest happiness for the greatest number—was the correct one that any variation of it must necessarily be inferior. Working-men socialists, she noted regretfully, were "specially afflicted with the theological temperament—the implicit faith in a certain creed which has been 'revealed' to them by a sort of inner light." Just as she had settled that "the personal element in social work is contemptible", and that the correct approach of the social worker to the recipient was not human sympathy but clinical detachment, so she believed that anyone moved by a burning desire to give the underdog his chance was suspect for that reason. In her estimation, idealism and fanaticism were interchangeable terms, most of the time. When men like the "new unionists" found her pragmatic approach to their shared aims repellent, she could only assume, wonderingly, that there must be some down-to-earth reason for it. Probably, she frequently concluded, it was because they had revolutionary tendencies. She thought of a fondness for revolutionary action in the same category as a fondness for whisky; as an addiction into which the addict was liable to relapse at any moment, and end up, ruined, in the arms of the S.D.F. The alternative reason she suspected, and one she found easier to comprehend because it was also a temptation of her own, was that the stubborn one must be working to get himself personal power and was afraid that the Webbs might get in the way.

On this basis she had no difficulty, from the first, in understanding John Burns, and had even thought that in spite of his "intense desire for notoriety" he might make a good fourth in the Fabian junta to balance the volatile Shaw. "What the Junta needs to make it a great power are one or two personalities of *weight*; men of wide experience and sagacity, able to play a long hand and to master the movement ... Burns is, in some respects, the strongest man of the four ..." (In fact he was playing even a longer hand than she credited and beat Sidney into the Cabinet by almost twenty years.)

At that time John Burns was a name to conjure with among working-class socialists and a nightmare to upper-class Tories haunted by visions of the tumbrils. He was the perfect image of a revolutionary agitator, huge, black-bearded, with a voice that could bring everyone within range around him when he started to speak at a street-corner. He always wore a striking white straw hat as Henry of Navarre wore a white plume in battle. He was strong, egotistical and assertive and had a magnificent command of racy, homely language. If the Trade Unions were to form their own political party, he was the most likely leader. He could not abide Keir Hardie, perhaps because he saw, in the incorruptible Scot, a *Dorian Gray* portrait of what he might have been himself. He was unfriendly towards Tom Mann and suspected Sidney was planning to make himself a rival Labour leader, to the point of trying to prevent Sidney from joining him as a colleague on the L.C.C.

Beatrice was shrewd enough to realise that Burns would at least not carry incorruptibility to the point of refusing help from the Webbs, if it seemed likely to pay him, and it was quite reasonable of her to think he might be persuaded to throw in his lot with them. She reflected impartially that "Burns, though unscrupulous, incurably suspicious and rather mean in his methods has some splendid moral and intellectual qualities. So long as he does not fear any diminution of his personal prestige his judgment is very fine." Unfortunately he feared it morning, noon and night. "He will not in any way consult us or explain his meaning; he is never open with us; in spite of our genuine desire to work with him both on London and Labour questions he always shows an undercurrent of jealousy and suspicion." But her hope of a Webb-Burns collaboration, which was high at one time—("Our relationship with John Burns has never been a cordial one; it promises to be more so in future") did not work out. The reason was not, in his case, because he was too loyal to working-class or trade-unionist socialism, but because he was determined not to be "got at by the Webbs", and in fact after the Labour Parliamentary party was born, he was returned to Parliament as a "Liberal-Labour" member.

By then, in any case, Sidney and Beatrice had decided there was no future in trying to amalgamate the various left-wing organisations into a political party under their own auspices. Instead, "We should continue our policy of inoculation—of giving to each class, to each person coming under our influence, the exact dose of collectivism that they were prepared to assimilate. And we should continue to improve and enlarge such machinery of government that came into our hands." As they had observed in their book, a trade union was "a continuous association of wage-earners for the purpose of maintaining or improving the conditions of their working lives",[2] and there, so far as they were concerned, it might as well remain. They did not even attend the conference that in 1900 federated the socialist groups, including those of the trade unions, into the Labour Representation Committee, which captured twenty-nine seats in the 1906 election. The Fabians, as Beatrice assured Keir Hardie, Tom Mann and Ramsay MacDonald, were "purely an educational body".

But although Beatrice observed contentedly that "it is so much pleasanter to investigate and write rather than organise and speak," it was almost impossible for dedicated socialists like themselves to keep out of the actual struggle. Their history of local government was started while the London County Council was making dramatic progress in real life and Sidney was deeply involved in it. Even if they had not been first "forced into the fight" (as they were long before they started the book) by ordinary political interest, the fact that Chamberlain personally was ranged against them was irresistible. He was one of the group that wanted to break up the L.C.C. again into the small pieces from which it had been assembled by the Local Government Act of 1888. Beatrice reflected, "It looks like sheer political idiocy to throw the trade unions and the London Progressives into the arms of the Liberals—but I suppose he thinks he sees his game." The immediate result was to provoke some energetic electioneering for the Progressives on the part of the Fabians.

The Progressive party was really Fabianism translated into local government and its election manifestoes read like paraphrased Fabian tracts. Sidney himself wrote, in *The London Programme:*

By himself the typical Londoner is a frail and sickly unit, cradled in the gutter, housed in a slum, slaving in a sweater's den and dying in the workhouse infirmary. Collectively he is a member of the greatest and most magnificent city the world has known, commanding all the latest resources of civilisation and disposing of almost boundless wealth.[3]

Sidney, who was otherwise detached from his background, without allegiance to his social class or troubled by family entanglement, had a deep loyalty to the city of his birth and thought of himself as a Londoner. (It was a part of him which Beatrice could not share. The gipsy Potters never identified themselves with a place. When Beatrice threw herself into L.C.C. politics it was because she thought, "The L.C.C. is a better platform from which to bring about collectivism than Parliament.")

The other subject on which Sidney was capable of being warm and eloquent was education. "The proper occupation of youth up to twenty-one is education and instruction," he declared. He himself owed his life's happiness to the educational chances he had been given, and he was passionate about other people having theirs. When someone objected that mass higher education would mean the community would have no hewers of wood and drawers of water, he answered angrily:

> I want no hewers of wood and drawers of water; no class destined to remain there and prevented from rising because we do not provide for it. . . . *Our* convenience! *Our* comfort! Our comfort is to stand in the way of enabling these people, our fellow-citizens, to attain anything better than being mere hewers of wood and drawers of water! I must apologise for having been betrayed into a little heat, but I do object to the notion that for our convenience we are to keep hewers of wood and drawers of water.[4]

He alarmed the prosperous by pointing out that Germany was overtaking Britain in trade and industry, and told them it was because Germany's system of technical education was so much better. On this basis he was able to set up the Technical Education Board which he then used to reform elementary, secondary and university education, by means of grants-in-aid and the establishment of a gigantic scholarship ladder. With Haldane, he transformed London university from a mere degree-awarding body (for those barred from the older universities because of being non-Anglicans) into a teaching one, and helped to get the Balfour Education Act passed, abolishing the School Boards and giving all powers to the local council. (This was the occasion of a quarrel with Graham Wallas who thought that Sidney, as an agnostic, ought to take the opportunity to crush the church schools out of existence instead of including them in a new 'dual system'. But Sidney kept them for their usefulness, believing that education was more important than any religious issue. Wallas tried to get Shaw on his side, but Shaw said that so far no one had produced a better alternative religion than Christianity.)

Sidney, at this time, was constantly being consulted by educationalists, bishops and cabinet ministers, as the foremost expert on public education, and a cartoonist pictured him hacking out steps on a mountain-side up which a poor child was climbing towards the peak marked "University". Beatrice wrote, "All this is in a way pleasant (I do not hide from myself that I am pleased and flattered that my boy is recognised as a distinguished man) but it means less intellectual absorption in our work." Like any other wife, she had to wait till her man came home from the office and listen to an account of the day's work in which she had no share. She decided, from

Sidney's description, that "the Council is a machine for evolving a committee; the committee is a machine for evolving one man—the chairman. Both alike a machine for dodging the democracy (in a crude sense) by introducing government by a select minority instead of the rule of the majority." The committee was Sidney's favourite instrument and he could make it play any tune he liked. When he wished to carry a point in committee he would draw up the agenda with the controversial point occurring twice. When the members had argued themselves into limpness on the first point, the second would be passed without opposition. On the L.C.C. he was known as "Wily Webb".

The L.C.C. was mainly a middle-class body, composed of men with sufficient means to spend most of their time on its work. But when Fabianism looked like becoming too powerful, the Moderates made a great election drive to get power over the Progressives. It ended in a draw, but Beatrice was struck by the improvement in the personnel of the Council since the "Labour and Socialist onslaught on London" had brought the upper-class hastily in to oppose them, and had thus made the L.C.C. "the most accomplished, distinguished and even the most aristocratic local body in the world!"

Sometimes Beatrice felt that she would not have seen any less of Sidney if he was actually in Parliament instead of only on the L.C.C., but "he is doing real work on the L.C.C., work which is not only useful to London but useful to him", and if he went into Parliament "it would take so much away from me." When they went into the provinces to do research for their book, Sidney had to leave her if there was L.C.C. business to do. "I am feeling somewhat lonely," she wrote, "in the little lodging—a whole fortnight away from him." One of the reasons why the founding of the London School of Economics was her dearest project was that she and Sidney did it together, and as far as was possible on their own.

The L.S.E. was, as Lord Beveridge said long after, the favourite child of the Webbs. Like the goddess Athene it sprang, fully armed, from the brain of its parent. But even the first two persons to learn of its conception, Bernard Shaw and Graham Wallas, could not have said whether it was Sidney or Beatrice who actually invented the project, because the Webbs first thought of it in bed, and informed the other two of their joint decision at breakfast.

Sidney had had a letter from a Derby solicitor informing him that he was named as executor to a recently deceased member of the

Fabian society named Hutchinson. Sidney had never met him, but
knew about him because he was a useful subscriber to the funds, for
which reason he was tolerated by everyone except Shaw. Hutchinson
was in the habit of trying to engage Shaw in a correspondence discussing the doctrines of Herbert Spencer, but Shaw said he could not
be bothered to write to the old fool, which was perhaps the reason
why Sidney was empowered to deal with the bequest and Shaw was
not mentioned. (If he had been, there would probably have been a
Fabian-backed Labour party in Parliament by the turn of the century but no London School of Economics today.)

Hutchinson had left the bulk of his money, apart from some
rather miserly annuities to his wife and children, to the Fabian
Society, to be expended within ten years "on the propaganda and
other purposes of the said Fabian Society and its Socialism and towards advancing the objects in any other way they deem advisable".
Having made that (as he supposed) clear, he put a pistol to his head
and pulled the trigger.

This "odd adventure", as Beatrice rather callously described it,
was not confided by Sidney to anyone but his wife when he first
learned of it, although—or perhaps because—it was bound to be of
immense interest to the two other members of the Fabian junta, currently sharing the same farmhouse in Surrey for their holiday. But
he told Beatrice, who took it for granted that she was in joint control
of the money with him, which would probably have surprised
Hutchinson, whose own womenkind were tractable and self-effacing
to a fault.

"Now the question is how to spend the money," Beatrice wrote
briskly. She and Sidney had discussed the suggestions which would,
they knew, be made sooner or later by interested parties; to place it
to the credit of the Fabian Society, and use it in the ordinary work of
propaganda, or to make "a big political splash" by subsidising members of the Fabian executive (not to mention the I.L.P.) to stand for
Parliament. "But neither of these ways seems to us equal to the
occasion". She dismissed the idea of saving the pockets of ordinary
Fabian subscribers as wasteful, if not bad for their characters. As for
the I.L.P., the Webbs had no intention of underwriting an organisation which believed that reform could be brought about "by
shouting". To the daughter of Richard Potter it was a moral principle that a windfall of money ought to be invested so that there
should be something to show for it in the future, in this case not

financially, but in the way of Socialist thinkers educated in Webb techniques of theory based on careful research. It was not a new idea. Since Sidney's chairmanship of the L.C.C. Technical Education Board, his dream had been to add to London's "technical" schools an establishment on the lines of *l'Ecole Libre des Sciences Politiques* in Paris, and now this became a possibility.

Shaw and Wallas were told of the bequest and that it was to be used to found such a school, and if either of them demurred at this point Beatrice did not think it worth recording. Neither was a trustee, and what Sidney had to do was to convince two of the five appointed and give his casting vote. In fact as Pease, who was one of them, reported later, "The other trustees were wholly guided by the initiative of Webb." Sidney asked Haldane (that "steadfast fellow conspirator for the public good", as Beatrice described him) for Counsel's Opinion as to whether the promotion of the study of economics and other branches of social science or political science could be regarded as a reasonable interpretation of propagating Fabian Socialism, and Haldane replied that if Sidney believed such studies would strengthen the case for Socialism, it could. Nine months after he had made up his own mind, Sidney explained to the Fabian executive how he was going to use the money. He added that in addition a part of the legacy would be set aside to appoint "Hutchinson lecturers" to go round the provinces spreading Fabian education. Ramsay MacDonald was offered one of the lectureships, and to the relief of the Webbs (who anticipated opposition to the L.S.E. part of the plan from him) he accepted it.

Graham Wallas, who had seemed a likely Principal for the school, said he would prefer to lecture at it only, and the Webbs appointed a young man of their own choice named Hewins whom they had discovered in the Bodleian library when they were searching for Trade Society records. Sidney, in his position at the Technical Education Board, was able to arrange for the Society of Arts and the London Chamber of Commerce to co-operate over lectures for the L.S.E. There was one difficulty. The Chamber of Commerce was (perhaps understandably) nervous in case it should be manipulated by Sidney into helping to spread socialism, and insisted that Hewins should assure them that the L.S.E. "would not deal with political matters and nothing of a socialistic tendency would be introduced." At this point of departure from the original terms of the will, even Beatrice began to get nervous. She confided to her diary, "Promises well just at present, but impossible to tell whether the old gang won't wake up and cry out before the institution is fairly started—which would delay, possibly baulk our plans."

They did. Shaw wrote furiously to Beatrice,

The general impression was that the Hutchinson trustees are prepared to bribe the Fabians by country lectures and the like to allow them to commit an atrocious malversation of the rest of the bequest; and that as the (Fabian) executive is powerless the best thing they can do is to take the bribe and warn future Hutchinsons to be careful how they leave any money they may have to place at the disposal of the Socialists. This won't do... Hewins must be told flatly that he must...speak as a Collectivist...the Collectivist flag must be waved and the Marseillaise played if necessary...the School has important endowments the conditions of which are specifically Socialist... we must be in a position at any moment to show that faith has been kept with Hutchinson. If Webb is ever publicly convicted of having served up the County Council and the Chamber of Commerce on toast to the ghost of Hutchinson everyone will laugh and think it is an uncommonly smart thing. But if he is ever suspected of having tampered with a trust of ten thousand pounds from a private benefactor, then we shall lose our character for being straight in money matters; and none of us can afford to do that. Please show him this letter and allow it to rankle.[5]

Shaw's protest was followed by another—or rather by a series of "furious letters" from Ramsay MacDonald on the "abuse of the Hutchinson Trust". Beatrice noted that the "brilliant young Scot" was simply "personally discontented because we refused to have him as a lecturer for the London School. He is not good enough for that work; he has never had time to do any sound original work or even learn the old stuff well."

They had some trouble in finding the kind of lecturers they had in mind. ("Advertised for political science lecturer—and yesterday interviewed candidates—a nondescript set of university men. All hopeless from our point of view...Finally we determined to do without our lecturer...It struck me always as a trifle difficult to teach a science which does not yet exist.") Long before Sidney had made public his plan for using the trust money to found the school, he and

Beatrice aged five

Potter Family Group. *(l. to r.)* Georgie, Mary, Mrs. Potter, Maggie, Beatrice, Mr. Potter, Theresa, Blanche

Photo: by kind permission of Rachel, Lady Clay

Herbert Spencer. A cartoon by "G.G."

Photo: National Portrait Gallery

Beatrice and Kate

Photo: by kind permission
of the Hon. Frederick Cripps and Odhams Press

The Sisterhood. *(l. to r.)* Standing: Rosy, Blanche, Lallie;
sitting: Maggie, Kate, Beatrice, Mary, Georgie

Joseph Chamberlain, 1886, by F. Holl

Photo: National Portrait Gallery

Beatrice at the time of her marriage

Photo: Underwood & Underwood, New York

Sidney before his marriage

Young Fabians by Bertha Newcomb.
(l. to r.) Bernard Shaw, Beatrice, Sidney, and Graham Wallas

Photo: by kind permission of The Sketch

The young Bernard Shaw

Photo: by kind permission
of Radio Times Hulton Picture Library

Working at Grosvenor Road

Photo: by kind permission of the Passfield Trust

"The Wrong Man in the Right Place."
A Cartoon of Sidney Webb by Max Beerbohm

Photo: by kind permission of Mrs. Eva Reichmann

Beatrice in her sixties

Photo: by kind permission of the Passfield Trust

Garden party at Passfield: the Webbs and Bernard Shaw.
Rosy wore the same dress when the Webbs were
reinterred in Westminster Abbey

Photo: by kind permission of Thomas Ponsonby

Stafford Cripps and the Webbs

Photo: by kind permission of Lord Parmoor

The Last Picture

Photo: by kind permission of Alan Chappelow, M.A., F.R.S.A.

Beatrice, sitting together by the fire in the evening had "jotted down a list of subjects which want elucidating; issues of facts which need clearing up. Above all, we want the ordinary citizen to feel that reforming society is no light matter, and must be undertaken by experts specially trained for the purpose." Beatrice herself was anxious that "we should concentrate on getting *research really done*. For that object I should like to gather round us all the able young men and women who are taking to economics, free their minds of prejudices and start them with a high ideal of accuracy and exhaustiveness in work."

The first students of the L.S.E. were depressingly inclined to be more interested in subjects which would help them to earn a living than in "pure learning and culture, such as the growth of political theory". But the Webbs persevered. "We are convinced it is worth while.... We want to create a centre of intellectual work and comradeship from which our views will radiate through personal intercourse."

Meanwhile, since "the funds of the Hutchinson Trustees are not inexhaustible", they had to find more money. They were introduced to an heiress who they had previously ascertained was "socialistic"—Charlotte Payne-Townshend—and interested her in their scheme. She subscribed £1,000, endowed a woman's scholarship and rented the top half of the premises in Adelphi Terrace, which the Webbs had taken for the school. "It was on account of her generosity to our projects and 'for the good of the cause' that I first made friends with her," said Beatrice with great simplicity. Charlotte got value for her money, since Beatrice then suggested that they should share a country house (and expenses) for the summer, and it was there that she met Shaw. After they were married the Shaws lived above the school, "Charlotte's attractive flat", as Beatrice benevolently described it. She and Sidney used to "dine sumptuously between our respective lectures" there, and observe Shaw in his new "environment of charm and plenty".

Charlotte continued to help them when they needed money, "My dear Sidney," she wrote after one request. "If you want university endowment from me you should not have married me to an anarchist . . . I have consulted G. B. S. as to whether I should send you a thousand pounds . . . On the whole he cannot conceive any method by which £1000 can be made to produce more widespread social mischief than the one you propose, but such is his affection for you that he urged me to enclose a cheque sooner than disappoint you."[6] A "brilliant idea" of Sidney's that the public would like to subscribe to a Library of Political Science was received (by the public) without enthusiasm. He wrote begging letters to politicians and Beatrice wrote to her old dancing-partners.

Whatever we get is so much spoil of the Egyptians. Not that we want to deceive the contributors. We are perfectly *bona fide* in our desire to advance economic knowledge caring more for that than for our own pet ideas. And anyone who knows us knows our opinions and all the money had practically been sent to *us* personally.

As the number of students crept up towards 300 the childless couple began to feel they had a stake of their own in the future at last.

We can now feel assured that with the School as a teaching body, the Fabian Society as a propagandist organisation, the L.C.C. Progressives as an object lesson in electoral success, our books as the only elaborate and original work in economic fact and theory, no young man or woman who is anxious to study or to work in public affairs can fail to come under our influence.

II

Salon on Grosvenor Road
1899–1905

"FORTY, FORTY, FORTY... I don't feel a bit old," Beatrice wrote a few weeks before their departure for a tour of the English-speaking world, half amused and half scolding her vanity as she surveyed the trousseau of gloves, furs, and elegant blouses she had collected to "inspire Americans and colonials with a respect for the refinements of collectivism". It was the first time for years that Beatrice had taken any interest in her appearance. The Webbs started off on their travels in high spirits. Their fellow Fabian, Sidney Olivier, was travelling with them on his way to Washington on official business, and so was Phillip Trevelyan, the young son of Beatrice's distant relative the historian. With the handsome youth in attendance, carrying rugs and seeing to her comfort, Beatrice envisaged an altogether delightful trip.

As soon as they landed in New York, the Webbs at once opened up their investigation of American municipal institutions. They went from city to city all over America, cross-questioning mayors, aldermen, politicians, professors and anyone else they happened to meet. In New York, undaunted by warnings from "good society" that he was a "low brute" and had "snubbed the commissioners of Education", they sought out and interviewed the mayor. They gazed through a glass door at a committee of Aldermen, mastered the principles of Tammany Municipal policy, learned that there were citizens in America who lived by the sword, and were disinclined to agree with a lawyer of good position (E. Eller Anderson) that Tammany Hall was a logical result of universal suffrage. In turn, Lawyer Anderson was politely sceptical when they told him that in England there were men prepared to go into public administration without hope of gain.

In Washington they met the engaging Theodore Roosevelt who was at the start of his political career. "My difficulty has been to live down to my ideas, not to live up to them," he explained. Despite ample means and belonging to New York's "good society" he had preferred to "fight in the ring". When he had first encountered a "mixed lot", some of whom sneered at his black coat and tall hat, his response was, "If you come in your shirts I don't care a damn, and if I choose to come in a speckled coat I shall do it." Beatrice judged him the most remarkable man they had yet met in America.

It was the height of the crisis of the 1898 war with Spain over Cuba —"an unfortunate time to be in Washington," Beatrice wrote to Kate. Everyone was preoccupied with news from Havana and the sheaf of introductions Sidney carried round with him remained, for the most part, undelivered, Their friend Phillip Trevelyan, however, "called out" Senator Cabot Lodge, one of the so-called *Brahmin* Cabot Lodges, the quintessence of New England aristocracy. He politely submitted to Sidney's cross-examination and then took their young friend home to dine, snubbing the Webbs by leaving them to return alone to their hotel.

In Princeton they met Professor Woodrow Wilson—the most intellectual man they had yet met in America, as Beatrice wrote to Kate; and in Boston, Mayor Jo Quincy, a blue-blooded New Englander (the most aristocratic), whose administration the Webbs approved. From "good society" America, they moved on to industrial centres, to Chicago, whose pavements they found unspeakably shocking, and to Pittsburgh, "a diabolical place with the corruptest of corrupt Governments", whose godforsaken citizenry worked in almost lethal conditions to make philanthropic millionaires. One was Andrew Carnegie, whom Beatrice dismissed as a "reptile". She declined even to ask him for money for the London School of Economics. Indeed, it was not until they reached Salt Lake City, the celestial city of Beatrice's girlhood memory, that they encountered a "self-respecting abode of municipal authority", and here they widened their enquiry to include the institution of plural marriage. Scientific breeding, Beatrice thought, might well include experiments in polygamy. Her final verdict on American cities as they sailed out of San Francisco Harbour was, "Noise, noise, nothing but noise."

During the enforced idleness of the five-day crossing to newly annexed Hawaii, she had time to collect her thoughts about the United States. Most of all, she had been struck by the good manners of American citizens. To her great surprise, not one person had ever asked her who she was before being civil to her. She recalled the keen eyes, chiselled features and "brows as though lined in thought" of her well-mannered hosts, according so ill with their banal conversation—which she called the "tyranny of the stale platitude". This levelling down to uniformity of an amazingly diverse people could be traced, she thought, to the fundamental fallacy accepted by every immigrant that "all men are born free and equal". The other fallacy devouring Americans, it seemed to Beatrice, was the assumption that, in the picturesque words of a senator from Montana, "Money was the king, everything else the servant." "No one in America," concluded Beatrice "seems to realise that good government rests on the growth of a new motive, that of Social Service."

The first stop on their voyage to the Antipodes was Honolulu. They sailed into the harbour with the ship's rigging dressed and cheerfully signalling, "Hawaii annexed to the U.S. The whole Spanish fleet sunk off Santiago." The English captain confided to Beatrice that "Americans never remember that they were two to one when they sank the Spanish fleet." It was too hot even for the Webbs to do any investigating, and they spent their time in Honolulu in "good society" with the descendants of missionaries and a charming surf-bathing princess, Kaiulini.

The only other stop on the long hot voyage to New Zealand was Samoa where Trevelyan went to look at Robert Louis Stevenson's house, while the Webbs paced up and down the coconut groves discussing their next step towards collectivism—their inquiry into Local Government. On board ship, Sidney read and read until he was down to the last encyclopaedia, while Beatrice discovered that Phillip Trevelyan's company fell short of her expectations. He spent his time writing long accounts of the trip to his mother. "What ails him?" she complained. "He does not interest me." Their brief stay in New Zealand left them with the impression of a country where there were hardly any slums and no millionaires, whose citizens, although regrettably apathetic about municipal affairs, were nonetheless refined and ready to take any amount of exercise in the open air.

And what of Australia, the one truly democratic country they visited? Seemingly it was inhabited, Beatrice noted with distaste on landing, by "a lower middle-class population suddenly enriched". Pursuing their enquiry in Sidney, Melbourne, Adelaide and Victoria, they reached the conclusion that political feeling in Australia was limited to a hatred of direct taxation, and that municipal government was backward. Beatrice could not, for instance, extract any

information whatever about municipal procedure from the mayor
of Sidney.

Mostly they met lawyers, journalists, the government-house
people and the well-to-do. They came to the conclusion that racing
and money-making were the national concern. Australian women,
Beatrice found, were inferior to the men, "the quintessence of vulgarity, ostentatious, with an absence of H's and snobbish." Her view
that they were the "idle companions of men on the race-course" was
endorsed by a Melbourne lady doctor, (Dr Constance Stone) who, as
one scientist to another, informed Beatrice that Australian women
had stronger passions than American, that illegitimacy was frequent
among the rich, that birth control meant more self-indulgence, and
that the use of contraceptives probably induced cancer.

The only socialists the Webbs met during their tour were members
of the Socialist party in Victoria, who, hearing that the two famous
Fabians had arrived in their town, invited Sidney to lecture to
them. He agreed, not very graciously, to talk to a few of them.
"We met our poor relations in a dirty ill-ventilated place," wrote
Beatrice. "The believers in socialist shibboleths." The chairman was
a young man with a "retreating chin, dirty coat and inevitable red
tie . . . 'Comrade'! 'revolution'! 'capitalist press', 'class war' and
all the rest of the socialist cant was showered on us . . . Sidney, in a
wily address, tried to explain the Fabian policy of permeation . . ."
The chairman, getting the message, suggested to members that they
should follow Sidney's advice and "take capitalists down a back
street and knock them on the head."

Before leaving the democratic shores of Australia, they investigated
the working of the crack Melbourne race-course, and the following
paragraph appeared in the Sidney Bulletin. "Mr and Mrs Sidney
Webb left Melbourne after seeing the Melbourne Cup . . . probably
. . . new-chum visitors have never asked so many questions. Mr and
Mrs Sidney Webb comingled with all sorts and conditions of men in
Melbourne. . . . The few who met the joint authoress of *Industrial
Democracy* were charmed with her."

On the voyage home, a letter reached them from Bernard Shaw,
announcing his marriage to Charlotte:

I found my objection to my own marriage had ceased with my
objection to my own death . . . She (Charlotte) had at last got beyond that corrupt personal interest in me, just as *The Devil's*

Disciple had relieved me of the appearance of a pecuniary interest in her. . . . Being cleared of all such illusions as love interest, happiness interest and all the rest of the vulgarities of marriage, I hopped down to the Registrar.[1]

The news was welcome. It was just what Beatrice had planned for him.

Back at Grosvenor Road, the Webbs settled down to their study of local government. Their elaborate investigations stretched back to the seventeenth century, and they employed three secretaries for the project. They travelled through the provinces, copying records and making notes, returning from time to time to store the precious information on the shelves in the little room on the half-landing at the back of the house. They rose early to pursue their sociological researches. Francis Galton, one of their secretaries, described their procedure. "Mrs Webb was fertile in suggestions . . ." When she had made a "a particularly far-fetched suggestion which Webb had smilingly dismissed, I ventured to quote the well-known remark by John Morley that 'Abstract thinking is thinking withdrawn from the concrete and particular facts' . . . and . . . Sidney so far unbent as to chuckle quietly to himself for some time afterwards."[2] While Beatrice coined the facts and Sidney recorded them, discarding any not up to mint standard, she would take his small hand, raise it to her lips and, hungry for love, nibble it affectionately. Marriage, she was fond of saying, is the waste-paper basket of the emotions. Their companionship was untroubled by passion, and Beatrice had never been so happy as in their joint search for truth. "This curious process," she described it, "This joint undertaking. We throw the ball of thought one to the other, each of us resting, judging, inventing in turn. And we are not satisfied until the conclusion satisfies, completely and finally, both our minds."

After lunch, Sidney repaired to the London County Council. On at least two days a week, Beatrice walked to St. Paul's Cathedral to pray earnestly and humbly for health, strength and guidance to bring about a society where the poor would cease to suffer and the idle be at work. Now and again she lectured to the students of the London School of Economics, "helping younger persons less fortunately placed than oneself to the pathway of research." Sometimes Beatrice longed for leisure and silence, and the beauty of the countryside and the ideal cottage she and Sidney had promised themselves when their work was done, with endless book-shelves and two spare bedrooms and a sunny verandah, and sometimes she was panic-stricken, afraid they would never finish their formidable task. So little time was left. Then Sidney, unperturbed, would reassure her with his, "keep your hair on, Missus."

When they were in the country Beatrice took exercise or meditated about the mystery of things, while Sidney, who hated exercise and meditation, would occupy his mind by memorising advertisements or counting spots on a wall. Sometimes his old craving for passing examinations would sieze him and he would do the *Times* puzzle competition. He was bitterly disappointed once at not getting the prize of £1,000. He had felt sure he would get it because his number added up to eleven, the "mystical symbol" of their partnership. Beatrice melted with tenderness at this example of "her boy's" simplicity. Sometimes three or four days would go by without either of them speaking a word. Then, when their silent companionship was broken by what struck Beatrice as a brilliant suggestion and Sidney merely muttered, "That's not new," she would flare up. But soon they kissed and made friends. They never discussed religion because it bored Sidney. In his view, you might as well talk about what train to take without being in possession of a time-table. His relation to the universe, he insisted, was his relation to Beatrice. Beatrice discussed it endlessly with her atheist friends, but their unbelief never impressed her as much as Emily Brontë's *Last Lines*:

> There is no room for Death.
> Nor atom that his might could render void:
> Thou—Thou art Being and Breath,
> And what Thou art may never be destroy'd.

In the summer of 1899 Beatrice was distracted by two public events. She was obsessed with the Dreyfus case, followed every detail in the papers and discussed it until Sidney grew impatient and would not hear another word about it. He also refused to get excited about the Boer War. (Even so, Beatrice founded the "Coefficients", a dining club where important personages, Haldane and Hewins among others, met to discuss questions of imperialism.) Beatrice's family, which covered every shade of opinion from jingoism to fanatical pro-Boer, used to visit Grosvenor Road when they wanted a refuge from the raging controversy. Leonard Courtney lost his seat in Parliament on account of his pro-Boer sympathies and he and Kate, accustomed to a lively social life, found themselves ostracised. Leonard, whose life was already darkened by his approaching blindness, remained philosophical. "We are passing through some smoke, but it will clear off," he remarked. Another brother-in-law, Alfred Cripps, was less philosophical. He was a determined imperialist and had been rejected by the electors of Stroud after an expensive election campaign.

The Fabian Society was split on the issue. The majority—including Shaw and Graham Wallas—according to Pease, "recognised that the British Empire had to win the war and that no other conclusion to it was possible." But a minority, which included Ramsay MacDonald, Bertrand Russell and H. T. Muggeridge, believed that the Fabian Society should "disassociate itself from the imperialism of capitalism and vainglorious nationalism and condemn war."[3] H. T. Muggeridge was stoned at open-air meetings for his outspoken pro-Boer views. MacDonald and Russell resigned from the society as a protest against the majority view.

Beatrice herself wrote afterwards:

I am struck with an extraordinary omission which seems to have passed unnoticed at the time . . . no one seems to have remembered that the various claimants to power, whether Boer or British . . . were only a minority, amid a vast majority of Kaffirs, five or six millions in number, among whom this variegated white minority had intruded itself.

But at the time, her feelings about the war were complicated by the harsh public criticism of Joseph Chamberlain, about the confusion over orders to Dr. Jameson, and the mysterious disappearance of a number of telegrams. One day, at the height of the public outcry against Chamberlain, his daughter came to lunch with the Webbs. Before leaving, when she was putting on her veil, she turned to Beatrice and begged her to congratulate her father on having successfully demolished his critics. Beatrice affectionately assured her that she and Sidney had never attached much importance to the telegrams. But she admitted to herself, privately, that his behaviour had been neither honourable, chivalrous nor even discreet.

She met him one evening on the terrace of the House of Commons, after one of Haldane's dinner-parties, and introduced him to Sidney. "I think you were in my office, Mr. Webb," said Chamberlain. Sidney replied quickly, "That is hardly quite correct. When I was there, you were not." Beatrice was conscious of amused stares from their fellow-guests as they talked together, and when she got up to leave, she realised that the bond between herself and "the man she loved but could not follow" was still unbroken. It was ridiculous, she told herself, as she walked with Sidney back to their "simple home". She was forty, and Chamberlain now over sixty. A year later, she met him again, and recorded sadly in her diary that "he saw a woman no longer young, living without the surroundings of wealth and social position, badly dressed and without any apparent distinction. And in spite of knowing that I loved him desperately, he turned away and left me."

In the early summer, when they were staying on the south coast, and Sidney had gone to London for the day, Beatrice lay on the beach in the sunshine, listening to "the slow withdrawing of the ocean swell ... like the inevitable withdrawal of a lover from his mistress ... and the bubbling ... of the tide in the caves ... spirits of children not yet born." Were their books worth more to the community than the children they might have had? she asked herself reflectively. Would the same man do as father of one's children and joint author? Should a man or woman have more than one lover? Then she thought of her "boy", writing "page after page, hour after hour", and pushing her bicycle uphill. The waves withdrew with "a sweet low moan" and she shook herself and got up to go back to her writing, remembering that she was over forty, and grey and wrinkled.

Periodically, the Webbs went off on their bicycles to some remote spot where they could work without distraction. They stayed with Mary Playne at Longfords and Beatrice rode over to Standish with Sidney. There they covered their bicycles with leaves in the woods as she and her sisters had once covered Herbert Spencer and wandered, hand-in-hand, past the village shops and cottages and rode back in the evening through the deep lanes, discussing grants-in-aid. Sometimes they visited Bertrand Russell and his American wife Alys—a sister of Logan Pearsall Smith—in Surrey. She was a "smiling Quaker" and Bertrand an "exact logician without a sense of sin". Both were Fabians.

Bertrand Russell admired and liked Beatrice for her ability and as a kind friend but he considered her undemocratic and arrogant. When he asked her if she ever felt shy she told him that if she did she would say to herself, "Why should I be? I am the cleverest member of the cleverest family of the cleverest class of the cleverest race in the world."[4] Sidney he esteemed less, calling him a "second-division civil servant who rose through immense industry to the first-division". But, he added, "To have some of the attributes of a human being is all you can ask." Russell disagreed with the Webbs' worship of the state, and, much later, with what he called their "absurd adulation of the Soviet Government". He never took them quite seriously and could not resist teasing them sometimes, as when he pointed out that the people who elect a member of parliament cannot be stupider than the man they elect. "That is the sort of argument I don't like," Sidney retorted irritably.

Again when Beatrice told Russell that starvation made her see visions, he replied, "If you eat too little you see visions; if you drink too much you see pink elephants." The Russells, Beatrice noted, were romantically attached to each other and "slept and dressed in the same room and had no children", just like Sidney and herself. She was mystified later when the Russells parted and wondered what could have interfered with that light-hearted companionship between her two friends who had so much intellect between them.

In London, Beatrice was seeing more of her sisters, who as they grew older were turning to religion and metaphysics as a refuge from their prosperous marriages, and all eager to meet their now successful brother-in-law. Rosy was again a worry to them all. As a wealthy widow, still young, she had spent the last few years wandering, with her little son and his governess, from Monte Carlo to Rome, from the Swiss Alps to Naples and Capri, picking up bohemian friends wherever she went. Now she had turned up in Chelsea with a handsome Irish husband. Beatrice alleged that she was again meeting former admirers. "Never any good," she wrote of Rosy. "Now positively evil ... mad or bad or both ... each successive development of her character more hateful than the other. ... She has gained in health and intelligence but this has increased her insane desire for flattery and physical indulgence, and her deceitfulness and passionate masterfulness." She added that Rosy—"terrible sister" —was a caricature of family characteristics, and that "each one of us recognises in her, family traits." Rosy, indifferent to her sister's opinion, was very soon subdued by matrimony, bore her husband five lusty children, lived with him in not unreasonable strife, and retained his affection to the end of their days.

Beatrice went through a period of deep dissatisfaction with herself.

[165]

She became subject to nausea and fatigue, obsessed with the idea that marrying without love was a mortal sin, or that she was dying of an incurable disease. She longed for emotional relationships, religion, and *douceur de vivre*. She even began to think of Rosy more charitably when she considered her own temptations. She met a doctor in Bradford who told her that eating was the cause of much illness and asked him how much an intellectual women of forty should eat a day. "At most one pound a day," was his grave reply. "Abstinence and prayer may prove to be the way to salvation in this world—at least for such as me," she wrote hopefully. She weighed herself regularly on Charing Cross station, and was jubilant when she lost a little weight and could manage a ride of thirty miles instead of only twenty on her bicycle. She was sure her brain was working better. A month after starting the cure, she was emaciated and apathetic but determined to "persevere short of ceasing to exist", but was forced to modify the treatment. In the end she was convinced that "poisons" were eliminated and "chatterings in personal vanity" ceased to trouble her and the mysterious ailment vanished. But she kept to the Spartan habit of diet to the end of her life.

"Wells' *Anticipations*. The most remarkable book of the year," Beatrice wrote at the end of 1901. She and Sidney, while on a bicycling holiday, called on the author and his wife, in their little house at Sandgate, and found him "a pleasant breezy person, eager to establish himself among interesting folk". Beatrice approved of the way that the Wellses, while being touchingly frank about their humble origins, had carefully trained themselves in dress and table manners and were "fit to associate with the greatest in the land". H. G. Wells said, "The Webbs are wonderful people. They leave me ashamed of my laziness." They were impressed with his imagination, and his being a "speculator in ideas . . . In one sense he is a romancer spoilt by romancing—but in the present stage of sociology he is useful to gradgrinds like ourselves in supplying us with loose generalisations which we can use as instruments of research." She gave a little dinner for him, "carefully selected". "The Prime Minister let himself go and, I think, thoroughly enjoyed the mixture of chaff and dialectic which flew from G. B. S. to Wells and round the table to Sidney, the Bishop of Stepney and myself."

The Webbs explained to Wells their idea of an official administrative class of experts—a modern Samurai to run the state. Wells, sending Beatrice a copy of his book, *A Modern Utopia*, told her, "The chapter on the Samurai will pander to your worst instincts." They became friendly enough for her to ask him why there seemed to be an anti-Webb current of feeling among the Fabians led by Graham Wallas. Wells suggested that Sidney was too much given to making an art of back-room tactics and gave a "foxy" impression and that she and Sidney played too much into each other's hands.

Wells joined the Fabian Society, but he was hampered by being a bad speaker. In later years he described his own delivery as "speaking haltingly on the verge of the inaudible, addressing my tie through a cascade of moustache that was no help at all, making ill-judged departures into parenthesis, correcting myself as though I were a manuscript under treatment."[5] When he gave an address on Socialism for the middle-classes, ending with a denunciation of the family, Beatrice turned to his novel *The Days of the Comet* to comprehend his argument. It ended "with a glowing anticipation of promiscuity in sexual relations," she noted.

> The argument is one that is familiar to most intellectuals—it has often cropped up in my mind and has seemed to have some validity. Friendship between particular men and women has an enormous educational value to both (specially to the woman.) Such a friendship is practically impossible . . . without physical intimacy; you do not, as a matter of fact, get to know any man thoroughly except as his beloved and his lover—if you could have been the beloved of the dozen ablest men you have known it would have greatly extended your knowledge of human nature and human affairs.

But, because Beatrice honestly admitted the attraction of Wells' theory, she was at pains to bring up equally passionate arguments on the other side; that the "perturbation caused by such intimacies" would leave a woman "no brain to think with", and that it would bring "a great increase in sexual emotion for its own sake and not for the sake of bearing children. And that way madness lies. . . ." After an argument with Wells on the subject she wrote in her diary:

> I cling to the thought that man will only evolve upwards by the subordination of his physical desires and appetites to the intellectual and spiritual side of his nature. Unless this evolution be the purpose of the race, I despair—wish only for the extinction of human consciousness. Without this hope—without this

faith—I could not struggle on. It is this purpose and this purpose only that gives a meaning to the constantly recurring battles of good and evil within one's own nature—and to one's persistent endeavour to find the ways and means of combating the evil habits of the mass of men. Oh! for a Church that would weld into one living force all who hold this faith, with the discipline and the consolations fitted to sustain their endeavour.

The other article of the Webbs' social faith which was "really repulsive" to Wells was their belief that the community owed moral training to children and "collective regulation of the behaviour of the adult". It was Sidney's pragmatic attitude towards church schools—tolerating them because they did provide elementary education—which usually sparked off this particular argument. Wells said, "I don't believe in tolerance, you have got to fight against anything being taught anybody which seems to you harmful, you have got to struggle to get your own creed taught." The mutual admiration society between the Wells and the Webbs was predictably short-lived. Sidney disliked Wells because he was brash, and threw out ideas merely to produce an effect; and Beatrice was too utterly opposed to him on her two most important beliefs—religion (of some kind) and chastity—to tolerate him for long, in spite of his scientific imagination. She suspected—correctly—that the disillusionment was mutual and that Wells resented the Webbs' "well-regulated prosperity". He was flippant about their monumental history of local government, asking how "investigating the methods of a Dogberry and a Shallow" could possibly contribute to the blue-print of a collectivist society.

Wells almost wrecked the Fabian Society. He told its members that it was "small . . . shabbily poor . . . collectively inactive", lived in a miserable cellar with an insufficient staff, did not welcome members and had private jokes. "Their supreme delight is to *giggle* and they permeate English society with their reputed Socialism about as much as a mouse may be said to permeate a cat." His remedy was that the Society should reorganise the executive, replacing the "old gang" with younger leaders, increase its membership and scrap the old-fashioned "basis", tax subscribers in order to get a "light, beautiful and hopeful" office and to publish plenty of bright new tracts, engage a large paid staff and organise an immense number of branches. The executive was aggravatingly reasonable about this attack. They printed Wells' address on "The Faults of the Fabians" in the *Fabian News* and formed a special committee, to be nominated by Wells, to discuss his proposals. Wells was elected to the executive, but the report of the special committee was subsequently rejected. In 1908 he resigned from the Fabians altogether, on the pretext that its "basis" allowed the non-Socialistic principle of mother and child being economically dependent on the father. In fact the firm entrenchment of the old leaders of the Society really defeated him. In any debate, Shaw could always make a fool of Wells, and though Wells was the idol of the younger generation, his increasing absorption in his own career and his private life occupied him too much for him to persist in trying to take over the leadership of the Fabians. Beatrice wrote crossly that Wells was engaged in

> an odd mixture of underhand manoeuvres and insolent bluster ... absolutely the first time he has tried to co-operate with his fellow-men and he has neither the training nor tradition to fit him to do it. ... I tell Sidney not to be too hard upon him and to remember that there was a time when 'the Webbs' were thought not too straight and not too courteous in their dealings (and that after a dozen years of men and affairs).

She reflected that if Wells had only

> pushed his own forward policy or rather enthusiasm for vague and big ideas without making a personal attack on the old gang he would have succeeded. ... There are fine qualities in the man of heart and intellect but he has no manners in the broadest meaning of them, is suspicious, insolent and untruthful ... it *is* training and the habit of public affairs that enables a man or woman to play fair when their passions are aroused.

The end of their friendship, she wrote later, was the "sordid intrigue" of Wells with the daughter of one of their old friends, an affair which Wells described glowingly in his novel *Ann Veronica*. The Webbs, learning that "Ann Veronica" was pregnant by Wells, felt "obliged to warn Sydney Olivier ... against letting his four handsome daughters run about with H. G. Wells. ... Olivier quoted us as his authority." This led to some abusive letters from Wells and scathing replies from Beatrice. Beatrice wanted to "stand by" the girl, in enlightened Victorian fashion. "We will make a real honest effort to get a hold over her and prevent the rot going further." But Ann Veronica "settled in the charming little cottage H. G. Wells has taken for her", was quite pleased with her own arrangements and only wanted to make sure her father would continue to pay her allowance. Beatrice prophesied that Wells would escape without "punishment and without financial liability", and visualised "poor little A. in the gutter, consorting in her despair with some other man ... doomed to sink deeper in the mire with every fresh adventure". She reflected that any sexual experiment involved so much deceit and secrecy that it was "this that makes any divergence from conventional morality so sordid and lowering". She added one of the strangest remarks she ever recorded in her diary. "That is why upright minds are careful not to experiment except in 'the accustomed way',"—that is, with prostitutes.

Wells' revenge was to write *The New Machiavelli*, a novel caricaturing the Webbs. He discribed the attitude of "Altiora Bailey" (that is, Beatrice) towards marriage as

something that happened to the adolescent and unmarried when you threw them together under the circumstances of health, warmth and leisure. ... The young people settled down, children ensued, and father and mother turned their minds, now decently and properly disillusioned, to other things. That, to Altiora, was the normal sexual life. ... I don't know what dreams Altiora may have had in her schoolroom days, I always suspected her of suppressed and forgotten phases, but certainly her general effect now was of an entirely passionless worldliness in these matters. Indeed so far as I could gather, she regarded sexual passion as being hardly more legitimate in a civilised person than—let us say—homicidal mania. She must have forgotten and Bailey—[that is, Sidney] too. I suspect she forgot before she married him.[6]

In the book, the hero's idyllic love-affair was destroyed by the spiteful scandal-mongering of a "set" which was so plainly the one which, in real life, gathered around the Webbs' ménage, that no one even pretended not to recognise it. Wells described the Grosvenor Road house as "a hard little house":

The place was almost pretentiously matter-of-fact and unassuming. The narrow passage-hall, papered with some ancient yellowish paper grained to imitate wood, was choked with hats and cloaks . . . we made our way up a narrow staircase past the open door of a small study packed with blue-books, to discover Altiora Bailey receiving before the fireplace in her drawing-room. She was a tall commanding figure, splendid but a little untidy in black silk and red beads, with dark eyes that had no depths, with a clear hard voice that had an almost visible pro-minence, aquiline features and straight black hair that was apt to get astray, that was now astray like the head feathers of an eagle in a gale. She stood with her hands behind her back, and talked in a high tenor of a projected Town Planning Bill. . . . 'Everyone comes here,' said Esmeer. 'Mostly we hate them like poison—jealousy—and little irritations—Altiora can be a horror at times—but we have to come. . . . It's one of the parts of the British machinery . . . that doesn't show . . . Two people who've planned to be a power—in an original way. And by jove! they've done it!' . . . Oscar Bailey was a short sturdy figure with a rounded protruding abdomen and a curious broad, flattened, clean-shaven face that seemed nearly all forehead. . . . He peered up with reddish swollen-looking eyes over gilt-edged glasses . . . and he talked in an ingratiating undertone with busy thin lips, an eager lisp and nervous movements of the hand. Altiora . . . had much of the vigour and handsomeness of a slender impu-dent young man, and an unscrupulousness altogether feminine. . . . She was neither uncertain, coy, nor hard to please, and altogether too stimulating and aggressive for any gentleman's hours of ease. . . . Yet you mustn't imagine she was an in-elegant or unbeautiful woman . . . but her soul was bony, and at the base of her was a vanity gaunt and greedy. When she wasn't in a state of personal untidiness that was partly a protest againt the waste of hours exacted by the toilet and partly a natural disinclination, she had a gypsy splendour of black and red and silver all her own.

This was the "salon on Grosvenor Road" which Shaw had sug-gested when Sidney first married Beatrice. He wrote to Sidney, "Webb, me boy, a wurd wuz yis. I am seriously of the opinion that what is wanted is a salon for the cultivation of the Socialist Party in Parliament. Will Madame Potter-Webb undertake it?"[7] Accord-ing to Sidney's fellow-Fabian, R. C. K. Ensor, the salon's "permea-tion" tactics developed away from their original idea.

Gone was the notion that Webb's career was to be that of a brilliant House of Commons man graduating to become a Socialist Minister in a Radical Cabinet. Instead had come the conception of him as a man purged of any desire to enter Parliament or hold office at all; a man personally disinterested in political wisdom (attested by a growing row of very solid books) which it was their delight to impart to anyone deemed capable of using it.[8]

The Webbs were now the recognised intellectual leaders of British Socialism in England and abroad. They set about fostering a socialist evolution by deliberately cultivating the acquaintance of those in positions of power and of authority in order to persuade or bamboozle them into putting socialist legislation onto the statute book. Beatrice first justified "permeation" as she called it when they were promoting the London Education Act.

> For good or for evil . . . we were compelled, if we wished to succeed to seek out those personages who could help to carry out our policy. How else can we explain our association with . . . Conservative cabinet ministers? . . . Why did our dear friend Haldane insist on introducing us to other members of the Liberal League?

The Webbs were also taken up by the exquisite "Souls", an aristocratic company of men and women, beautiful intellectual butterflies whose reputation for wit is a tradition to this day. They visited Stanway, the home of Lady Elcho, the Archdeaconess of the Souls and met Mrs. Pat Campbell, to whom Sidney took a great dislike. He was no longer susceptible to beautiful women and thought Shaw's infatuation with Mrs. Pat a sign of senility. He complained when the lovely Lady Desborough (one of the great beauties of Edwardian society) sat next to him at lunch that she had a "silly trick of shutting her eyes at you". The Elchos came to Grosvenor Road in return and dined off Welsh mutton and rice pudding. There were grand parties, too, at the Asquiths. Beatrice thought that Margot Asquith's "sparkling sallies" and Lady Dickson Poynder's "pretty folly" were an unsuitable background for a democratic Minister like Asquith, and when Margot and Lord Hugh Cecil asked her in blank amazement, "But *why* change anything?" —she had to check an indignant retort. "Brilliant but silly Souls," she and Sidney agreed on their way back to their "shabby little home". The Prime Minister, Arthur Balfour, was also one of them, and at a dinner Beatrice took him in. "I say 'took' because he was so obviously delivered over into my hands by my kindly hostess who wished me to make as much use as possible of the one and a half hours he had free from the House." Beatrice was delighted with Balfour. "I set myself to amuse and interest him but seized every opportunity to insinuate sound doctrine and information as to the position of London education. Sidney says I managed skilfully, but then he is a partial judge!" She glowed under his flirtatious eyes and called him "Prince Arthur" and they "talked and laughed and showed off". He invited the Webbs to stay. "What shall I say of our visit? Too self-consciously Arthur's 'latest friend' to be quite pleasant, the party each night becoming a watched tête-à-tête between us two—the rest of the company sitting around, as Sidney said, 'making conversation'." Beatrice added reflectively, "For philanderer, refined and consummate is Prince Arthur, accustomed always to make others feel what he fails to feel himself. How many women has he inspired with a discontent with their life and life companion, haunted with the perpetual refrain—'If only . . .'"

Beatrice enjoyed this social life so much that she began to fear that her weakness of personal vanity and love of admiration was getting out of hand. "How any mortal with resources of their own and a few intelligent friends can exert themselves to get into 'Society' passes my comprehension. And yet I have just expended twenty-one guineas on an evening dress!" Sidney was repressive about their increasing social round. "You won't be able to work next morning and I don't think it is desirable that we should be seen in the houses of great people. By all means be courteous, but keep clear of them." Beatrice "recognised the better voice" and tore up her invitation-cards.

But the Webbs were in fashion, "strange to say not as reformers and experts but as persons with a special kind of *chic*".

The Duchess of Marlborough wrote note after note to Beatrice because she "apparently has been seized by a whim to hear Sidney lecture and get us to dine with them afterwards." The Webbs wondered why the Duchess insisted on dragging the Duke to a technical lecture and to entertain "two dowdy middle-class intellectuals uncomfortably at a restaurant—for quite obviously they had

come up to London on purpose." She came to the depressing conclusion that they were angling for an invitation to meet Bernard
Shaw.

Even we have a sort of reflected glory as his intimate friends . . .
whenever he is free there is such a crowd of journalists and
literary hangers-on around him that one feels it is kinder to
spare him one's company. . . . What a transformation scene
from those first years I knew him; the scathing, bitter opponent
of wealth and leisure—and now! the adored one of the smartest
and most cynical set of English 'society'. Some might say that
we, too, had travelled in that direction; our good sense preserve
us!

The Webbs were particularly irritated with Shaw, because of his
intractability over the L.C.C. elections. Shaw had stood as candidate
for St. Pancras, and Sidney had gone all out on wire-pulling to get
him elected, taking charge of Shaw's committee-rooms, writing
round to the twenty-one clergy in the constituency "imploring them
to go hard for Shaw", and calling up the whole of the Fabian
Society on Shaw's behalf. Sidney even resorted to "puffing him out-
rageously in the *Daily Mail*," Beatrice recorded crossly. But Shaw
would run his election his own way, insisting that he was an atheist,
and that, as a teetotaller, he would force every citizen to imbibe a
quart of rum to cure any tendency to intoxication. He laughed at the
nonconformist conscience, chaffed the Catholics about transub-
stantiation, abused the Liberals and contemptuously patronised the
Conservatives—until nearly every section was equally disgruntled.
Beatrice was "not wholly grieved" when he was badly beaten at the
polls.

In 1903 Herbert Spencer died, an unresigned atheist. "Why
should I be resigned when I have nothing to hope for in return?"
he asked. He was glad to see Beatrice, who loyally visited him
during his last months. "Poor old friend; I verily believe that he
thinks it a treat for me to spend so many hours in his stuffy house,
subsisting on his stingy housekeeping, so stingy that I sometimes
spend no little time in considering whether I can manufacture an
excuse to get a good meal out."

"It is goodbye, dear old—or is it young?—friend," he said with
a glimmer of his old facetiousness. "My oldest and dearest friend,
let us break bread together. You and I have had the same end. It is

only in methods we have differed." She kissed him on the forehead and took his hand in hers as they shared a plate of grapes together on the bed.

He was buried in Highgate cemetery, near to Karl Marx, and the last words were spoken by Leonard Courtney to a few friends gathered round the grave. He was deeply mourned in France and America, and in Italy the Deputies arose and adjourned the Chamber for an hour to commemorate the passing of a great thinker. In England the news of his death was received with indifference although only *The Times* actually published an attack on him. His philosophy of individualism was already half-forgotten and the State was creeping up on Man.

Already Beatrice's political nose began to sniff changes in the Liberal air around her. New names were cropping up in the Liberal Party. Rosebery was disclaiming social reform; Campbell-Bannerman was coming to the front ranks and Lloyd George, behind him, was emerging as a brilliant parliamentarian. "A worthy little person of honest conviction, but without a notion about national administration," Beatrice thought. Winston Churchill impressed her even less favourably. He was "restless, egotistical, bumptious, shallow-minded and reactionary", disqualifications redeemed by a personal magnetism and pluck which even Beatrice could detect. But he drank and talked too much and thought too little and seemed utterly ignorant of social questions. "I never do any brainwork that anyone else can do for me," he told her. Beatrice disapproved and advised him to stick to the Tory Party. There was more office in it, she said.

Politicans were getting a little tired of being managed by the Webbs. Campbell-Bannerman, who had never liked them, wrote, "We have had the benefit of instruction from Mr. Webb and have survived it." Nevertheless, permeation had achieved one thing. It was through her friendship with Balfour that Beatrice was appointed to serve on the Royal Commission on the Poor Law, giving her the opportunity of becoming a reformer in her own right. It was an important event in her life; it also heralded the break-up of the Salon at Grosvenor Road.

12

Poor Law
1905–1912

IF YOU WANTED TO PIN-POINT the moment in time when the very first foundation of the Welfare State was laid, a reasonable date to choose would be the last fortnight of November in 1905. During it, a young journalist and social worker named William Beveridge was co-opted onto a committee for dealing with unemployment; Shaw's *Major Barbara* had its first performance and Beatrice was appointed to the Royal Commission on the Poor Law—an appointment which set her on the road to the great achievement of her life. She lived to see most of her ideas accepted, in the Beveridge Report of 1942, but died before they were implemented in post-war Britain.

Beveridge's co-option onto the unemployment committee was important, because through it he first began to work with Beatrice and Sidney, and, as he said himself, "The Beveridge Report stemmed from what all of us had imbibed from the Webbs."[1] *Major Barbara* was important because it put the new twentieth-century attitude to poverty into dramatic form and hurled it into the face of the upper and middle classes. The "time-spirit" of the nineteenth century had been its consciousness of sin about the linking of progress with poverty, and a belief that it was a moral duty to reform the characters of the poor. The twentieth century aimed at reforming their physical condition, neither out of pity nor morality, but from enlightened self-interest. As Shaw put it, "Poor people, abject people, dirty people, ill-fed, ill-clothed people poison us, morally and physically; they kill the happiness of society, they force us to do away with our own liberties and organise unnatural cruelties for fear they should rise against us and drag us down into their abyss."[2] Beatrice's appointment to the Royal Commission was most important of all, because through it she laid down the first blue-print of cradle-to-grave social security which could wipe out destitution without toppling the whole social structure in the process of removing its feet of clay.

The Prime Minister, Balfour, who had appointed the Commission, went with the Webbs to the opening performance of *Major Barbara*. Both he and Beatrice were extremely shaken by "the force —the horrible force" of Shaw's theme. (Sidney was placidly immune to the pity and terror experienced by more susceptible playgoers.) It upset Beatrice so much that she was driven to call on Shaw to reason with him about it. Shaw told her that the middle classes would not face up to the fact that the only way to convert the poor is to make them comfortably-off, that if they are better-fed, better-housed and better-clothed, they will be better-behaved; but it is the material advantages, and only the material ones which matter. "I found it difficult to answer him," Beatrice admitted. "But he did not convince me. There is something lacking in his presentment of the crime of poverty." And although it was Beatrice herself who put the twentieth-century "time-spirit" into its most concrete form, in the Welfare State, something in her remained sturdily Victorian to the very end. "What has to be aimed at is not this or that improvement in material circumstances or physical comfort but an improvement in personal character,"[3] she wrote. She believed that citizens who were given benefits by the community ought to make an effort to improve themselves, or at least submit themselves to those who would improve them. She wanted to have social services on a scale never dreamed of before—but with strings attached—For instance:

> When the visitor from the Children's Care Committee discovered an underfed child . . . it would be no use for the man to say he was out of work . . . he would simply be required to be at the Labour Exchange where he would either be provided with a job or found the means of improving his working capacity while he was waiting for a job. If it was discovered by actual observation of the man's present behaviour that there was in him a grave moral defect not otherwise remediable, he would have to submit himself, in a detention colony, to a treatment which would be at once curative and deterrent . . .[4]

She wanted medical aid to be available to all—but with an obligation on the sick person to get well and stay healthy. (Since Beatrice firmly believed that if she was strong-willed enough she could manage this herself, she assumed that other people could.) She was against patients in a national health service having a free choice of doctor, because they would be liable to choose the "kindest"; that is, the one "least censorious about personal weaknesses and most indulgent in dragging out convalescence", the one who would allow the patient whatever diet, personal indulgences, home sanitation and going out at night that he liked, instead of disciplining him. She wanted money to be diverted from the rich to the poor, "so long as it is accompanied by an increase in personal responsibility on the part of the benefited classes". The Charity Organisation Society embodied the Victorian idea of using alms-giving as an instrument to make the poor reform their ways. Beatrice wanted to use welfare services to make them into better citizens; that is, to make people good by Act of Parliament. She had not travelled as far as she thought she had from the C.O.S.'s theories about the "deserving poor", and it did not occur to her that being coerced by a Local Authority official or by a voluntary do-gooder feels much the same at the receiving end.

Like Shaw, she was unwillingly attracted by the Salvation Army's mystical belief that if you drew sinners into the fold by ministering to their bodily need, you could keep them there to save their souls. Shaw said (meaning it as a compliment) that the Salvation Army with its fervour and love might lead the poor to turn round and burn their own slums. Beatrice, visiting a Salvation Army farm colony for the unemployed, and comparing it with the state-run variety, was troubled by the difference in atmosphere between the two, and even wondered if Salvation Army officials might turn out to be the *Samurai* caste she was always looking for, who would rule society for its own good. But she turned down the idea, like "Major Barbara" herself, because 'it is cheap work, converting starving men with a Bible in one hand and a slice of bread in the other."[5]

Beatrice, in her twenties, had made a deliberate decision to study "the chronic destitution of whole sections of the people" as her life-work. Being appointed to the Royal Commission was the ideal opportunity. It was odd, in a way, considering the Victorian obsession with the problem of poverty, that no government arranged for an enquiry into the poor laws until the beginning of the twentieth century. The previous one had been the Royal Commission of seventy years before. It had at least broken new ground by suggesting that pauperism (that is, throwing yourself onto the mercy of the community, to be supported by it) was preventable, and not just an unavoidable misfortune imposed by a mysterious Providence. But the 1834 Commission's idea of prevention was to goad the very poor person into struggling against this final surrender. This was the object of the notorious "less eligibility" principle on which the law was based, that you must always make sure that the pauper's lot was less eligible than that of the worst-paid workman, so that he would try to support himself at all costs. In order to make this principle effective, all Boards of Guardians, throughout the country, were supposed to give exactly the same severely restricted relief, which must never take the form of a hand-out, but only of board and lodging in the workhouse.

Sidney and Beatrice, suspiciously discussing Tory motives in appointing a commission about the poor at all, came to the cynical conclusion that it was probably for the purpose of getting the 1834 laws tightened up. Over the years, the severities had been relaxed in some districts, which meant that it was worth the pauper's while to shop round for an easier billet, or for an unmarried mother to be careful about which side of a parish border her child was born on. Before the Commission's proceedings started, Beatrice called on a zealous official who had been recently appointed to the Local Government Board and "extracted" from him the admission that he and his colleagues meant to coerce the commission into making the administrative changes they wanted, and also into preventing private charity from softening the harshness of the legal regulations. Much gratified at having her very worst suspicions confirmed, she hurried off to Charles Booth who had also been appointed a commissioner (and who greeted her as amiably as if there had never been any coldness between them about her marriage). They agreed that they would head off any attempt by permanent officials to sway the commission for their own purposes.

There were only two commissioners, besides herself, of Labour or Socialist persuasion—the secretary of the Carpenters' Union, and George Lansbury, who was at that time an east-end borough-councillor and (as always) an idealist and a humanitarian. Beatrice described him as a "thoroughgoing sentimentalist". Octavia Hill, Beatrice's former preceptor in housing reform, was also a member. Apart from these, the commission was conventional and conservative, and heavily weighted with supporters of the Charity Organisation Society, including its secretary, Loch, with whom Beatrice (over-optimistically) expected to see eye-to-eye on questions of investigation. Other omens were unpromising. The English officials meant to turn the enquiry to their own ends, the Scottish and Irish ones did not want an enquiry at all, Charles Booth wanted it to find out the "right treatment" for paupers, and George Lansbury wanted to know why anyone should be condemned to be a pauper at all. Besides this divergence inside the Commission, the President of the local Government Board, who had been instrumental in getting it all started (Gerald Balfour, the Tory Prime Minister's brother), lost his post when the government lost the election, and in his place was the unaccountable John Burns. (There was a story circulating that when Campbell-Bannerman offered him the post, he clasped the new Premier by the hand and said, "I congratulate you Sir Henry; it will be the most popular appointment you have made.")

From the first meeting of the Commission onwards, Beatrice was as restive as a race-horse compelled to run in harness with a team of lumbering dray-horses. But the majority faction deserves a modest niche in history for the part its individual members played as devil's advocates, since it was their stubborn opposition to Beatrice's ideas that clarified the issues in her own mind, and made her build up a series of concrete proposals out of them. Before the Commission, her ideas for dealing with the problem of poverty were limited to her own belief in the value of "real" research and Fabian theories—such as taking the sick poor out of the poor law. But because the battle was so hot, she took to making all kinds of exhaustive surveys into various aspects of poverty herself, and in the end constructed a detailed blue-print of a (then) imaginary society, in which different public services would meet the different human needs, on the principle that "prevention is not only much better but much cheaper than cure". It was, in essence, her contribution to the "Utopia" literature so popular among her contemporaries, but unique because hers was worked out in practical detail. H. G. Wells might have imagined such a state, but he could not have added the handbook of instructions for the reader to set about constructing the model himself.

At the beginning of her battles with her fellow-commissioners Beatrice prayed for patience. "To be single-minded in pursuit of truth, courteous in manner and kind in feeling . . . modestly persistent in my aim must be my prayer," she told herself severely. "It will need all my self-command to keep myself from developing a foolish hostility and becoming self-conscious in my desire to get sound investigation. I was not over-pleased with my tone this afternoon and must try to do better." She found listening to the pedestrian recitals of witnesses so boring that she could hardly bear to waste time at the meetings, but when she was allowed to cross-examine them she was so pertinacious that the other members stopped her. She retorted by drawing up, with Sidney, a memorandum about methods of enquiry and circulating it round the Commission. Charles Booth scolded her for arousing hostility unnecessarily. "He may be right. On the other hand if one begins by being disagreeable one may come in the end to a better bargain," meditated the daughter of hard-headed Richard Potter.

In the first months, the quarrels centred round the question of whether it was Beatrice or the chairman who was supposed to be running the Commission, but presently an ideological battle began to take shape. The majority considered that the issue was how to relieve destitution, while to Beatrice it was—increasingly—to find out the causes of it. Although Balfour had confided to her that he had deliberately avoided including "any politicians" on the Commission, the battle was really between a Conservative point of view, bent on making the original structure good enough to continue working, and a Socialist one, aiming at fundamental reform. As a sub-plot to the main conflict, there was one between rival methods of investigation—the conventional way of listening to evidence or the Webb-style interview. It was this that made Loch, of the C.O.S., her most implacable opponent. To Beatrice, the causes of poverty were economic and social; to Loch they were always in the character of the individual. He believed that "Poverty is principally the result of a moral failure and indiscriminate charity...aggravates the failure", and that pauperism was "a habitual reliance on others due to want of self-control and foresight and of the goodness that underlies these things".[6] What sparked off the Loch–Beatrice quarrels was usually a competition in the cross-examination of witnesses. On one occasion, as Beatrice reported in her diary, Loch turned "white with rage" and protested that she was introducing "misleading statements of economic doctrine".

The room was cleared. 'Now, Mr. Loch,' I said in my blandest tone, 'I have listened to you cross-examining a series of witnesses and...however ignorant of the whole subject-matter these witnesses may be, they invariably come out at your conclusion. So long as you pursue this policy, I shall continue to make each successive witness say the exact contrary of what he has said to you.'

Halfway through the first year, when the chairman was beginning to calculate how soon they could complete their work, Beatrice
started a new hare. The C.O.S. contingent was arguing that
medical relief should be restricted to those who were "completely
destitute". At this point, "it suddenly flashed across my mind that
what we had to do was to adopt the exactly contrary attitude"; that
is, to make medical treatment not a favour granted to those in desperate need but to compel all sick persons to submit to it, "to treat
illness, in fact, as a public nuisance to be suppressed in the interests
of the community." (This idea of illness being anti-social had been a
feature of Butler's *Erewhon*, one of the "Utopia" books of the
eighteen-seventies.) She invited a medical member of the Commission to dinner and she and Sidney convinced him of their point of
view, which he obediently produced at the next meeting and then
tried to retract. The chairman agreed "in a frightened way" that
Mrs Webb might as well present a memorandum on the subject.
She organised an exhaustive private inquiry into medical aid, sub-
sidised by Charlotte Shaw. By the end of the year she had actually
succeeded in driving the Commission, reluctantly, towards enquiring
into the causes of destitution. This was not at all the same as finding
the reasons for pauperism. Being destitute was being short of the
necessities of life. Becoming a pauper was going "on the parish",
being a burden to the community. Once you began to trace the
cause of destitution, you were dangerously near to the radical
question asked by the very first Fabian tract—*Why Are the Many
Poor?*

Beatrice's answer to it, and her great contribution to the social
history of the twentieth century, is that "the poor" are not a separate
race, with common characteristics, nor even a separate class, but
groups of persons suffering from identifiable misfortunes; some
sick, some handicapped, some orphaned or widowed, old or
mentally ill, some either temporarily or continually unemployed
and some on starvation wages. All these varied disabilities resulted
in their ending up destitute, just as patients suffering from different
complaints all end up prostrate in bed. But that does not mean that
the same remedy is right for them all, especially since some can only
be given a palliative while others can be cured. Most important of
all, she suggested that a great many of the misfortunes which lead
to poverty can be prevented from occurring at all. Her solution was
to distribute the destitute among local authority departments which

dealt with their kind of need, not with the "pauperism" which had developed because of the need. For instance, at that time a patient could not see a Poor Law doctor until he was technically "destitute", which meant that none of these doctors ever saw a case of tuberculosis until it had gone too far to cure, because the patient had to wait until he was too weak to work and had sold up everything in the house.

Pauper children, instead of being brought up in a General Mixed Workhouse should be turned over to the education department, which would train them up to be useful citizens. Widows, instead of being supported with their children in the workhouse, should be paid "boarding-out" fees to look after them in their own home. The "healthy and deserving aged" should receive a pension which would liberate them from having to spend their last years in the dreaded "Union". "Only by re-distribution of the services can you get curative and restorative treatment,"[7] Beatrice summed up. But in 1905 this was a concept which the Commission could not—or would not—grasp. The Charity Organisation Society said that what was needed was one nation-wide voluntary body, with local agencies and increased powers, to distribute "relief" (it is not difficult to guess which voluntary body they had in mind.) The representatives of the Boards of Guardians were firm. "We must mark off for stigma the dependents of the state," they said, "there must be no blurring of the lines between persons who were supporting themselves and those that were being supported out of the rates whether on account of old age, sickness or unemployment." They put great faith in this "stigma" as a deterrent, because apart from that it was almost impossible to make the workhouse more disagreeable than a very poor person's own home. It was useless for Beatrice to reiterate that it only kept the self-respecting destitute away, while to the carefree cadger one stigma more or less was all in the day's work. What she wanted was to lift all the non-able-bodied poor out of the Poor Law once and for all, and classify them not by their dependence, but by their need.

The non-able-bodied were, in any case, the lesser problem. "I am blest if I know what to do with the able-bodied," Beatrice reflected, as she drew up the plans for her Utopia. The able-bodied pauper or "sturdy beggar" who could work but did not had been the chief villain, to be feared and disciplined, ever since the first poor law was framed. But by 1894, it was becoming increasingly clear that being out of a job was not necessarily pure perversity on the part of the unemployed person, and the word "unemployment" was added to the dictionary to describe a set of circumstances, as opposed to a lack of personal action. By 1905, the Unemployed Workmen Act was passed, which directed local authorities to provide relief works for them. But the work created for the purpose only helped a tiny fraction, and in any case by the time the borough had acquired some land for the unemployed to till and hired spades and horses and carts it would have been cheaper to make the men a present of their money instead.

Beatrice—though considerably hampered by there being no figures about the number of unemployed in the country—nevertheless classified them in types, each with a different reason for having no job; the respectable workman who had lost his through no fault of his own; the under-employed, who lived on casual or seasonal work, and the unemployable. She was clear that the unemployable—whether work-shy or simply inadequate—would have to be put in colonies and trained and disciplined according to their shortcoming. (Problems which involved the improvement of other people's characters always seemed comparatively simple to her.) But the respectable unemployed and the under-employed were more difficult because, as George Lansbury put it, "there is simply not enough work to go round," and its distribution was completely unorganised. She visualised the government launching on relief work on a large scale; and taking married women and children under fifteen out of the labour market altogether. But what was needed was an elaborate scheme of national organisation—a "Ministry of Labour", she suggested—which would be responsible for preventing or minimising unemployment. This, she wrote, might seem to many persons "Utopian". But

the average citizen of the middle or upper class takes for granted the constantly recurring destitution among wage-earning families due to unemployment as part of the natural order of things and as no more to be combated than the east wind. . . . Fifty years hence we shall be looking back with amazement at the helpless and ignorant acquiescence of the governing classes . . . in the constant debasement of character and physique, not to mention the perpetual draining away of the nation's wealth that idleness combined with starvation plainly causes.[8]

[184]

(She was right, but it had to become the overriding problem of a whole generation first).

Meanwhile, the Webbs consulted William Beveridge—"an ugly-mannered, but honest, self-devoted, hard-headed young reformer of the practical type"—who was working at the Central Unemployed Body for London, and the three of them "formed an alliance to prepare an assault on the authorities". According to Beveridge's own account. "My pet scheme was labour exchanges."[9] Beveridge was asked to Sunday luncheon with the Webbs to explain his plan for "substituting a market for unguided hawking from door to door as the means of bringing the would-be buyer of labour and the would-be seller together". Beatrice, he recounted, tore his ideas to pieces, and delivered

> an eloquent expression of her own views. At the end of her harangue I heard Sidney pipe up from the other end of the table, "You are absolutely right, my dear, and I agree with every word you have said. But—there is just this in what Mr Beveridge has said." There followed an exposition of my views in Sidney's language and a complete acceptance of them by Beatrice.[10]

When Churchill was appointed President of the Board of Trade, his first action was to send down to the Labour department for literature about labour exchanges. Beatrice was hopeful:

> I am not sure that he is not beginning to realise the preposterousness of the present state of things—at any rate he is trying hard to do so, because he feels it necessary that he should do so, if he is to remain in the Liberal ranks. Will he remain in the Liberal ranks?

The Webbs told Churchill, "If you are going to deal with unemployment you must have the boy Beveridge," and arranged a dinner-party so that they could meet, which also included one of Beatrice's researchers and a Radical M.P. named Masterman. Beveridge wrote to his mother:

> My dinner last night was of course very interesting and mainly about Labour Exchanges. Mrs Webb had sent their scheme (which is founded on me) to Winston Churchill before and he has been converted and is now at work converting Asquith. I

don't think he is at all points clear as to what Labour Exchanges mean—as Mrs Webb said afterwards you never quite know what he's going to hand back to you afterwards as his version of your idea—but still so long as he talks about the name it doesn't matter . . . Masterman is rather horrified at Mrs Webb's zeal for disciplining people and prayed that above all things he might never fall into her hands as an unemployed.

Churchill's only reservation about Beatrice's scheme was that he jibbed at the idea of labour exchanges being compulsory.

Lloyd George—at that time Chancellor of the Exchequer—also welcomed the chance to pick Beatrice's brains. He invited the Webbs, with Haldane, to breakfast at 11 Downing Street, to thrash out the question of how social insurance would fit in with her scheme. There was a heated discussion, because Beatrice's objection to insurance was that it gave the authorities no chance to discipline the insured person. She reported, "I tried to impress on them that any grant from the community to the individual . . . ought to be conditional on better conduct, and that any insurance scheme had the fatal defect that . . . the persons felt they had a right to the allowance whatever their conduct." Haldane, shrewdly realising that the irrepressible Puritan in Beatrice was, as usual, ruining her case, hastily intervened with a lawyer's compromise that "insurance had to be part of a big scheme with conditional relief for those at the bottom and insurance for those struggling up."

Haldane also advised Beatrice to try for a rapprochement with John Burns. "He is vain and ignorant and in the hands of his officials . . . if you could get him to take up the scheme as his own, then I could follow, but he is at the head of the department concerned and would resent a lead-off by another member of the Cabinet." (Haldane was in charge of the War Office.) Beatrice, who by now had high hopes of "the break-up of the poor law" being "quietly taken for granted by both front benches" by the time the Commission got round to making a report at all, did call on Burns, although she always found that "almost unconsciously one treats him as a non-responsible being—a creature too unintelligent to be argued with, too crazily vain to be appealed to . . ." She suggested to Burns, "You read my scheme, and if you agree with it, you might give a sort of lead-off to your colleagues on the question of poor law reform."

Lord Elcho (of the "Souls") was "captivated" by Beatrice's report and told Arthur Balfour he ought to read it. Beatrice said to Balfour she would lend it to him if he would promise to read it and remember to return it. "I promise on both counts, Mrs Webb," said Balfour, and kept it for some weeks, then returned it with an encouraging letter. "So having reported to H.M. Government, I report to H.M. Opposition," Beatrice reflected jubilantly. Labour men were less co-operative because they had reservations about re-training the chronically unemployed. Beatrice recorded, "They sometimes suggest unemployed benefit paid by the state *with no conditions*. That is, of course, under the present conditions of human will, sheer madness . . ."

But the difficulty of solving the question of what to do with the permanent surplus of labour market oppressed her. "I dream of it at night, I pray for light in the early morning, I grind, grind, grind, all the hours of the working-day to try to get a solution. . . . Also, though in a way the fight between my colleagues" (on the Commission) "and myself adds to the excitement and amusement it also adds to the strain." By now they were—perhaps understandably—getting restive about Beatrice's activities. The chairman sent her a "curt and crude" request that she should stop running a one-woman Commission, independent of theirs. "I politely but firmly said I intended to continue." Haldane applauded her. "Splendid, they won't encounter you in a hurry again." By now she was becoming indifferent to their hostility. "At first I was so horribly sensitive to their dislike. Now I watch the chairman's expression of puzzled displeasure or listen to Loch's rude ejaculations (I heard him say— 'What cheek! . . .') and find myself coolly calculating how much they will stand." At home, Sidney had amiably retired into the background. "Just now our positions are rather reversed; it is he who sits at home and thinks out the common literary work; it is I who am racing round dealing with men and affairs!"

She was riding high, just as she had been when she first got into the public eye over her anti-"sweating" campaign, and once again her own officious conscience struck her down. One of the pillars of the C.O.S. on the Commission was Mrs. Bosanquet, who, like Beatrice, was a writer about social problems but in a rather different vein. "The remedy against pauperism does not lie in the liberalities of the rich. It lies in the hearts and habits of the poor," she wrote. "Plant in their bosoms a spirit of independence. Give a higher tone of delicacy to their character. Teach them to recoil from pauperism as a degradation."[11] After two years of simmering resentment against Beatrice, she suddenly suggested, blandly, that Beatrice should produce the correspondence with the Medical Officers of Health on which she had based her report on the medical services. Beatrice had not admitted to the Commission that there had been a number of "stupid, conservative" M.O.H.'s who had emphatically not taken to her ideas, but it was evident that Mrs Bosanquet suspected they had written to that effect. Beatrice hurried home, with her heart in her mouth, to look through the letters. Guiltily, she took out all the "anti" ones, hesitated, then put all but a few of them away, and made up a bundle of the "pro" ones with a small selection of the other kind to add verisimilitude. She sent off the bundle as though it were the whole correspondence. "To be frank," she admitted to her diary, "I had qualms of conscience." Mrs. Bosanquet suggested that the bundle should be printed and circulated, which would have exposed its incompleteness to those who had written. Beatrice sent a "dignified refusal" and promptly collapsed with a nervous breakdown. She went down to Beachy Head on sick leave, and tormented herself with remorse over "my little lack of straight dealing", just as she had on a previous occasion. But happily, by the time she got back, it had all blown over, and she let the Commission know that "what with offended feelings and delicate health" she proposed to withdraw herself from "the silly business of endless cross-examining and devote my whole energy to solving the question of able-bodied destitution".

By now, there was so much outside interest in her schemes—even leading members of the Labour Party, apart from MacDonald, coming round to it—that she had decided to produce a minority report of her own, knowing that the Commission would only, at the most, agree to a part of her proposals ("It will be amusing to see how much 'Webb' this Commission will stand—what exactly will be saturation point?"). Haldane borrowed copies of her report and told her that he had been deputed by the Prime Minister to prepare a comprehensive scheme of reform. "They would bring in some portions of it next year and the year after (I understand Winston's labour exchanges and Lloyd George's invalidity pensions) and go the year after that to the country on the whole scheme" Beatrice reported happily. She noticed, though unsuspectingly, that Haldane seemed "rather woolly" about it and chaffingly told him that if the Liberals did not want her scheme the Tories would. "Which I should prefer in many ways—there would be no nonsense about democracy!" She amused herself by laughing at the rest of the Commission as they struggled to get their majority report composed.

Are all men quite so imbecile as that lot are? I sit and watch them and wonder.... If I ever sit again on a Royal Commission, I hope my colleagues will be of a superior calibre—for really it is shockingly bad for one's character to be with such folk—it makes me feel intolerably superior.

They signed their various supports and dissents, were photographed together and parted. "My colleagues will now melt back into the world at large and we shall know each other no more. The relation has not been a pleasant one for either side." There was one last battle. Beatrice's report was all ready "in a fine blue cover ... 300 pages of reasoned stuff with a scheme of reform at the end," and she was proposing to have it published by the Fabian Society and by Longmans. The Treasury forbade it, on the grounds that it would infringe the crown copyright. Sidney wrote back that in 1887 the Lords Commissioners of the Treasury, in a minute which was never rescinded, had disclaimed copyright in government blue-books. This was news to the Treasury solicitor who subsided forthwith, leaving the Minority Report to become a best-seller among government documents.

But Beatrice was bitterly disappointed when the two reports appeared.

We turned out to be quite wrong as to the reception of the Majority Report. So far as the first day's reviews are concerned, the majority have got a magnificent reception. We have had a fair look in but ... the majority hold the platform. Perhaps we feel a trifle foolish at having crabbed the Majority Report to our family and intimate friends and exalted our own. That has certainly not proved to be the estimate of public opinion.

The fact was that the Majority Report, contrary to all expectations, had emerged as a reasonably enlightened document. The reason was that after four years' constant exposure to Beatrice's constructive imagination, backed by methods of investigation which made those of the C.O.S. look slipshod, the nineteen other commissioners were (temporarily at any rate) reformed characters.

(Lansbury and the Carpenters' Union official had been with Beatrice from the start, and one of the Church of England persons came over officially to her side. These three signed the Minority Report with her.) The Majority party, hypnotised into enlightened thinking (according to their lights) did draw up a document which would have seemed wildly radical to themselves four years earlier. In 1905 they had been quite prepared to fall in with the views of the permanent officials that what the Poor Law really needed was to change its administration (from Boards of Guardians to county and county borough authorities) so that its strict regulations could be tightened up. By 1908 all of them—even including Loch—were convinced that the spirit of the old Poor Law had got to be swept away. They threw the cherished principles of deterrence and less eligibility overboard without a backward look. But they still jibbed at Beatrice's vision of an entirely new social system, in which the community was responsible for keeping its socially inadequate members with their heads above water, as one of the regular duties of the state. They proposed that the business of relieving the poor should still be shared between voluntary bodies and statutory authorities. Beatrice reflected:

> In our depreciation of the Majority Report and our false expectation of its failure to catch on, we overlooked the immense step made by the sweeping away of deterrent poor law *in name at any rate*. . . . Every now and then I realised this but . . . I lost sight of it in my indignation at their attempt to present a new appearance while maintaining the old substance underneath. In a sense the Majority Report meant success to our cause but not victory to ourselves.

Twenty years before she had been faithful to the Fabian creed— "We want the things done and we don't much care who does them." But now, for the first time, she had (almost) tasted the heady experience of pushing through a major reform of her own, just as she had conceived it, and after that, the normal slow process of permeation and compromise and manipulation, of fighting every step and giving way when necessary, looked unbearably drab. She could not quite resign herself to it.

After the first depression, she decided to turn her attention to the young hopefuls of the Fabians and the London School of Economics, and to "keep the flag flying for levelling up the bottom-most layer of society" by launching a campaign, with their help, for the "break-up of the Poor Law". The Webbs formed an organisation, with Beatrice at the head of it, to crusade against destitution. "It is rather funny to start, at my time of life, on the war-path, at the head of a contingent of young men and women," she wrote, deprecatingly. But she loved it. Old friends joined in—Graham Wallas, H. G. Wells, her brother-in-law Leonard Courtney; the Liberal press was friendly; the office they took as headquarters was always crowded with workers.

Beatrice warned herself, in parenthesis, that

It is a curiously demoralising life, if one did not . . . guard one's mind from . . . the subservient and foolish admiration of followers. Just as during those last months on the Commission I was working in the atmosphere of perpetual hostility and disparagement, here I am working in the atmosphere of admiration and willing obedience to my will.

One of the young workers later described the "joyous enthusiasm and, often, a passion of hero or heroine worship" with which they spent "hour after hour, day after day, in folding or addressing circulars . . . to be amply rewarded by a brilliant if rather vague smile"[12] from Beatrice herself when she looked in. The young poet Rupert Brooke had poor-law-reform leaflets piled under the table in his (subsequently legendary) "Old Vicarage, Grantchester", and himself cycled round all the Cambridgeshire villages distributing them, presumably collecting the list of village names which he used in the poem. ("At Over, they fling oaths at one, And worse than oaths at Trumpington; and Ditton girls are mean and dirty, And there's none in Harston under thirty.") "We are not much interested in the treatment of the aged and infirm—we don't want to study *them* —we want to find out what's wrong with the whole damned Poor Law," Brooke wrote to his fellow-undergraduate, Hugh Dalton. Beatrice, carrying on a "raging tearing propaganda, lecturing or speaking five or six times a week", began to think that the Majority Report would win after all and "commit the country to a policy of complete communal responsibility for the fact of destitution". The Minority Report party, alarmed, formed a matching organisation of its own and impudently named it the National Poor Law Reform Association, and from then on the two rival campaigns trailed each other up and down the country, like travelling circuses competing for an audience. Manchester University conferred a doctorate on Beatrice. ("Manchester, the birthplace of my family as members of the governing class. Dear old Father, how pleased he would have been.") Arthur Balfour came to dinner and "egged us on, evidently vastly interested and amused", and invited them to stay at his ancestral home when the campaign took them north. They started a magazine, *The Crusade*, as the organ of their committee, in which distinguished medical men, education officers and social researchers pleaded for the Webb scheme for breaking-up the poor law. "It is clear that we are making great headway in the country, we are rolling up a great body of enthusiasm. And it is all centering round our joint personality," wrote Beatrice.

But meanwhile the Webbs were being "quite strangely dropped" by their distinguished acquaintances and the Liberal Ministers in particular. Their invitations dwindled, and even Haldane began to avoid them. Once, when he had felt obliged to make the gesture of asking them to an informal dinner, he was markedly chilly when they described the success of their campaign. Halfway through the evening, he maliciously attacked Beatrice on her most tender point, about her own habit of private prayer. "Both the Haldanes turned round and openly scoffed at me, Haldane beginning a queer kind of cross-examination in law-court fashion as to what exactly I prayed to, or prayed about, and Elizabeth scornfully remarking that prayer was mere superstition." Beatrice herself was incapable of permanent malice and was always incredulous when she met it. Friends who turned hostile and said unforgivable things found themselves welcomed back as her friends, as if nothing at all had happened. "Being well-bred persons we all saw our mistake—I in introducing a note of too great intimacy and they in scoffing at it," she wrote afterwards, with characteristic fairness.

But the jar produced between us lingered through the remaining part of the evening and I went away with somewhat hurt feelings.... For some reason which we do not appreciate, the Haldanes are constrained or estranged. Possibly because they feel obliged to go back on their former agreement with the Minority Report, possibly because they have heard that we admire Lloyd George and Winston Churchill and openly state that they are the best of the party. (I always put in a saving clause for Haldane, out of old affection.)

She met Churchill on the Embankment one afternoon and asked him whether the Cabinet really meant to do anything about the Poor Law. Churchill said, "Oh yes, they do. You must talk to Haldane about it. We are going in for a *classified* poor law." Beatrice, turning the conversation over in her mind, suspected that it meant that Haldane and Asquith had turned against her and her report. Next time she saw Asquith personally, at a dinner-party where they were fellow-guests, he was "somewhat marked in his non-recognition of either of us", and spent the evening ogling pretty women and discussing the latest Society scandal, while two other Ministers who were there did not even speak to her. "Each of them would, I think, have been supremely bored to have exchanged one little word about poor law or any other socio-economic question."

What really defeated Beatrice, in the end, was not the government's disapproval of her ideas for reform, but their approval of part of them. While she was still drafting her Minority Report, and six months before the appearance of either that or the Majority one, Churchill, according to Beveridge, "not in ignorance of their respective contents", had obtained the consent of his colleagues to the establishment of a system of labour exchanges and they were introduced in 1909. "The business of the labour exchanges was to render a service to citizens—not to extract money from them as the Revenue Departments did."[13] But although both Reports "blessed labour exchanges", the Webbs were bitterly disappointed that they were not made compulsory, as a way of bringing the work-shy into line. At the same time as Beatrice was writing her study of the "able-bodied", Lloyd George was making a trip to Germany for the purpose of examining the schemes of sickness and invalidity insurance invented by Bismarck. In his budget speech the next year, he announced plans for introducing a British version of them, and also a British-invented extension of Bismarck's scheme, in compulsory unemployment insurance. Since the government had already introduced old-age pensions (5s a week), it became increasingly obvious, as Beatrice commented ruefully, that "the big thing that has happened in the last two years is that Lloyd George and Winston Churchill have practically taken the *limelight*, not merely from their own colleagues but from the Labour Party. They stand out as the most advanced politicians."

When at last the day arrived on which the Poor Law was to be discussed in Parliament, the National Committee was in a state of tremendous excitement and the House was packed, but the result was a very damp squib. Balfour made what Beatrice described gratefully as an "extraordinarily friendly" speech, Asquith made a "coldly appreciative" one, and John Burns was "as hostile as he dared be". The net impression of the debate was that though the majority proposals were dead, "the *status quo* had the hot approval of John Burns and that Asquith was sceptical of the possibility of change and Arthur Balfour hesitating as usual". No division was taken, but after the debate there was a private discussion about the Minority Report in Balfour's room. Joseph Chamberlain's son, Austen, who was there, said that Balfour disclaimed even having read Beatrice's report— (so much for his assurance to her and his returning it with an encouraging letter)—but that he knew the Webbs were keen on it. Austen was not. He said that its plan would cost £5m, would make the position of the State-aided better than that of the "ordinary decent working man" taxed to support them, and would establish "an intolerable bureaucratic tyranny", in which five separate Local Authority inspectors might descend on any working-man's home with a right to interfere in his family affairs. The supporters of the Majority Report had also attacked Beatrice's scheme on the grounds that it would break up the family by shuttling its members from one department to another. (Half a century later, when much of the scheme had been implemented, a Fabian tract pointed out that it still required "that the needs of the family as a whole should be the central point of the personal Social Services", and related the story of the "exasperated over-visited mother, who on hearing yet one more knock on her front door threw up her first-floor window, flung out the front door key and cried, 'Here, you hang it up at the Town Hall, it will be more use to them than to me.'")

The general opinion of the Webb scheme was summed up by the *Morning Post* correspondent who said, "The Webbs carry you on logically and imperceptibly from one point to another, but when you look at the whole, it's moonshine!" Loch, of the C.O.S. said, "Their achievement was to alienate the government, bore the public and postpone reform."[14] (It was also to dissolve the ideology of the original C.O.S., which was later rehabilitated with new ideas and a new name.) But the final blow to the crusade itself was dealt when Lloyd George's "rotten scheme of sickness insurance"—as Beatrice called it—had a splendid reception in Parliament. *Punch* pictured

Lloyd George bowing on the stage while a crowded audience threw haloes to him. But when the country began to realise what his scheme meant there was a tremendous and noisy opposition. The unemployment insurance provision (which was very restricted in scope anyway) was accepted without fuss, but the Health Insurance part made Lloyd George the most unpopular man in the country. The Friendly Societies suspected it and so did the insurance companies; the doctors resented it; there was a mass meeting of ladies protesting against having to stick on stamps for servant-girls and everyone except the socialists thought it too socialistic. The Tory press called it the "cheat's charter" and the "malingerer's millennium". Loch said, "If we have sickness insurance we must be prepared to pay for it, not only in money, but in the mettle that makes the strength of men and women."[15] Beatrice wrote in her diary:

> The sickness insurance is wholly bad and I cannot see how malingering can be staved off . . . what the Government shirk is the extension of *treatment* and *disciplinary* supervision—they want merely some mechanical way of increasing the money income of the wage-earning class in times of unemployment and sickness. No attempt is made to secure an advance in conduct in return for the increased income.

But public opinion "takes the sloppy and sentimental schemes and dislikes anything that looks like efficiency and control."

Beatrice's disappointment was partly the natural one of seeing a carefully worked out and exhaustive plan scrapped. But it was also because she had failed to impose her deeply felt moral views on the nation. Her plan for welfare was not to provide social security only as a safety-net for the unfortunate—the non-able-bodied poor and the compulsorily unemployed. She wanted to use social services as the 1834 law had used "relief", that is, as a means of disciplining the recipient into self-improvement, where possible. Octavia Hill had used housing reform to coerce tenants into becoming better people. Beatrice wanted to use unemployment relief to coerce the unemployed into becoming more employable, and sick relief for making the sick person do what the doctor told him. The voluntary worker of the Charity Organisation Society had opposed "indiscriminate alms-giving" because it offered loopholes to the undeserving poor. The Minority Report laid down that "no encouragement whatever should be given to any distribution of money, food or

clothing in the homes of the poor by any private person or charitable societies whatever'',[16] because it might provide a loophole by
which the inadequate citizen could get benefits without undertaking
to make an effort to become adequate. The idea of using social
insurance as a means of enforcing good behaviour dies hard, and
Beatrice had her spiritual successors who felt that the Beveridge
Report itself failed to do so. Shaw said that one reason why the
Minority Report was not adopted was because of the folly of young
journalists who ''revolted with all the petulant anarchism of the
literary profession against the Ideal Interfering Female as typified
in their heated imaginations by poor Mrs Sidney Webb'',[17] but it
was true that, as she had told Chamberlain, she was firm in wanting
''sternness from the state and love and self-devotion from individuals'', and became more rigid about it as she grew older.

In the meantime, the security against poverty caused by sickness,
without her moral factor as part of it, seemed to Beatrice to be
adopting her idea with the spirit of it left out. ''All the steam went
out of the movement,'' she admitted sadly. Balfour, who was ostenta-
tiously less friendly than he had been before, told her that he thought
it a good idea of Lloyd George's to ''make the wage-earners pay''
and in any case if it made the government unpopular so much the
better for the Opposition. Masterman sneered to Lansbury, after
Lloyd George's triumphant exposition of the scheme, ''We have
spiked your guns, eh?'' John Burns went round explaining happily
that insurance had finally ''dished the Webbs''.

13

Middle-aged Fabians
1912—1918

AFTER TWO YEARS OF POWER AND POPULARITY, it was hard to accept total failure. Beatrice had enjoyed leadership "because I have the gift of personal intercourse and it is a gift I have never, until now, made full use of.... How shall we be able to retire? is what I ask myself." She had believed she was on the way to the "conversion of England" and felt that *The Times* was not exaggerating when it suggested that the Minority Report was the French revolution in another form. When she went to see John Galsworthy's new play, *Justice*, she was quite sure it was based on the Report's philosophy. When the King died, she was impatient because the public turned all its attention, for the moment, to the "royal wake, slobbering over the lying-in-state and the funeral procession". When she was asked out to dinner, she expected the conversation to revolve around her campaign. "The Liberal Ministers' indifference, not to say distaste, is amazing and makes one wonder exactly what is happening to the leaders of the Liberal Party. Here we are making the bed they will have to lie in and yet they seem wholly unconcerned with this happening. Strange!"

But now the campaign was over, the young volunteers were beginning to melt away, and she was tired, "deep down tired". She wondered whether she could draw the remnant of her followers into the Fabian Society and go on leading them there. She was irritated with Shaw, because he chose this moment to withdraw from the Fabian executive, and to suggest that other members of the "old gang" should also resign, to make way for younger men. She concluded—correctly—that Shaw was getting anxious about his own career and losing interest in Fabianism. He was, in fact, at the end of his period of turning out sociological plays based on Fabian-type philosophies which also aimed at commercial success, and on the verge of two more lasting ones (*Androcles* and *Pygmalion*) which had nothing to do with Socialism. In any case he was a born rebel and most at home in the Fabian Society when it was a small group of idealists and bored when it began to develop into a cast-iron bureaucracy.

Shaw, inviting his old friends the Webbs to spend Sunday at Ayot St. Lawrence, before they went abroad for their holiday, was interested only in reading them the text of *Fanny's First Play* and in getting Sidney apart so that he could talk to him about Mrs Patrick Campbell. Sex, as Beatrice observed sharply in her diary that evening, was a topic which did not interest Sidney and G.B.S. had "nothing constructive to propose". Beatrice, left alone with Charlotte, had to listen to her troubles, her account of how much she disliked the theatrical set, and how much she wished that the Webbs would get Shaw interested in Socialism again. Beatrice decided crossly that "he and Charlotte are getting every day more luxurious and determined to have everything just so"—a singularly unjust remark considering the drab discomfort of the Shaws' house—and realised that it was no use trying to get Shaw back into the fold. Possibly it was her irritation with him that made her decide, on this occasion, that he must really be the illegitimate son of G. V. T. Lee, "that vain, witty and distinguished musical genius who lived with them", because, looking at Lee's photograph, she found the expression on his face "quite amazingly like G. B. S. when I first knew him".

The Webbs went off to the Far East, in the summer of 1911, still undecided about their own future plans, now that Beatrice's National Committee had folded up and Sidney had "slipped quietly out of the L.C.C.". But they were inclined to think that unless some masterman emerged in the Fabian Society or the Labour Party, they were "doomed to offer themselves as officers of the larger crusade to conquer the land of promise". They visited Japan, where they were delighted with the efficiency, cleanliness and courtesy of their hosts, though they regretted that they were short on infant health and child development in rural areas. Sidney visited a brothel, booked a prostitute's time and spent it with notebook and pencil cross-questioning the astonished young woman about her hours of work, pay and prospects. They found the Chinese lacking in cleanliness and moral values, also on the verge of a revolution, so that the Webbs counted themselves lucky to get the last train out of Peking. In India they found it difficult to get much attention from the government, which was absorbed in a royal visit; they were not invited to the Government House garden-party and Beatrice had chronic catarrh. She came home so exhausted with tropical climates and perpetual journeyings that it took her two months to get over her holiday. But she brought back with her a new idea for meeting

> the clear call to leadership in the Labour and Socialist movement to which we feel we must respond. For that purpose we are starting a new weekly next spring and the planning-out of this organ of Fabianism is largely devolving on Sidney.... To the experienced journalist it must seem a mad adventure and we ourselves hardly expect more than a run for other people's money and our own hard work.

Massingham, the editor of the *Nation*, prophesied that any rival run by Beatrice and Sidney would consist of "the Webbs, flavoured with a little Shaw and padded with the contributions of a few cleverish but ignorant young men." Shaw was, at first, lukewarm about the product.

> Unless you can find a team of young lions (coaching them to some extent at a weekly lunch or dinner) and give them their heads, the job cannot be done. Sidney is wonderfully young—hardly in full flower even yet—but he hasn't the smallest intention of making himself fascinating and nothing short of that will delight the sixpenny public.... None of the brilliant people will be quite likeable, any more than Wells is ... or for that matter I am ... and I am quite an angel compared to most of them. And you know what Sidney is to people whom he doesn't like. He will quarrel with you like mad over them.[1]

All the same, Shaw subscribed £1000 and undertook to write for the paper. They got the promise of another £4000 from friends and calculated that they would need 5000 subscribers to make it pay. They built up a card catalogue, starting with the clientele of the Fabian Society and the National Committee, and circularised them and got 2,400 postal subscribers before the first number appeared. Clifford Sharp, who had edited the National Committee's journal, *The Crusade*, was editor, John Squire, the poet, was literary editor and Desmond McCarthy, the author and journalist, was dramatic critic. Arthur Balfour's suggestion that it should be called *The Statesman* was at once accepted by the Webbs, until S. K. Ratcliffe (one of its prospective writers) pointed out to the recently returned travellers that this was the name of India's most widely circulated paper, and it was re-christened the *New Statesman*.

The first issue appeared in May 1913 and announced that it was not an organ of the Labour party, that its policy was Fabian Socialism, that it had no axe to grind nor panaceas to advocate, but believed in applying the scientific spirit to social problems. It had a long article (the first of a series) on "What is Socialism?" by the Webbs, and two by Shaw, one on the Marconi scandal, the other about the forcible feeding of suffragettes.

It was a set-back that Shaw refused to sign his articles. Clifford Sharp told him that if he wrote anonymously he would be subject to editorial alterations like anyone else. Shaw agreed, but—predictably —was unable to live up to it and for the next three years there was a continual duel between Sharp and himself. He told Beatrice that like the old Thames Steamboat Company and the *Westminster Review*, the *New Statesman* would "struggle on long after all creation shrieks for its internment. But if you and Sidney put a violent end to it I shall not be greatly grieved."[2] Sharp confided in her that she and Sidney did not realise how Shaw treated the rest of the world. "His personal attitude refuses one not merely the liberty of criticism but the right to possess any view of one's own at all. I believe you and Mr Webb are probably the only people in the world towards whom this intolerance is modified by, as it were, a long inbred habit of affection and respect." At one point in the paper's development, Beatrice felt that Shaw, though meaning to be kind and loyal to them

> had in fact injured the N.S. by his connection with it; we have had the disadvantage of his eccentric and iconoclastic stuff without the advantage of his name . . . persons who subscribed for their weekly portion of Shaw are angry and say they were got to subscribe under false pretences. The N.S. is, in fact, the only weekly in which Shaw's name never appears and it is his name that draws, not his mind.

As Shaw had suggested, the Webbs held a regular weekly lunch at Grosvenor Road to discuss policy but the young lions were given their head. Sharp was allowed so much independence that he protested he was in danger of thinking that the paper was more his affair than the Webbs. But they were in entire agreement that the *New Statesman* should be deliberately detached from the emotional concerns of the earlier Socialists. At first it was also detached from Europe. (As Leonard Woolf said, foreign policy was not one of the Webbs' subjects.) During the fifteen months between its foundation and the outbreak of war, it had only one regular foreign correspondent, in Berlin, and he wrote mostly about German administration and industry and hardly mentioned German militarism. From the beginning the Supplements were, as Beatrice said, a permanent attraction. The first ones dealt with the theatre, the widening activities of women, the medical profession, teachers, insurance and Ireland. The two most famous ones of all time were Shaw's *Common-Sense About the War* in 1914 and Leonard Woolf's on *International Government* in 1915. Although at the beginning of the project Beatrice said, "If I were forced to wager, I should not back our success," the *New Statesman* not only survived their estimate of three years' life but eventually outlived the *Saturday Review*, outdistanced the *Spectator* and swallowed up the *Nation*, although as Ratcliffe said, its lifetime "is strewn with the wrecks of weekly journalism". With the London School of Economics it was one of the Webbs' two outstanding personal triumphs. They needed it, because, at the time of its foundation, their popularity was at its very lowest ebb.

In 1913, the Webbs, as Beatrice recorded ruefully, were hated. "We are extraordinarily unpopular today—more disliked, by a larger body of persons, than ever before." They had alienated their powerful friends by the poor-law campaign, since "you cannot at one and the same time exercise behind-the-scenes influence over statesmen, civil servants and newspaper editors, while you yourself engage in public propaganda of projects which those eminent ones may view with hostility or suspicion." At the same time, "the revolutionary Socialist and fanatical sentimentalist see in us, and our philosophy, the main obstacle to what they call enthusiasm and we call hysteria." They had come back to a climate of opinion in which the militancy which had been growing for the last few years had suddenly sharpened up. While Beatrice was still immersed in her campaign she had noted briefly that her old acquaintance Tom Mann, who had gone out of her life when he emigrated to Australia, was back again, spreading the new doctrine of Syndicalism—that is, of industry controlled by the Trades Unions (or *syndicats*). "We most certainly favour strikes," he said. "We shall always do our best to help strikers to be successful and we shall prepare the way as rapidly as possible for a General Strike of national proportions." In 1909 there were two million working days lost through strikes; by 1912 it was thirty-eight million. Beatrice commented: Syndicalism has taken the place of old-fashioned Marxism.

The angry youth, with bad complexion, frowning brow and weedy figure is now always a Syndicalist; the glib young work-man whose tongue runs away with him today mouths the phrases of French Syndicalism instead of those of German Social Democracy. The inexperienced middle-class idealist has accepted with avidity the ideal of the Syndicalist as a new and exciting Utopia.

It had spread to the Fabian Society in the form of Guild Socialism, which added a flavour of William Morris's neo-mediaeval Utopia, and of the "distributivist society" favoured by Hilaire Belloc and G. K. Chesterton, as opposed to what they called the "servile state" favoured by the Minority Report.

In the new Fabian Research Department, which Beatrice had launched when she returned from the Far East, and which she was now finding "extraordinarily useful in providing Supplements for the *New Statesman*", the "new group of rebels" as she called them, backed by Shaw, suggested that the Fabian Society should in future limit itself to the work of research, but "what the little knot of Rebels are after is not Research at all, but a new form of propaganda and a new doctrine which they believe themselves to be elaborating with regard to the Control of Industry." The new group was led by three young men, G. D. H. Cole, Mellor and Gillespie. Mellor—later editor of the *Daily Herald*—was at this time secretary of the Fabian Research Department. Gillespie—later an official of the Mining Association—was Honorary Secretary. Cole (who eventu-ally was four times chairman—or president—of the Fabian Society) had at this time just written the first of his many books on Socialism and trades-unionism. In it he lamented that British intellectuals had too little influence on the Labour movement because

a single and very practically-minded body of them long ago carried the day. The first leaders of the Fabian Society, and in particular Mr and Mrs Webb, were able so completely, through the Independent Labour Party, to impose their conception of society on the Labour movement that it seemed unnecessary for anyone to do any further thinking.[3]

From Beatrice's point of view, this disruption of the Fabian Society by the Guild Socialists could hardly have happened at a worse moment. She had just been elected to the executive and was hoping to channel the activities of its younger members into research and to lead them herself. She had told Shaw that it was no use for the "old gang" to step down from leadership "with the view to making room for young men who are not there!" Now, it appeared, they were not only there but "fanatical and one-idea'd" and personally hostile towards her. When the "Guild Socialist clique" attacked the Executive and tried to get control of the Fabian Society for themselves, Beatrice wrote:

It is all the more annoying to us, as we are honestly anxious to find successors and if these rebellious youths and maidens had only refrained from asking for a public execution of the old people we would gladly have stepped down from our position directly they had secured some sort of respect from the members at large. But these young people delight in 'frightfulness' for its own sake; they do violent and dishonourable acts just for the sake of doing them.

Since they were first married, Beatrice had felt that she and Sidney ought to find their most important disciples among the "clever men from the universities". She had let it be known at Oxford and Cambridge that "anyone coming up who is interested in economics will have a warm welcome at Grosvenor Road", and in the early years of the London School of Economics they were "perpetually entertaining . . . students whom we feel it our duty to see and talk to". During her campaign, the enthusiasm of the university Fabians had been unflagging. Rupert Brooke, the poet, who was president of the Cambridge Fabians, had taken with him into "Arcady" (otherwise a holiday cottage in the New Forest) the works of Shakespeare, Aristotle and the *Minority Report*. But when the crusade began to wilt, so did the young people's enthusiasm for poor-law reform and Fabianism alike. Brooke was a romantic, who had been first converted to Socialism by reading William Morris's *News from Nowhere*. He and some other Cambridge Fabians (including Hugh Dalton who became Chancellor of the Exchequer in the Labour government in 1945) went to the summer school at which Beatrice had specially organised a conference of university Fabian societies, but it turned out a failure. Beatrice wrote that the young men are inclined to go away rather more critical and supercilious than they came. Quite clearly we must not attempt it again unless we can ensure the presence of twenty or thirty leading dons and attractive celebrities. 'They won't come unless they know who they are going to meet,' sums up Rupert Brooke. . . . They don't want to learn, they don't think they have anything to learn. They certainly don't want to help others, unless they think that there is something to be got in the way of an opening and a career, they won't come. The egotism of the young university man is colossal. Are they worth bothering about?

Brooke wrote to Lytton Strachey, "We all loved Beatrice, who related amusing anecdotes about Mr Herbert Spencer over and over again." The group of Cambridge Fabians whom he represented had, in fact, a Herbert Spencer of their own in G. E. Moore. His book *Principia Ethica* propounded a new rationalist and scholastic religion, which aimed at determining what things are good in themselves. Beatrice tried to understand it, although as Brooke reported, "She'd a long story about handing *Principia Ethica* to Mr Arthur Balfour, who skimmed it swiftly and gave it back, saying 'Clever, but rather thin. The work of a very young man.'" The Cambridge group teased her and founded an "anti-anthletic league" when she tried to organise long, uphill walks, but at least they were eager to talk to her and explain their point of view. Lytton Strachey described "a remarkable scene in which Rupert and I tried to explain Moore's ideas to Mrs Webb while she tried to convince us of the efficacy of prayer". By contrast the "Oxford boys" at subsequent summer schools were rebellious and hostile. "Why must these young men be so *rude*?" she wrote of them in her diary.

These young men struck against the rules and demonstrated against a religious convention which was being held in the neighbourhood, so that the police called on the Fabian School authorities to complain. If any one of them was called to order during a meeting, they all swept out in a body. Shaw found them amusing, but Beatrice found it exhausting to have to stand between them and the hard-worked establishment. She was only thankful that "fortunately they do not tamper with sex conventions—they seem to dislike women. But all other conventions they break or ignore."

But although neither the Fabian Society nor the Research Department seemed to promise a harvest of future leaders to take over from

Sidney and herself, the *New Statesman*, at least, had "attracted a group of able young men, and if once it can be put on a safe financial basis we shall be able to retire quietly from it." Looking for talent, the Webbs found Leonard Woolf, as they had found Beveridge six years earlier and with equally important results. Woolf had become a Socialist by the same path as Beatrice herself—through working in the slums for the Charity Organisation Society and resigning from it because he became convinced that there was "some vast, dangerous fault in the social organism which could not be touched by paternalism, charity or good works. Nothing but a social revolution, a major operation could touch it."[4] Like Beatrice, he decided to examine the Co-operative movement, as at least a practical experiment in socialism, and the Webbs first noticed him when he wrote an article about it for the *Manchester Guardian*. Woolf described his first acquaintance with them.

> The Webbs, sitting in the centre of their Fabian spider-web, always kept an eye watching for some promising young man who might be ensnared by them. They read and were impressed by my article and the result was an invitation to lunch. . . . I ate my first of many plates of mutton in Grosvenor Road. . . .[5]

They introduced him to the *New Statesman* and eventually started him on an enquiry into possible developments of international law. Woolf and Sidney drew up a draft for an international treaty for the establishment of a supra-national authority. Both studies were first published as supplements to the *New Statesman* and were combined with Woolf's blueprint for a League of Nations in his book, *International Government*, which was the basis of the British government's brief at Geneva and which lay on President Wilson's desk when he was first drawing up his plan.

During the twenty years in which Woolf was the established authority on the subject, both in the Fabian Society and the Labour Party, he got to know the Webbs very well. Sidney, he observed was

> all the way through exactly what he appeared to be on the surface. He had no doubts or hesitations (just as he never had a headache or constipation) for he knew accurately what could be known about important subjects or, if he did not actually know about it, he knew that he could obtain accurate knowledge about it with the aid of a secretary and a card index. . . . But you could not see much of Beatrice without realising that, beneath

the metallic façade and the surface of polished certainty, there was a neurotic turmoil of doubt and discontent, suppressed or controlled, an ego tortured in the old-fashioned religious way almost universal among the good and the wise in the nineteenth century.... She had, too, the temperament strongly suppressed, the passion and imagination, of an artist, though she would herself have denied this. Her defence against these psychological strains and stresses was a highly personal form of mysticism, and in the consolatory process prayer played an important, if to me incomprehensible part.[6]

This difference between Sidney's temperament and that of Beatrice was never clearer than during the years of the 1914 war. Like Woolf, who found that "the horror of the years 1914 to 1918 was that nothing seemed to happen, month after month and year after year, except the pitiless, useless slaughter in France", she never succeeded in adjusting herself to it, as Sidney did. A few days before the declaration, Sidney was still refusing to believe in the possibility of war among the great European powers because "it would be too insane", but two days after it had begun he had settled down to devising plans for increasing employment during wartime. Even when the uncertain optimism of the first few months had collapsed, Sidney went on placidly,

doing every job as it comes along, leaving the result, as he often says "on the lap of the gods". He is far more philosophical about the war than I am. "It is a sag back, but presently there will be a sag forward, and Humanity will move forward to greater knowledge and greater good-will; the Great War will seem to future generations a landmark of progress."

From the outbreak onwards, Beatrice never succeeded in identifying herself either with the patriotic fever of the majority, nor the dedicated pacifism of the tiny minority. On the day after the declaration of war, she and Sidney went to watch the demonstration in Trafalgar Square which had been summoned by the *Daily Herald*, and listened to George Lansbury and Keir Hardie declaiming against "this needless horror". She was untouched. "It was an undignified and futile exhibition, this singing of the Red Flag and passing of well-worn radical resolutions in favour of universal peace." She took the resignation of John Burns from the Government and of Ramsay MacDonald from the Chairmanship of the Labour party as "both desirable events", and approved when "even such pacifists as the Courtneys are agreeing that we had to stand by Belgium". But she was distracted by depression and anxiety, "drifting between letter-writing and reading successive editions of papers", while Sidney was busily drafting memoranda for Government Departments and resolutions for Labour meetings. "It is almost impossible to keep one's mind off that horrible Hell a few hundred miles away," she wrote despairingly.

The "disgusting misuse of religion" in stimulating patriotic militarism shocked her. "To those who aspire to faith and holiness and love as the end of purpose of the evolution of life—this horrible caricature of religion is depressing." But she was equally disturbed when she reflected that "war is a stimulus to service, heroism and all forms of self-devotion". She reproached herself for neglecting her work in order to moon over the newspapers and puzzle over the paradoxical morality of war, and tried to believe that a little brisk effort on her part would conquer her sense of hopeless tragedy. "The root of my trouble is, of course, a bad conscience; I am neither doing my share of emergency work, nor yet carrying forward, with sufficient steadfastness, my own work."

Haldane came to dine, "full of his past participation in diplomacy and military organisation . . . greatly admiring of Kitchener and anxious to tell us that it was he who insisted on 'K' going to the War Office. 'K' says we must prepare for a three years war and is expecting initial disasters. The Germans expect to walk through the French army 'like butter'." At Haldane's house they met Lloyd George, and Sir Edward Grey, who had spoken of "the lamps going out all over Europe—we shall not see them lit again in our lifetime," knowing that he himself was likely to be blind before the war ended, and suffering, Beatrice sensed, "from an over-sensitive consciousness of personal responsibility". Lloyd George "showed at his best in his lack of self-consciousness, his freedom from pedantry, his alert open-mindedness and calm cheeriness." They all agreed that the war would mean political disaster to one side and financial disaster for everybody. Haldane visualised "we well-to-do" living on half their income in future. Grey prophesied that war would bring the Labour Party to power.

MacDonald and Henderson had formed a Worker's Peace Emergency Committee, to unite workers against war, but by the time it assembled the war was already two days old. The name was changed to War Emergency Committee and its aim to protecting the workers' interests in wartime. It included representatives of the seventeen important left-wing organisations and was the most comprehensive Labour body yet formed. It needed someone to draft agendas and look after committee work—some committed Labour man who was yet not too closely bound to any of the different sections. In fact it needed Sidney, as though a far-seeing Providence had created him for this very purpose, some half-century before. Within a week, he had drawn up its first pamphlet, *The War and the Workers*. Eventually he was responsible for much of the emergency legislation that put the new social morality, which grew up in the 1914 war, into practical form; in regulating food-prices, freezing working-class rents where there was hardship, and getting allowances for servicemen's families. It was Sidney who exposed the scandal of the Kitchener Army huts (cost to the producer £10, price to the government £150). Richard Potter's fortune—which provided the Webbs' own income—had been founded on an exactly similar deal, during the Crimean War. But it was not until the 1914 war that "profiteering" was established as an unpatriotic activity.

Sidney, suddenly finding himself needed and busy, as he had not been since he left the L.C.C., had neither the time nor the urge to brood, as Beatrice did, over "the horror and insanity of the killing and maiming of millions of the best of the human race. I cannot bear to look at the fresh young faces in each week's 'Roll of Honour'" (which in the spring of 1915 included Rupert Brooke, and later three of her own nephews).

Since MacDonald's withdrawal, Arthur Henderson had moved into his place and was chairman of the War Emergency Committee. He and Sidney formed a close working friendship, more like the one Sidney used to have with Shaw than any male friendship since his marriage. Henderson profited, as Shaw had done, by Sidney's willingness to surrender the credit if he could only do what he wanted to behind the scenes. Beatrice was indignant that the Labour party should make so much use of his ability, and "all they ask is that Sidney's name should not appear". But Sidney knew what he was about. By 1916 he had been given a place on the National Executive Committee of the party; by the end of the war he was the brain behind its new constitution. As Shaw had said, he was hardly in full flower yet.

Beatrice was lonelier than she had been for twenty years. More and more she reverted to the reflections and self-questioning which she used to pour out to her diary. "The war is a world catastrophe beyond the control of my philosophy," she wrote despairingly. "Such social philosophy as I possess does not provide any remedies for racial wars. Today I feel like the fly, not on, but under the wheel."

She began to cling to close friends. Haldane had been dropped from the Cabinet because he was suspected of being "pro-German". All sorts of legends were in circulation about him; that he had used his position to conduct secret negotiations, that he was secretly married to a German wife, or alternatively that he was himself the illegitimate brother of the Kaiser. He was more friendly to the Webbs than he had been for years, eager to have them to dinner so that they could listen to his side of the case.

> He says that he had reported to the Cabinet in 1911 that Germany was preparing for war. His advice was to prepare secretly for war whilst doing all that could be done to keep on friendly relations with Germany. . . . He did not look a physical wreck but perpetual over-eating and over-smoking has undoubtedly dulled his intellect.

One day Beatrice met Arthur Balfour in the park and stopped to talk to him about the Prince of Wales' Fund, in which the *New Statesman* was currently taking a suspicious interest. "But it was clear that neither the person approaching him nor the subject interested him . . . so I ceased to trouble him." Shortly afterwards, she met his sister-in-law and received a deliberate snub. (In the days of the poor-law campaign Lady Betty had written to her, "You have been an Egeria to me ever since that first visit of yours to Whittinge-hame and my reverence and admiration for you has gone on growing, but it is hard to believe that in our intercourse I can give as well as get for I am such a desperately ignorant, untrained and inefficient person.") Now, being cut by Lady Betty hurt Beatrice so much that she felt physically faint, and that night she lay awake thinking about the absence of any "ethic of friendship . . . the few troubles of my life have arisen from broken friendships"—and remembering how she had been hurt in exactly the same way by both Charles Booth and Joseph Chamberlain.

Maggie had three sons at the front and the eldest in prison as a conscientious objector. Beatrice went to a meeting of the No-Conscription Fellowship but found only a "muddled mixture of motives" which repelled her. When Roger Casement was condemned for treason, she tried to get Shaw to help him but Shaw "as usual had his own plan" which was that instead of wasting money on lawyers he would himself write a speech for Casement which would "thunder down the ages". "And yet the man is both kindly and tolerant," Beatrice commented. "But his conceit is monstrous and he is wholly unaware of the pain he gives by his jeering words and laughing gestures. . . . He never hurts my feelings because I am as intellectually detached as he is."

Her sister Georgie died, and she reproached herself for feeling no grief, only that it was "yet another break with the past—a past which is rapidly becoming the greater part of my personal life". She began to write in her diary about her longing for a personal faith, as she used to forty years before.

> Why do I believe that the heart of man, if it is to remain sane, if it is to rise to higher things, must concentrate on the emotion of Love? I can give no reason for this faith—it remains an Act of Faith. Why do I believe that this concentration of the mind on Love is furthered by Prayer, by the attempt to attain the consciousness of communion with a spiritual force outside oneself?

When she gave a lecture on the War and the Spirit of Revolt, she tried to explain her faith with regard to the purpose of human existence and was dismayed, afterwards, when the religious papers hailed her as a convert to Christianity.

> As a matter of fact, the Christian religion as set forth in the Bible or as developed in the dogmas of the Churches attracts neither my heart nor my intellect. The character of Jesus of Nazareth has never appealed to me . . . it would not be true to say that this faith in love with its attendant practice of prayer is a continuous state of mind. If it were, I should be a consistently happy person, which I am not.

Halfway through the war, Beatrice's health broke down, and she confessed to Sidney that she thought she had cancer. Sidney, terrified, took her at once to a specialist, who calmed her fears and prescribed more food and more sleep. She was relieved, but ashamed.

> With millions of young men facing death and dying on the battlefields of Europe, it seems contemptible for an old woman

who has had a full and happy life to shrink miserably at the inevitable end . . . but I have always been a prey to fear. As a child I would suffer mental agony over some trifling incident, fear of physical pain, fear of the exposure of some wretched little delinquency or a state of emotional misery arising out of the presumed dislike of someone I cared for. Oddly enough, I never feared death as a child. I sometimes longed for it and even contemplated suicide. These occasional and temporary obsessions are my 'Mr Hyde . . .' To most persons, who think they know me well, like my sisters, I think I present an even surface of impersonal attitude and equable temperament. That is due to my will-power which, in spite of mental agony remains supreme so far as outward behaviour is concerned.

She was ill for six months and did not recover fully for almost two years. The reason, she summed up afterwards, was

partly war neurosis, partly too persistent work to keep myself from brooding over the horrors of war, partly, I think from general discouragement arising out of our unpopularity with all sections of the political and official world. Sidney, with his sublime unselfconsciousness was wholly unaffected by the coldness with which we were regarded. But the hostile atmosphere undoubtedly lowered my resistance to neurasthenia . . . Once aware that my disorder was more mental than physical I took myself in hand . . . But the breakdown proved to be the turning-point from middle to old age. I now feel I am packing up so that I may be ready to depart when the time comes.

In fact Beatrice was "packing up" for thirty years—over a third of her lifetime—perpetually telling herself that she would achieve one last aim before she died, and that now she really was on the last stretch.

During her convalescence, after trying to fall in with the patriotic custom of knitting soldiers' socks, without much success, she bought herself a cheap typewriter and began to copy out and edit her own diaries, with the idea of making a "Book of My Life". She enjoyed it so much that it made her feel guilty. For years she had wanted to sum up her experience "in its larger and more intimate aspects". At first she found that she had lost the art of writing as she wanted to write, after so many years of curbing herself to match Sidney's dry

and agenda-like style. Now that she was on her own, free to crystal-
lise thoughts instead of always recording proven facts, writing became a pleasure instead of a grind. Still she dreamed of the ideal life
"in a comfortable small country house, noiseless except for birds and
the rustling of water and wind—with my diaries to type", while
Sidney occupied himself with "those endless volumes of historical
material . . . But until the war is over I suppose that Sidney and I
ought to render national service." When Lloyd George—now prime
minister of the Coalition Government—invited her to join a "Re-
construction Committee" she agreed cheerfully and put her diaries
away. She found herself sufficiently in her old form to coerce her
colleagues on the Local Government panel of the committee into
accepting many of the recommendations of her original Minority
Report. At the same time she was helping Sidney to draw up a pamphlet on Labour's war aims, and the new constitution for the
Labour Party. "Sidney and I have plenty of work before us," she
wrote happily, at the beginning of 1918. "Sidney in the Labour
Party, and I on government committees." They began to see more
of Haldane again, and of Lloyd George. "The little Welsh conjuror
. . . is so pleasant and lively that official defence and personal respect
fade into the atmosphere of agreeable low company . . . of a most
stimulating kind—intimate camaraderie with a fellow adventurer."
Lloyd George said flatteringly that he knew that the recent success
of the Labour movement was due not to Henderson but to someone
else—waving his hand towards Sidney. At Grosvenor Road, the
Webbs entertained the representatives of foreign socialist organisations, and gave a series of dinners for Labour leaders. Beatrice began
to realise that Henderson was hoping that after the war he would be
the Prime Minister of a Labour government, and assuming that
naturally Sidney would be in the Cabinet.

The Twenties
1918—1929

THE NINETEEN-TWENTIES were the years of harvest-time for the Webbs, when much of their planning and propaganda of the last thirty years was at last put into practice. Labour came to power; Sidney became a Cabinet Minister; the poor law was broken up. They finished their monumental work on Local Government, sending out circulars to Local Government authorities about it, pointing out that their book could be legally purchased on the rates. They revised their book on trade unions, wrote a tract on the decay of capitalism and their own blue-print for a Utopian society, *A Constitution for the British Socialist Commonwealth*. Beatrice fulfilled a long-standing ambition of her own, and produced a work of literature, as opposed to works of information, in *My Apprenticeship*, the story of her own youth, woven into a study of Victorianism and Victorian ideals. The period of Webb unpopularity, which had distressed her so much, was over. Instead, they found themselves on an eminence of old age and respected service, as elder statesmen to the infant Labour governments. A great many personal slights of the past were now compensated for. As a girl, Beatrice had been snubbed by aristocratic hostesses. In old age, she was embarrassed by unwanted invitations to Buckingham Palace. As a young woman, she had failed to marry the kind of rising politician favoured by her sisters, and settled on a suitor whom they thought ludicrously ineligible. Now he had left her brothers-in-law behind. But she never learned to bask in the sunshine of this Indian summer. All through it, she was reluctant and uneasy, protesting that it had all come too late, and that what she really wanted, now, was to withdraw into the ideal "life of learned leisure" for which her mother, eighty years before, had also sighed in vain.

The period of the twenties opened sadly, with the death of Maggie, the person whom she still loved better than anyone else except Sidney. During Maggie's last few months, when she knew she was dying, she turned back again to Beatrice and to the intellectual companionship in which they were so much at one that explanations were unnecessary. Beatrice alone could understand why Maggie had turned to Spiritualism after her youngest son had been killed in the war, when none of the various intellectual creeds which denied personal immortality offered any comfort. Maggie could confide to Beatrice that she had provided herself with a means of voluntary and easy transit from life, if it should become unbearable, and discuss whether or not to use it, with cool detachment. This late reunion with Maggie affected Beatrice deeply. It made her less afraid of death herself. "How difficult is the art of dying," she wrote, meditating on Maggie's courage and philosophical outlook. "I often wonder whether one will be able to "live up" to death so that one's last act shall be good and an inspiration to others. . . . But when the time comes, I will try to." It was difficult to switch her attention from this preoccupation with death to Sidney's prospective new career as a member of Parliament, but she consoled herself with the thought that if she should die first, and leave him alone, it would be a good thing for him to have so many new calls on his time and attention to get him through the first few months of loneliness and grief.

Sidney, who had agreed to be one of the "stage army" of Labour candidates at the immediate post-war election, without any serious idea of getting elected, afterwards acknowledged that he would really like to be in Parliament, but disliked the idea of pushing himself forward and claiming a winnable constituency. The impetus from outside was eventually provided, by his being appointed to the Sankey Commission on the Mining Industry. The Miners' Federation, led by Robert Smillie, had put forward demands for higher wages, shorter hours and nationalisation of the mines, and the Commission was set up to pacify them. Through meeting Lloyd George privately, at Haldane's house, the Webbs discovered that he meant to pack the Commission with persons known to be against nationalisation. They promptly confided their discovery to Smillie and advised him to stand out for the miners having their own representatives on it. The three experts chosen by the miners were typical intellectuals of the Labour party, R. H. Tawney, of the Workers' Educational Association, the Fabian Sir Leo Chiozza Money, and Sidney himself.

On this Commission, Sidney was in his element, and the other side, as Beatrice reported jubilantly, were absurdly outclassed. The majority of the Commission did report in favour of nationalisation, but Lloyd George temporised and refused to act on their recommendation, on the grounds that it was not unanimous. But the results for Sidney personally were far-reaching. Every miner devoured the press reports of the proceedings of the Commission and Sidney became the miners' hero. When the mining constituency of Seaham, in County Durham, wanted a parliamentary candidate, they begged Sidney to stand.

From the first, the Webbs liked Seaham. It consisted of a long narrow strip of coast, with pit villages grouped around new mines and the port in the centre. The Webbs took up residence at a modest hotel (7s 6d a day) on the seashore. Beatrice wrote:

> I was exhausted with the winter's work on the book and with sorrow, and I was glad to escape with Sidney to this quiet little place with the North Sea to look at, sometimes in dead calm and sometimes surging in on a north east gale. The sea is always to me a tonic and a sedative, inspiring with new energy and calming down earthly fears. For the last week has been one of panics, foolish panics, fears now for Sidney's safety in Herron's side-car, then of some quite imaginary ailment of my own. But the sight of the sea and the bracing walks along the strip of sand and rock, have swept the panics away by sheer shame at my own weakness. . . .

She had no difficulty in making friends with their prospective constituents. As miners went, these were prosperous, living fairly well, though in overcrowded conditions, and with their own flourishing, though rather drab, clubs and pubs, betting and chapel-going. She felt at home among them, as she had among the weavers of Bacup, and they accepted her as the Bacup community had. Sidney, too, found them sympathethic, because of their eagerness for education. The Webbs set about nursing the constituency with an efficiency which awed the miners and profoundly irritated the sitting member. They became experts on mining history generally and produced a pamphlet, *The Story of the Durham Miners*, for their own flock. They lectured in every single village, "giving decidedly stiff discourses on difficult subjects to little meetings of 40 to 50 miners, in bitterly cold miners' halls, starting off at 6 o'clock and getting home at 10 . . . rather an ordeal for a woman over sixty," wrote Beatrice, who, for the next ten years, had to keep on firmly reminding herself of her age, and who rather enjoyed playing the part of a philosophically resigned old lady—a part which did not in the least correspond with the reality, and which she abandoned, when necessary, at the drop of a hat. 'We hear so much at your meetings—it is as good or better than a tutorial class," her listeners told her. Shaw came up to speak for Sidney. Afterwards, Beatrice told him, "If I'd known you were such a spellbinder, I would have used you more in the movement, instead of letting you waste your time on writing plays." As the 1922 election approached, Sidney's constituents—experienced punters to a man—backed him so heavily that the best odds you could get, three days before the poll, were 7–3 on Webb. Sidney won the seat with a majority of 11,200 which so bewildered *The Times* that his result was recorded simply as a row of noughts.

"To enter Parliament for the first time at sixty-three years of age is a risky adventure from the standpoint alike of health and reputation," Beatrice wrote repressively, and anticipated trouble from the different economic creeds and clashing temperaments within the Parliamentary Labour Party, which was now the official Opposition. Its career opened with a struggle for leadership which ended unexpectedly in Ramsay MacDonald being chosen. "He now has the opportunity of his life, and it remains to be seen whether he is a big enough man to rise superior to his personal hatreds and personal vanities and sectarian prejudices and do what is wisest for the cause in its largest aspects." MacDonald treated Sidney as an important and valued colleague and invited him to sit on the Front Bench. Sidney, Beatrice reported, was "like a boy going for his first term to a public school!... How long this phase of youthful keenness will continue...it is difficult to foresee...to be happy in Parliament he had got to be successful as a debater." Sidney never learned to shine in the House, as Beatrice, who had been a connoisseur of Parliamentary performance since she was a girl, frankly admitted. His maiden speech went well enough. *Punch* remarked affably that, "Needless to say...he would like to place everything and everybody under the benevolent direction of the State." But the young Tories were apt to tease him, keeping up an audible hum of conversation and then shouting that they could not hear his rather weak voice, and telling him to "Sit down, Nannie!" (referring to his goatee beard). "Speak out and speak more slowly; you are too accustomed to talk to small classes of people who *want* to listen to you," a friendly colleague advised him.

But if Sidney was only an indifferent M.P., Beatrice was an unqualified success as "our member's wife". She never put a foot wrong in her relationship with his constituents and found the miners' wives, "gathering round me with a sort of hero worship", very touching. She wrote them a monthly letter and started a circulating library for them. One of the miners, Jack Lawson, who later became an M.P. himself, said that although in time Sidney "got" his audiences in his own quiet way, Mrs Webb gripped the women much more than he ever did. There was the real stuff of the north when she addressed meetings and she left a memory which will never be forgotten by those living. (In fact, to this day, "Beatrice Webb" is a legend in the district.) If she was not as completely successful with the wives of Sidney's colleagues in the Parliamentary Labour party, that was not entirely her fault. She saw her part in the blossoming new party as helping it to create a social life of its own, quite different from the London Society in which other politicians and their wives and daughters moved. In their book *Socialist Commonwealth*, the Webbs had condemned the functionless rich, not only because they were economic parasites, but for their futile occupations, often licentious pleasures and their inherently insolent manners.

Beatrice passionately wanted the party of her adoption to found a new social system based on equality and simplicity of manners. She realised, too, that the wives of Labour members who had come to power through the Trade Unions were apt to feel lonely and lost; cut off from their own background, but not part of the world in which their husbands worked. It was for these wives that Beatrice formed the "Half-Circle Club", which she hoped would provide a centre for a Labour social round. The sober and realistic Henderson whole-heartedly approved the idea, and talked of getting a grant from the Party to extend it. But the husbands of the women concerned were hostile from the first. One of them told Beatrice, "Not even your genius for organisation, Mrs Webb, will make the wives of Labour men come out of their homes and hobnob with the women organisers and the well-to-do women." Herbert Morrison (who as Mayor of Hackney made a point of wearing a tweed suit and red tie with his chain of office when receiving a visit from Queen Mary) accused Beatrice of wanting to "teach working-class women how to behave". Robert Smillie talked about a "school for snobbery". In fact, Beatrice was absurdly misjudged for her effort to make a stand against the kind of class-ridden society which she knew better than anyone else and now profoundly disliked. Perhaps the truth was that the rising Labour hierarchy understood that this was what she aimed at better than they pretended to. But they were secretly eager to try out the exact kind of social life she had experienced and discarded. The trade-union members' wives did come to the social evenings of the Half-Circle Club (where the literary editor of the *New Statesman* gave talks, and there were musical recitals of negro poems, with the company sitting on the floor and joining in the choruses), but what they really liked best was to have tea on the terrace of the House, just as the womenfolk of the "class that gives orders" always had done, and it was no use for Beatrice to assure them that it was all a hollow sham.

Those who had sneered at Beatrice's club were the very ones who were most enthusiastic about the offer of Lady Warwick (originally the "darling Daisy" of Edward VII, now a sentimental convert to Socialism) to lend her stately home for Labour conferences and weekends. In *Socialist Commonwealth*, the Webbs had suggested that the country houses of the functionless rich should be turned over to this very purpose, but they had not visualised, in their wildest dreams, that the owner would remain in residence and raise eyebrows at the manners and habits of the visiting socialist representatives. Lady Warwick did. Also, she invited the press and newsreel camera-men to record the democratic picture of Labour entertained by aristocracy, which caused exactly the kind of amusement in upper-class circles and resentment in puritanical working-class ones which Beatrice had hoped passionately they might avoid.

In fact she had to force herself to take part in it all, because she was always longing to get back to the country to write her own book, and only persevered out of loyalty to Sidney and the Party. She did her duty as a political hostess, holding dinners and lunches at Grosvenor Road, and taking an interest in Sidney's colleagues and new acquaintances. "We have made the acquaintance of the most brilliant man in the House of Commons—Oswald Mosley," she noted.

"Here is the perfect politician who is also a perfect gentleman," said I to myself as he entered the room (Sidney having asked him to come back to dinner from the House). If there were a word for the direct opposite of a caricature, for something which is almost absurdly a *perfect type*, I should apply it to him. Tall and slim, his features not too handsome to be strikingly peculiar to himself, modest and yet dignified in manner, with a pleasant voice and unegotistical conversation, this young person would make his way in the world without his adventitious advantages which are many—birth, wealth and a beautiful aristocratic wife. He is also an accomplished orator in the grand style.... So much perfection argues rottenness somewhere.... Is there in him some weak spot which will be revealed in a time of stress— exactly at the very time when you need support—by letting you or your cause down or sweeping it out of the way?... This question is a pertinent one, as it seems that he will either now or in the near future join the Parliamentary Labour Party. J.R.M. is much taken with him, and he with J.R.M....

Beatrice was herself beginning to concede that even if MacDonald was not a born leader of men he was at any rate "an *accomplished* leader of a Labour Party...nothing ragged or obviously defective in him...it is certainly marvellous how the achievement of his ambition has improved his manners and swept away his rancours."

In the autumn of 1923 Baldwin announced that the Conservative party would go to the country to demand a national mandate for protection as a cure for unemployment. Labour's election slogan was, "The Labour Party alone has a remedy for unemployment", and Ramsay MacDonald was eloquent about its intention to "make the land blossom like a rose and contain houses and firesides where there shall be happiness and contentment and glorious aspirations." Sidney was returned with an increased majority. Over the country, the Conservative vote fell, the Liberals decided to support Labour and Ramsay MacDonald was invited by George V to form a (minority) government. The Webbs held a dinner-party of Labour party leaders at Grosvenor Road, to discuss whether to take office and what to do if they did. Sidney reported to Beatrice that everyone had cold feet, except Henderson, who thought they should certainly take office and concentrate on unemployment. The Webbs also held a reception for the Half-Circle Club and the victorious and defeated candidates. Beatrice reflected:

It was a funny thought, this first gathering of the victorious Labour Party at the house of Altiora and Oscar Bailey—H. G. Wells ought to have been here to describe it! Funniest of all is the cordial relationship between J.R.M. and ourselves—all the more cordial because there is no pretence of personal intimacy or friendship. We have learnt not only to accept each other, but to respect and value our respective qualities.

MacDonald invited Sidney to be in the Cabinet, and offered him the Board of Trade. "What a joke, what an unexpected and slightly ludicrous adventure," said Sidney to Beatrice,

for a man of sixty-four to become, first a member of Parliament, and, within a year, a Cabinet Minister; and that with colleagues none of whom have held Cabinet office before; whilst only three of them have been in the Government—and those three do not include the Premier! If anyone had prophesied ten years ago that J.R.M. would be Prime Minister and would invite me to be in his Cabinet, I should have thought the first extraordinarily unlikely, but the two combined a sheer impossibility.

Haldane, who at the previous election had, as Beatrice put it, "courageously come out for the Labour Party", was asked by MacDonald to join the government as Lord Chancellor and Leader of the House of Lords. Beatrice's brother-in-law, Lord Parmoor, was the only other "outsider" in the Cabinet. "So there will be two "Richard Potter" husbands in the Labour Government—the Tory and the Socialist!" Haldane, "our old diplomatist", was in his element, holding a secret dinner at his house to discuss procedure, lending his spare frock-coat to the ex-miner War Minister for the Buckingham Palace ceremony, and generally "beaming and telling anecdotes about the Campbell-Bannerman and Asquith and other Cabinets; our old friend is literally revelling in his Heavy Father's part." Beatrice dug out the frock-coat and tall hat which Sidney had brought home from Japan in 1912 and never looked at since. "We were a jolly party," Beatrice reported. "All laughing at the joke of Labour in office."
    It was a perverse irony of fate that those who had resented her efforts to found a new kind of Labour "Society", based on Socialist ideals, now turned to her eagerly for instruction about upper-class habits. Beatrice was justifiably irritated.

Just at present there are two questions—clothes and curtseys. A sort of underground communication is going on between Grosvenor Road and Buckingham Palace which is at once comic and tiresome. . . . My latest job has been to help Mrs. Clynes to get her establishment fixed up at 11, Downing Street. I have provided her with housekeeper, cook and butler; no I forgot, the *very* latest task has been to soothe the feelings of Mrs. Snowden, deeply offended at being excluded from occupying the usual residence of the Chancellor of the Exchequer. . . . She is a "climber", refusing to associate with the rank and file and plebeian elements in the Labour Party. . . .

At the Foreign Office, the permanent officials were pleased with MacDonald. "They say they have got rid of a Cad in Curzon and found a gentleman in MacDonald. . . . And of course that is the danger. J.R.M. is a born aristocrat and he will tend to surround himself with 'well-bred men' in spite of their reactionary attitude towards affairs . . ." Even Sidney grumbled about the lack of real contact between the Cabinet and the Premier. Beatrice meditated about the "unlimited autocracy of the British P.M. . . . It was MacDonald who alone determined who should be in his Cabinet; it is MacDonald who alone is determining what the Parliamentary Labour Party shall stand for in the country." His pose as an "aristocratic charmer" began to exasperate his supporters. "MacDonald is no Labour man, he is one of us. He is the illegitimate son of the Duke of Argyll," said the Duchess of Sutherland to Lady Warwick. Beatrice noted bitterly that "all the other Labour men and their wives who accept invitations to great houses are flattered to their faces but sneered at when they have left the room." Six months after Labour took office, she wrote:

Unemployment is the crux—and up to to-day the Labour Party has not succeeded in putting forward a practicable policy. . . . Where I think the Labour leaders have been at fault—and we among them—is in implying, if not asserting, that the prevention of unemployment was an easy and rapid task instead of being a difficult and slow business involving many complicated transactions and far more control of capitalist enterprise than anyone has yet worked out.

All through this period of Beatrice's life, unemployment was the insoluble problem which overhung everything, just as poverty had been when she first began to be interested in politics. She looked back on her own Minority Report and decided that she had gone seriously wrong in "suggesting that we knew *how to prevent unemployment. We did not. All we knew was that it was high time to set about getting this knowledge . . ."*

During its eight months of minority government, Labour did improve unemployment benefits and make plans for public works to provide jobs, and also put through housing and educational reforms. MacDonald persuaded the French to evacuate the Ruhr, worked for disarmament and planned treaties of friendship with Soviet Russia. But, perhaps because of his success in foreign affairs, he became, Beatrice wrote, "even more aloof and autocratic towards his Ministers." Sidney began to think it would be a good thing when this first Labour administration ended, and meditated writing a book about the Cabinet as an institution. Beatrice told him that what was really needed was a plan to prevent the complete autocracy of the British Prime Minister.

The two oppositions decided to kill the Labour government on the issue of a sedition case, with the Russian treaty as background. MacDonald suddenly announced that he wanted the King's Speech, ready for dissolution, that afternoon ("Webb, you had better go and do it."). Labour lost the subsequent election on the "Zinoviev letter" scare—supposed to be a call from the Communist International for an armed insurrection in Britain. "Here ends the episode of a Labour government," Beatrice wrote. Sidney "having no career before him to be injured by MacDonald's errors will remain benign and philosophical." She herself was relieved to have him back in opposition.

> The next few years will see him more and more inclined to retire from the fray and spend the few years left to us in finishing up the researches we have begun. We must not allow ourselves to become depressed because our careers are behind us; when you are nearing seventy that is inevitable. The bitter fate is to feel baulked when you are young and in the prime of life; we have had our cake and we have thoroughly enjoyed eating it. Now we must be content to help others to do likewise.

All through Sidney's term of office, she had been longing to be able to devote herself whole-heartedly to writing her autobiography, "this little book of my own—which is a big book in its high endeavour to explain my craft and my creed." She had never had as much time as she had hoped for, and though she neglected her diary for it, the work went slowly. Often she told herself that it was ridiculous to mind so much about whether it was a success. When she asked Sidney to look at what she had written so far, he clearly disliked it.

There is something about it that he—not exactly resents—but which is unsympathetic. In his heart he fears I am over-valuing it, especially the extracts from the diaries ... and all that part which deals with "my creed" as distinguished from "my craft" seems to him the sentimental scribblings of a woman, only interesting just because they are feminine. However I have enjoyed writing it and the book as a whole will have *some* value as a description of "Victorianism".

When Shaw came to stay she hoped that he would take an interest in her manuscript, but he was absorbed in his own affairs. "His prestige, since the publication of *St. Joan* has bounded upwards; everywhere he is treated as a 'great man' and his income must be nearer thirty than twenty thousand a year. Charlotte purring audibly ..." Shaw was determined to write his own summing-up of Socialism, in a way that would make it clear even to the most stupid woman. It was published later under the title, *The Intelligent Woman's Guide to Socialism and Capitalism.* When he glanced at Beatrice's work, he said, like Sidney, that there were too many extracts from her personal diary in it. Beatrice, in her character of a philosophical old woman, scolded herself for minding so much. "Old people ought to be *less* anxious for applause." Sometimes she was embarrassed at the thought of how much she had given away about her real self in the book—"like an actress or an opera singer—you lose your privacy." Underneath it all, she had the triumphant certainty of the artist, and knew it was the best thing she had ever written. "*Done it!*" she wrote exultantly, in the small hours of an autumn morning in 1925, as she finished it at last.

When *My Apprenticeship* was published the reviews were "unexpectedly good; and my self-esteem ought to be satisfied." Outsiders did it more justice than her own friends did. Haldane reviewed it in the *Observer*, but it had clearly raised some antagonism in his mind, perhaps because he himself did not figure in Beatrice's autobiography as much as he felt he had a right to expect. Shaw praised it, but added:

> The Victorian reserve about your love-affairs is funny in these shameless psycho-analytical days. It even suggests that they were affairs of states of mind ... had you ever an intellectual hero and a great lump of a fleshly hero simultaneously? Did you ever tell your love ... ? ... how far did you find yourself a critically self-controlling agent and how far the helpless instrument of a force that landed you in interests that appalled you by the incongruity of their objects?[1]

Charlotte said patronisingly that she saw nothing particularly original about Beatrice's struggles to find a faith in place of Christianity, since that struggle had been the common experience of thoughtful girls of that period. "Original and distinguished" was the general verdict, and Beatrice, on the whole, was relieved. "My panic that the book would fall dead, on the one hand, or on the other my delusion that I was going to make a little fortune out of it seem to-day about equally ridiculous."

The other absorbing interest was their new home at Passfield Corner. They had advertised for a site, in the *New Statesman*. "It must be relatively high, with a pretty view; and above all completely isolated from houses harbouring cocks or dogs." They found one, near Hindhead in Surrey, with a cottage to which they added several rooms, and some dozen acres of ground. Beatrice wrote gaily:

> Shocking sight—the aged Webbs adding acre to acre ... laying out these acres in park-like avenues, cutting down trees to make vistas, discussing with the expert from Kew ... what trees and shrubs to plant—good to look at. We salve our consciences by assuring each other that we are preparing a country residence for the staff and students of the London School of Economics, but in our heart of hearts we see pictures of two old folk living in comfort, and amid some charm, writing endless works, and receiving the respectful attention of an ever larger public.

Meanwhile, she found the solitude restful and took to listening to music on the wireless and enjoying it so much that she warned herself against allowing it to become a "drug" in her old age. She also had time now for reading novels, and was interested and disturbed by the modern young writers' "utter absence of any ethical code" and the current preference for "men and women who combine a clever intellect with unrestrained animal impulses". Graham Wallas's niece, who came with him to visit the Webbs, explained to Beatrice that "Contraception renders chastity quite unnecessary". While Beatrice read D. H. Lawrence and Aldous Huxley, Sidney was deeply absorbed in A. S. M. Hutchinson's *If Winter Comes*, the story of a meek and martyred husband which had a tremendous (and inexplicable) success in the early twenties.

"The General Strike will fail," she wrote, on the day it started. "When the million or so strikers have spent their money they will drift back to work and no one will be any the better and many will be a great deal poorer and everybody will be cross." Towards the end of it she went up to London and accompanied their old friend Susan Lawrence round strikers' meetings. Susan, who was usually calm and hard-headed, was in a state of emotional excitement, addressing the strikers as "comrades" and referring to them as heroes and martyrs. Beatrice had always disliked revolutionary emotionalism among actual workers, but she found it most distasteful of all in romantic intellectuals. "What is the use of having professional brain-workers to represent you if they refuse to give you the honest message of intelligence and treat you to a florid expression of the emotion which *they* think the working-class are feeling or ought to be feeling?" When the strike collapsed, she concluded gloomily:

The Government has gained immense prestige in the world and the British Labour Movement has made itself ridiculous. A strike which opens with a football match between the police and the strikers and ends nine days later with densely-packed reconciliation services. . . . will make the continental Socialists blaspheme. . . . We are all of us just good-natured stupid folk. The worst of it is that the governing classes are as good-natured and stupid as the Labour Movement.

She was depressed by the idea that European civilisation was nearing its end. ("There is always the U.S.A.—a self-confident and overwhelmingly prosperous race," said Sidney cheeringly.) But Beatrice was haunted by the thought of "Russian communism and Italian Fascism—two sides of the worship of force and the practice of cruel intolerance—with the still more penetrating idea that this spirit is creeping into the U.S.A. and even creeping into Great Britain."

Shaw was feeling disillusioned about Socialism. He had been stung by the icy reception among his friends of his *Intelligent Woman's Guide*. Beatrice and Sidney decided that "the less we discuss the book either with G.B.S. or with others, the better. In Socialist circles this kindly 'passing by' is what is going to happen." Shaw went to stay in Italy and came back announcing that he admired Mussolini.

His argument seems to be that either the Haves or the Have-Nots must seize power and *compel* all to come under the Fascist or Communist plough. It is a crude and flippant attempt at re-construction, bred of conceit, impatience and ignorance. It will injure G.B.S.'s reputation far more than it will the democratic institutions of Great Britain. But it re-inforces the Italian Tyranny. It is only fair to add that this naïve faith in a Super-man before whose energy and genius all must bow down is not a new feature in the Shaw mentality . . .

Shaw gave a Fabian lecture on "Democracy and Delusion". Beatrice reported:

The audience became more and more bewildered and when he sat down . . . there was the feeblest clapping I have ever heard at Kingsway Fabian lectures—and a hurried and silent departure of depressed men and women. . . . Poor Charlotte looked gloomy and suggested that we should discuss the subject with him when we go to Ayot next week-end. But it will be useless; he is too old and too spoilt by flattery and pecuniary success to listen to criticism.

She began to watch herself for signs of any similar "senile Vanity" and was reluctant when the London School of Economics asked Sidney and herself to have their portrait painted, to hang in the Founders' Room there. "All that one can say to oneself is that it is not worth the fuss of refusing." She borrowed a pink blouse from the gardener's wife at Passfield in order to pose for it.

But it was impossible not to feel triumphant when, exactly twenty years after she had composed her Minority Report, the poor law was at last broken up, just as she had suggested. "To be able to *make* history as well as write it—or to be modest—to have foreseen, twenty years ago, the exact stream of tendencies which would bring your proposal to fruition is a pleasurable thought. So the old Webbs are chuckling over their chickens!"

From the moment when they first found the cottage, Beatrice had been firm that this was definitely the last lap of the Webbs' life, even picturing a "funeral procession wending its way down the new drive, a few years hence, perhaps a few months hence of one of us, leaving the other desolate and alone." She was taken aback when Henderson, spending a week-end at Passfield Corner, spoke of the Labour Party being called to office again soon and assumed that Sidney would be required in the House of Lords. "I should very decidedly prefer *not*," she wrote. "... But we still think that the occasion will not arise in the remaining few years of health and strength." Meanwhile, they agreed that the safe Labour seat at Seaham should be handed over to MacDonald. "Who would have thought that the embittered vendetta of former years would terminate in such a model manner!"

In the spring of 1929, the Webbs went for a two-month holiday abroad, and called on Leon Trotsky, in exile on the island of Prinkipo. "We were alone with the great revolutionary for a couple of hours," Beatrice reported. They discussed the possible advent of the British Labour party to power. Trotsky said that as soon as a new Labour government was formed, he was going to demand a visa from Ramsay MacDonald. Sidney said he might not get it, to which Trotsky replied testily that a Party not strong enough to answer for its actions had no right to power. "I don't think we impressed each other with our respective arguments," noted Beatrice. "Beneath his polished intellectualism he has the closed mind of a fanatic who refuses to face the fact of Western democratic organisation." When they got back to England, preparations for a general election were already in full swing.

15

In Love with Russia
1929—1955

ON ELECTION-DAY the Webbs were staying at Cheyne Walk. Kate Courtney was dead, and Beatrice was winding up the estate, distributing the treasures collected by the Courtneys during their married life among the hundred and fifty-five Potter descendants. It was in her late sister's drawing-room, with all its Liberal associations, that Beatrice and Sidney first heard the news of the final collapse of the Liberal party and the Labour victory. Harold Laski—then a young professor at the London School of Economics—and his wife sat up with them listening to the wireless until the small hours and became "almost hysterical" at the prospect of Labour having a majority in the House.

The Webbs discussed whether Sidney should accept a Cabinet post, or refuse a peerage if Cabinet office was not included. They were disconcerted when almost a week went by without a message of any kind from MacDonald and when Beatrice's brother-in-law, Lord Parmoor, called to tell them that he—Parmoor—had been allotted a Cabinet post. At last there was a midnight telegram, summoning Sidney to see the Prime Minister. "He wants you to accept a peerage without office," said Beatrice. "I shall not do it," said Sidney. He returned from the interview having won his point and accepted a peerage, but with office as Minister for the Colonies. The position completed the curious parallel between Sidney's career and that of Joseph Chamberlain, but now Sidney had outstripped his famous rival by a peerage. He decided to call himself Baron Passfield.

Beatrice debated with herself and discussed with Sidney about using the title. She admitted that there had to be Labour peers in order to form a government and that it was Sidney's duty to go to the House of Lords. But there was no such obligation on her part and if she made the gesture of refusing the title herself she could undermine the institution of nobility, a part of the "paraphernalia" of aristocracy which she regarded as one of the evils of the capitalist society, an evil to be swept away rather than encouraged to spread in the democratic ranks of the Labour movement. Having examined her conscience for motives of pride or superiority, Beatrice reached the conclusion that "an honour ignored is an honour deflated", and reflected ironically that the social ostracism which would follow her refusal would be extremely convenient, because she did not in the least want to be forced into the social obligation of London Society again. "I respect our King and Queen and I acquiesce in a Constitutional Monarchy," but she would be glad to be dropped from the Buckingham Palace list.

Her gesture was, on the whole, well received. The public took it as a demonstration of feminism rather than as an attack on the "prestige of titles and an insult to the fountain of honour", which was the view held by the Tories and expressed by Mrs Baldwin when she shouted out (or so it seemed to Beatrice) at the Royal garden party, "Lady Passfield we shall call you, whether you like it or not." Friends who teasingly addressed her thus got a playful box on the ear. At a reception, she suddenly found herself being presented to the Duke of Connaught. He was a kindly old man and as he hobbled up to her she had not the heart to disappoint him. "She curtseyed!" announced the press and the B.B.C. news bulletins. "So that's that, and curtsey I must on all future occasions," said Beatrice resignedly. (In Durham, to this day, elderly miners remember that while Sidney "let us down", Mrs Webb "stayed one of us".)

Beatrice was highly critical of the Snowdens, who would retail in deferential tones every detail of their visit to Sandringham. She even called Shaw's *Apple Cart* (in which Susan Lawrence was pictured as "Lysistrata") "Shaw's annoying satire on democracy", because the character of King Magnus struck her as an excessively loyal tribute to the Monarchy from a socialist. She deplored such "romancing about the Royal family" as a symptom of the "softening of the brain of socialists enervated by affluence". At an informal dinner at York House, the Prince of Wales, with royal courtesy, deferred to her wishes and addressed her as Mrs Sidney Webb. He asked her earnestly what she believed in and what she thought of Russia. She was strangely concerned about the young prince, as though she sensed how short-lived would be his role in the monarchy. Her second royal encounter lacked sparkle. "Where do you live?" asked Queen Mary. "In a cottage near Liphook, ma'am,"

Beatrice replied. "Liphook," repeated the Queen, looking about for one of her subjects who could explain.

Other aspects of Sidney's high office troubled Beatrice's conscience. She asked herself how far such life-long advocates of an egalitarian state were entitled to the social prestige and luxurious living which were the way of life of great personages. Was such an environment compatible with the "equal sharing of available commodities" to which the Labour Party was pledged? And how could she herself, as the wife of the Colonial Secretary, guard against the subtle flattery of London Society and the evil glamour of political power, or combat her ever-present enemy, personal vanity—"a devil not yet laid by old age"? At seventy-two, Beatrice still had a silvery beauty. These dilemmas brought on insomnia and the old "whizzing" in her ears and made her afraid of not being able to survive Sidney's term of office without a nervous breakdown. Sidney shared none of her misgivings. Old age and happiness had made him complacent about his good fortune and dulled his desire to change a social order from which he had so greatly benefited. He tolerated the world and its "dark places". He enjoyed being a peer and Secretary of State in the office where he had once worked as a clerk. To Beatrice, this was the one redeeming feature in their new circumstances and her one care, now, was to concentrate her remaining strength on helping him. Nothing else, she felt, was of any consequence.

In the autumn of 1929 she handed over the lease of 41, Grosvenor Road to Susan Lawrence, now under-secretary to the Minister of Health. ("Susan is enjoying herself vastly, she loves the exercise of power; she has visions of glorious changes...") Beatrice had no regrets about leaving the little house by the Thames where she had spent forty years of "amazingly happy and full life" with Sidney. She looked round with relief on the dingy dining-room and the three narrow flights to the garret bedrooms. But she was sorry to say good-bye to her old servant, Emily Worsley, who had chosen to remain on in the house rather than follow her old mistress into the country. A service flat in London, for Sidney's work, was all that they needed and they rented one in Whitehall Court for what seemed an exorbitant rent (fourteen guineas a week). But it was next door to the Shaws' flat, and only a few steps from the Colonial Office, and they had their annual salary of £1,500 to spend on entertaining Sidney's colleagues and creating a social centre for the Parliamentary Labour Party.

Eight Fabians were in the Cabinet, and ten others in Parliament. But there was an increasing prominence of the governing class in the Party, which Beatrice did not like—men such as Hugh Dalton, Noel Baker and the arrogant—though able—Oswald Mosley, and among their leaders a growing tendency to be "gobbled up" by fashionable society. Jimmy Thomas, a favourite among suburban Conservatives and race-goers, adored for his genial wit and cockney accent, often publicly disowned socialists. The distinguished Philip Snowden, who appealed to the banking world, had become "the champion of the moneyed classes". Ramsay MacDonald's popularity in aristocratic circles was reflected in the court circulars announcing, "The Prime Minister left after his visit to the Duke and Duchess of Sutherland, for Loch Choir, where he will be the guest of the Marquis and Marchioness of Londonderry." Nor was there much of the social reformer about the gay Lord Thompson, the ill-fated Air Minister, with his amusing court anecdotes. He recounted to Beatrice when he had attended the King during the presentation of the bishops, "He turned to me at the end of the ceremony and asked me what were my views about this religious business. I told him that in my youth I fervently believed in Mars and Venus. Today I put my faith in Minerva tempered by Bacchus." (Before Thompson left on his fatal flight on the R101, Beatrice had "a presentiment" that she would never see him again.)

The Shaws' environment was far from socialist. They seemed to be continually surrounded by royalties, or consorting with the Astors, or the Sassoons, or actors, actresses and prize-fighters. Even the Webbs themselves, though "leaning towards a simple life", found themselves entertaining coming Conservatives, attending Mansion House lunches and receiving pressing invitations from the rich and influential who wanted to be governors, ambassadors or simply peers. Beatrice was convinced that the Labour Party would have to dissociate itself from "the paraphernalia of court and diplomatic circles" if it was to carry out any serious measures of social reform. Permeating days were over, now that socialists were in power.

Beatrice only came into the Colonial Office picture on official occasions. She did once give a democratic dinner at Lyons' Corner House, to which the whole of Sidney's administrative and clerical staff, much to their surprise, were invited. The seating was arranged democratically by drawing names from a hat, at which there were some mild grumblings from some of the older civil servants, and Beatrice gave a little talk. But the occasion was not a success and was not repeated. Mostly, she was in the country and Sidney in London. She did not like this arrangement but solaced herself with the thought that the episode would soon be over and that once Sidney was out of office and the "business of the street no longer interested" them, they would "sink together in the everlasting night, grateful for a love-lit day," in the dear little cottage she had transformed, thanks to their official salary, into a house "fit for a peer to live in".

During her lonely days at Passfield, Beatrice scribbled in her diary, and began her new book *Our Partnership*, in which she planned to sum up her experience of life and the conclusions she had reached, as frankly as Sidney's susceptibilities would allow. Her opening chapter was a charming tribute to the "Other One". She prepared broadcasts and lectures—one to the Oxford Union on the Perplexities of an Old Woman—and took exercise (her walks were now reduced to four miles a day) with a little companion, Sandy, a white dog on whom she lavished demonstrative affection in Sidney's absence. As the only surviving Potter sister—Rosy, she considered, did not count—she took over the responsibility of an aunt to her numerous nephews and nieces, now, except for Rosy's children, middle-aged men and women. She was apt to silence the expression of unauthorised opinion with, "That, my dear, is a subject about which you know nothing".

At meals, impatient to get on with the talk, she would wolf down the scrap of food on her plate with one snap like a starved animal, leaving everyone else awkwardly swallowing nourishment. But all the same the nephews and nieces were all fond of their delightful, astringent, kind "Aunt Bo". She fostered a motherly interest in all their doings and even "brilliant but proletarian" Malcolm Muggeridge, Rosy's son-in-law, whose views she strongly opposed, was gathered into this family embrace. So was vagabond Rosy, who still roamed about Europe, her enthusiasm for the beauty of nature and "free love" undiminished by age. Beatrice visited her neighbours, the Balfours, old souls who had forgotten their feud with her, and Bertrand Russell, now an earl. "Poor Bertie"—as Beatrice called him—had lost his sardonic humour and was working out his modern ideas on marriage—not very happily she thought—with a new wife, Dora. H. G. Wells came to tell her of the crusade for

"Peace and a World State" which he was working on with Lloyd George. Lloyd George himself floated into her orbit again. All were voices from the past, like their own and that of Shaw, who was broadcasting "constructive proposals"—such as testing the blood of candidates to see whether they were worthy of being M.P.s, and imposing a political creed on children, as in Russia. Whence would come the heralds of the future? Beatrice wondered wearily.

Sidney was not an effective Colonial Secretary. His White Paper on Kenya scarcely departed from traditional Imperial policy and was not implemented until he was out of office. Palestinian matters were taken out of his hands by MacDonald because Zionists complained that his policy was too pro-Arab. When his friends urged him to preserve his dignity and resign, he stoutly refused. Beatrice only picked up a vague idea of how things were going when she listened to an occasional remark he made about his work as he sat in his armchair, at the end of the day, meditating, his finger-tips pressed together.

His awkward predicament was not to last long. Gandhi was clamouring for Dominion status in India, promised during the Great War, and the Government, having lost faith in Britain's right to rule there, was puzzling over how, not when, to grant it. Beaverbrook was clamouring for Empire Free Trade. Even MacDonald was clamouring, in the United States, for Universal Disarmament. At home there was a clamour for higher wages, shorter hours and more dole, and nothing was done about the steady rise of unemployment. Beatrice began to doubt whether Labour was fit to govern. How much longer could this ghost of an Empire continue? she wondered. Where could a leader be found "who will be fervent in faith and scientific in method and equalitarianism?" Not in the ranks of the Labour Party, or among the clever young men at the School of Economics, nor yet to be discovered in the Labour Research Department, now run by Douglas and Margaret Cole.

Discontent in the Labour movement was growing, with a socialist government which could not even deal with the question of unemployment. Even Shaw no longer believed that socialism was essential to the continuance of civilisation—a counsel of despair and against freedom, which Beatrice was not yet prepared to accept. With reforming zeal, she struck her last blow for egalitarianism in a free democracy. She gallantly set about campaigning for the reorganisation of Parliament. She had broken up the Poor Law, why not

Parliament? In order to meet the new demands of socialism there were to be two parliaments. One was to deal with foreign affairs and matters of general policy, and the other with home affairs. The Webbs had already elaborated the idea in their *Socialist Commonwealth for Great Britain*. Beatrice addressed a meeting of members of Parliament on "How to Make Parliamentary Institutions Equal to their Task", lectured the Fabian Society, gave broadcasts and wrote an article in the *Political Quarterly*. Shaw thought it was a capital plan and if carried out might save England, but there was sharp criticism from her friends at the School of Economics, and a discouraging apathy in the air. It had all been so different in the nineties, Beatrice reflected sadly, and her faith in political democracy began to falter.

If she was gloomy about politics, she was even more disturbed by the moral chaos prevailing among the younger generation, and expressed by her nephew-in-law, Malcolm. Sexual morality was being undermined, to the ugly sound of Jazz music, by the repulsive animalism of D. H. Lawrence. "My only religion", he wrote, "is a belief in the blood and flesh being wiser than intellect. . . . I am not sure if a mental relation with a woman does not make it impossible for me to love her . . . essential drama is essentially phallic . . . it is the death of the phallic consciousness which is making us go withered and flat."[1] It is not surprising that his message—and the fact that Rosy's views on free love, which had so shocked herself and her sisters years ago, were now the general rule—did not appeal to Beatrice. The lack of belief in religion and the absence of a "common opinion about the right use of the sexual impulse" were destroying society, Beatrice believed. Birth control, with its inevitable companion, "death precipitation", would soon be blessed by Anglican Bishops. "The human race has disgraced itself. It has shown neither intelligence nor good will," Beatrice lamented. Capitalist civilisation seemed to be decaying under her very eyes, just as she and Sidney had predicted, ten years ago.

Nothing interested Beatrice which was not successful. She turned her attention to the two countries of the future, capitalist America, with its violence and crime, and puritanical, communist Russia. What if the communist experiment were to succeed? The thought prompted her to invite the Russian Ambassador, M. Sokolnikov, and his wife to dinner at Whitehall Court. Neither of them spoke a great deal of English, but the evening was saved by Shaw's wit and some

French. Beatrice was delighted to find that the Ambassador was a puritan, neither smoking nor drinking his wine. In return, the Sokolnikovs invited the Webbs to lunch where Beatrice was delighted by an example of egalitarianism—she could not tell who were diplomats and who servants. They saw an exhibition of photographs of life in the Soviet Union, which Beatrice promised to get Shaw to open, and the Sokolnikovs urged them to go and see Russia for themselves. Down at Passfield, they discussed the Russian Five Year Plan with their new friends and Philip Snowden. The Ambassador described the enthusiasm with which workers in Russia were accepting low wages and hard conditions in order to save money for the state. "That's sound," said Snowden. "Our workers want more wages and shorter hours." "Ah," retorted Beatrice, "you will never get the British workman to work harder for less." The Sokolnikovs followed up their visit with a beautiful basket of flowers which they sent to Beatrice on her 72nd birthday.

The political situation had now become critical. MacDonald no longer consulted his ministers, and his dislike of his colleagues had become a joke in the Labour party. Snowden was ill, and Oswald Mosley had resigned. So had Trevelyan and Ponsonby. There was no more money and the condition for an American loan was cutting the dole. At Passfield Corner on August 24th, 1931, Beatrice heard the news of the resignation of almost the whole Labour Cabinet and the formation by MacDonald of a National Government. It was an inglorious end, but "what I wished to hear". She wrote off to the women of Seaham instructing them not to vote for MacDonald in the coming by-elections.

A little dazed by their taste of power, the Webbs resumed their old routine of work and exercise and a strict diet, the evenings now made beautiful with the strains of classical music from the wireless set, their companionship shared with their little dog Sandy. They attended a lack-lustre Labour Party Conference at Scarborough at which Beatrice's nephew, Stafford Cripps, was the important person. Beatrice completed the first chapter of *Our Partnership*, with which Sidney was delighted, and they were visited by friends who had been neglected during their two supposedly glamorous years of office. Week-ends were conversational marathons—five hours' talk, for example, with the Maiskys, with "Kingsley Martin intervening". Kingsley Martin, then editor of the *New Statesman*, described a loquacious visit to Passfield Corner:

One got to Passfield Corner, where the Webbs had been working intensely all the week, for tea on Saturday. The condition of the world, and the Labour and Socialist Movement in particular and the immediate topics of the day were systematically dealt with. One could almost hear Mrs Webb putting a mental tick after each item when nothing further of importance was likely to be said on the subject. The long, meaty conversation would continue at night by the fire; Mrs Webb sat ... with her elegant hand warming by the flame, and her authoritative voice emphasising, with confirmation at intervals by Sidney, just those morals which she thought arose from reminiscences. At half past eight the next morning you would be having breakfast and Mrs Webb, who had already been up for several hours and done a lot of work, would be standing between you and the window, lecturing. ... At 11 there was the walk. ... There was always the incident with Sandy, the white dog ... when he would bark violently at Mrs Webb, while she beat the ground with a walking stick and scolded him until he was silent. At lunch, there would be distinguished visitors ... the topic of the morning talk ... would be pursued during tea, when the taxi would arrive to take one home, so full of mental food that only the strongest digestions were not somewhat exhausted. ...[2]

They were getting old and the inevitable end and separation approaching; but only of the body, and for a short while. Their ashes were to be mingled together under the ash tree in the grove at the bottom of their garden. Their word and thought would live on in the London School of Economics and Passfield Corner would be a resting place for professors of sociology and their wives and little ones, heirs of the scientific spirit to which she and Sidney had dedicated their lives. The song of the birds, too, which each morning had brought them back to consciousness, would be perpetually renewed each spring. Thus "strolling down the slope of life" together was very pleasant, but they still had a little energy and will left to work for the cause of socialism. How were they to use the remnants of their wits now that neither of them any longer believed in the inevitability of gradualism? The question always uppermost in Beatrice's mind was—what if the Russian experiment were to succeed?

She was getting tired of opening books which began or ended "Whither Mankind?" and prophesied doom. Worship of money and love of luxury were undermining capitalist countries and disillusionment existed everywhere. Only Russia was hopeful, and the Webbs decided in favour of communism and resolved to visit the Soviet Union. "For sheer common sense give me my little Bee," Beatrice remembered her father saying. He had been right, she thought.

The Webbs, with characteristic thoroughness, devoted the next few months to preparing their minds for the visit to Russia. They read *Humanity Uprooted* and *Red Bread* by Maurice Hindus, and *Soviet Russia* by W. H. Chamberlin, both of whom challenged the inevitability of gradualness, and described the zeal for public welfare among Soviet citizens. They read the works of Lenin and two novels, *Sot* [sic] and *Free Love* which described the "immense straining upwards... in morality of the Soviet citizens". They heard favourable reports of the Five Year Plan from the Ambassador in Moscow, Sir Esmond Ovey, and some less favourable from less important members of the English mission. They were told the facts about Soviet Russia by the Russian Ambassador, and Mme Sokolnikova told them of the strict moral discipline and almost religious fervour of the members of the Communist Party, who had instructions not to waste their time and energy on sex. They listened to Shaw, converted to the egalitarian state after his visit to Moscow with Lady Astor. They heard the other side from Rhea Clyman, a young Canadian journalist living in Moscow, who disliked the régime because the Russian people were enslaved and everyone was wretched except the party bosses. The collective farms were a failure, she said, and there was famine throughout the land and party leaders were intriguing against each other. Miss Clyman was an anarchist by temperament, Beatrice decided, and discounted her unfavourable testimony.

Beatrice believed that the Communist leaders were dedicated men, subject to strict moral discipline, and that although chasity was not a rule, members were advised not to waste time indulging their sexual appetites. Even Miss Clyman had never accused them of self-indulgence. Russia, it seemed, was ruled by a religious order in which the would-be mystic in Beatrice discerned the quality of soul noticeably lacking in their own blue-print for a Socialist Commonwealth. That was the magnet which drew her to Russia. Of course, she regretted the absence of the love of God and Christian humility and freedom of thought, without which the soul of man and the scientific spirit would wither away. But, after all, was the denial of God also the denial of man? Had not the religion of humanity come into its own at last in Soviet Russia? And was it not possible for State Socialism to exist without the incentive of profit? She and Sidney were going to Russia to find out.

Beatrice had just had the honour of being elected the first woman member of the British Academy, when on May 7th, 1932, she and Sidney, with a draft of their foregone conclusions (the result of months of scientific investigation) safely stowed in their luggage, set out on their pilgrimage to Moscow after a week's anxious delay caused by ice in the Gulf of Finland. M. Bogomolof of the Soviet Trade Mission was on the quay to see them off, and their faithful friend Shaw, surrounded, as usual, by a mob of photographers, waved farewell. The two disillusioned old Fabians, with a combined age of one hundred and forty-seven, steamed out of the port of London with renewed hope, Beatrice fervently praying that the Communist experiment would turn out to be a success.

On board, the captain paid them much attention, and at the end of the voyage graciously presented them to the pilot and the customs-house representative. He invited Beatrice to criticise the ship's appointment and appeared grateful when she complained that there were no chamber pots, nothing to vomit into, no menus, no drinking water and that the door handles were hard on delicate hands. Having assured her that all would be put right, he presented her with a large portrait of Lenin, and set his important passengers ashore on Soviet soil. It was cold and raining and the sombre city of Leningrad seemed half in ruins. This unfavourable impression was redeemed by the reception committee waiting to greet them on the quay, consisting of trade union representatives, consumers' co-operatives and various other officials. "We seem to be a new type of royalty," Beatrice said to Sidney. They were whisked off to a luxurious hotel, to await the departure of their train to Moscow. In Moscow, they were put up in a palatial mansion reserved for important foreigners, with imperial crested crockery, and were given excellent food for the only time during their stay in Russia. Their guide and interpreter, it appeared, had read their works and was on the tenth volume of their book on Local Government. She was a cheerful woman except for a note of strain and tragedy which Beatrice noticed in her conversation.

The Webbs spent their time in Moscow interviewing influential officials. Beatrice observed that they sometimes got answers which did not agree with the facts. Once she asked a comrade what the communist ethic was. "Any action hostile to building up socialism is against the communist ethic," he replied irritably. They did not interview Stalin who was, they were told, away in the Caucasus; and "in any case," wrote Beatrice, "an interview with a great personage is of no consequence." She visited an elementary school where there were not more than forty in a class, and where the children were wrapped in fur bags in the winter and the delicate ones given a special diet. They were taken to the theatre, where they saw a popular drama called *Fear*, about a conflict between an old professor and a young communist. It lasted for four hours. The hall was crammed with cheering workers. Beatrice was struck with the enthusiastic spirit of social service everywhere, and if the Park of Culture and Rest seemed rather gloomy, at least there was no sign of any "spooning" there.

They journeyed down the Volga, interrogating authorities in every port. As they went south, although Beatrice only found one bug, conditions became less comfortable. For instance, there was no food in the hotel at Stalingrad, where they interviewed comrades for two days. Meals were brought up to their room. At Rostov, a "specialist" refused to move out of their reserved room. Their guide was particularly incensed because the "specialist" had only recently been a "wrecker". However, they were lavishly entertained by a crowd of comrades who showed them the collective farms. As they gazed round the famine-stricken land they marvelled at the mechanical developments and the advance in education of the Russian peasant. They noted with interest the enthusiasm of the new governing class and the liquidation of the old, and listened to some remarkable statistics of what had been achieved. Russia, indeed, seemed to be one of the wonders of the world, thought Beatrice. After seeing the farms she fell ill. The doctor diagnosed "stomach fever" and she went off to a resort in the Caucasus for a few days, leaving Sidney to complete their scientific investigation in the Ukraine.

When they got back to Moscow they lunched with Sir Esmond Ovey, who seemed to them a little uneasy about the favourable impression Russia had made on them and diplomatically reminded them that their visit had been very short. How entirely cut off from Russian life he was! thought Beatrice. He had never even heard of the Associations of Producers and actually believed that the State was the only employer. By then, their old eyes had grown accustomed to the heaps of rubble, crumbling walls and grey faces of a terrorised population, and when the time came for them to leave the "Mecca of the Egalitarian State", the city of Leningrad, which had seemed so gloomy on their arrival, looked beautiful in the summer sun.

Their visit had lasted three weeks. It had been an intense experience and Beatrice was more than ever aware, when she came back, of the spiritual desert of their capitalist environment. It seemed to her that leaders of socialism, like Stafford Cripps, Hugh Dalton and Clement Attlee, lacked the revolutionary spirit. They were far too well off, and, although Shaw was a wonderful "weedkiller in the sociological garden", he had nothing whatever to plant. Both he and Wells had "succumbed to their royalties". None of them, not even themselves, had any intention of exchanging their easy circumstances for the hard life of a revolutionary. What was the good of talking about revolution when no one meant it? Sidney was moved to ask; and Beatrice recalled the small sardonic figure of Lenin lying silently in the Red Square, and reflected how soft their own lives had been compared with his.

Beatrice was worn out, but she preferred to "wear out than rest out". So she settled down to ponder over her conclusions about the Soviet Union and to help Sidney sort the information they had brought back with them from Moscow in preparation for the book they were going to write. They had seen little of the dark side of Russia—"the trap-door disappearance of unwanted persons"—but the suppression of freedom had not altogether escaped their notice and they were haunted by the question of how it could be reconciled with the free spirit of scientific investigation without which an egalitarian state could not flourish.

That autumn, Beatrice broadcast about Russia, while Sidney wrote six articles on current history for America in order to recuperate the cost of their Russian trip. By the end of the year, Beatrice began to weary of the task they had undertaken in their old age, and it was only with an immense effort of will that she was able, on Christmas Day, to summon up her energy to plan the opening chapter of their book, *Soviet Communism, A New Civilisation?* In the New Year the Soviet atmosphere was brought too close to be entirely welcome, by the sound of the Kremlin bells followed by the *Internationale* and details for the Five Year Plan from Radio Central Moscow, together with birthday greetings on her 73rd anniversary from M. Maisky, the Soviet Ambassador who had replaced M. Sokolnikov. She was tired of it all, and wondered if they would ever rid themselves of the thought of communism. She and Sidney went off in the spring to Porto Fino in Italy, for a complete change. Sidney wanted to take the first chapter with them. "Let us keep our brains a vacant plot for awhile. I am dead tired of wondering what is going to happen to our little world of human beings and trying to make sense out of the confusion of thought," pleaded Beatrice.

She invited her fashionable friend, Lional Phillimore from the British Embassy in Rome, to join them, handed her two books on Communism, which she had no desire to open, and settled down to enjoy a gossip about the Vatican and Mussolini. They went on to Cannes, Sidney acquiescing, and visited Odette Keun, a chic, audacious friend of Wells. With her, they met Somerset Maugham, whose books Beatrice had always admired. He wrangled with his hostess over the stories they both wanted to tell and Beatrice came away with the impression that he was a coarse and unsavoury character.

This brief trespass onto capitalist playgrounds refreshed them for another start on their book *Soviet Russia, A New Civilisation?* Later they dropped the question mark. They spoke and thought of little else. Every evening the air in their sitting-room was filled with the sounds of propaganda from Moscow Central Radio. Some of their friends were disturbed, some agreed with them and some were bored. On one occasion Arthur Henderson, the leader of the Labour party, mildly protested. Beatrice reacted by dancing wildly to the strains of the *Internationale* in defiance. Despite this obsession, her thoughts often strayed from the problems of man in the Soviet Union to the meaning of existence and the mystery of death, and she wondered why humanity had not acquired a more realistic outlook on death as they watched it happening to trees and animals and human beings all around them. Certainly, in Soviet Russia, the hairs of a man's head were never counted. There, if the death of one man were to profit the masses, die he must.

Sidney, meanwhile, wrote with boyish glee, sending off each chapter as it was finished to be checked for errors by the Soviet

Embassy. M. Vinogradof, the press secretary, while approving of their chapter "Man as a Citizen", suggested that they should change the title of "Man as a Believer" to "Man as an Organiser"; and M. Guinsberg, of the Trade Mission, suggested one or two slight amendments to "Man as a Consumer". The Soviet Ambassador confined himself to congratulating the Webbs on their vitality. "You complain of feeling very old," wrote M. Maisky. "To be quite frank, I am very much impressed by the great vitality displayed by Mrs Webb and yourself. My wife and I cherish the hope that we may be as strong as you are when we reach your age. But, alas, I do not think we shall attain it. The Russian revolutionaries of the old generation do not live long as a rule. Could you perhaps send me the page proofs of the chapter on liquidation?"[3] Sidney himself checked the one on collective farms by new facts from *Moscow News*. Only M. Turin—and he was a Russian exile, who translated all their Russian documents—had a serious criticism. He complained that the Webbs had invented the Soviet Constitution. Beatrice replied: "Telling the truth about things which you cannot tell until you have discovered it, is always invention."

In November 1934, Beatrice fell ill. She had a severe haemorrhage at the Labour Party conference and her doctor advised the removal of a kidney which, at that time, was often fatal to anyone of her age. She faced the ordeal with her usual stoicism and, on the eve of her operation, spent three hours drafting a scheme for their chapter on "In Place of Profit", which described how in the Soviet Union devices for "shaming the sinner" and self-criticism replaced profit-making incentives as the driving force in industry.

As she lay recovering in a nursing home in London, unable to sleep more than three hours in twenty-four, she imagined Sidney, who could not endure distressing scenes, down at Passfield Corner, sleeping in his little room, drinking his coffee, walking with Sandy and getting on with their book. She recalled the research and writing of each one of what she called their "unreadable books", and reminded her resentful soul of how happy she had been. In three week's time, she had recovered sufficiently to come home and, summoning up her courage and remaining strength, struggled to get back to work with her dear one.

Reports of the trial of British engineers in Moscow, at the beginning of Stalin's reign of terror, of the failure of the collective farms, and of financial collapse were now reaching them on every hand.

Even the Soviet press did not deny a food shortage, and accounts of widespread famine in the *Manchester Guardian* bore out Malcolm Muggeridge's denunciation of the Soviet Union. He had gone there appalled, like so many young men of his generation, by the condition of England, believing that Communism could be the salvation of the world. He had returned utterly disillusioned. Beatrice dismissed his accusation that Russia was a slave state, and she wrote and asked him the reason for his anger and bitterness. He replied:

> Angry and bitter, aunt Bo, because something I believed in has turned out to be a fraud.... Not a fraud, though, because of its deplorable economic consequences, but because of what it is trying to do.... The most encouraging thing about the Soviet régime was its failure. If it had succeeded.... I should have known that there were no limits to the extent to which human beings could be terrorised and enslaved....[4]

Beatrice's comment on her disillusioned nephew-in-law was, "Why did he imagine he would like Soviet Russia? He ought to have smelt a rat... and carefully avoided discovering its stinking body." She excused Malcolm as an "Artist, anarchist and aristocrat by temperament".

It was an uncomfortable atmosphere in which to be writing their book on Soviet Communism, but they continued undaunted. The thought of famine did not disturb their faith. They had a heated argument with Walter Citrine, the Trade Union Council Secretary, who asserted that oil, grain and gold production had decreased according to Soviet figures. Sidney was able to correct him by showing him the "official" Soviet figures.

It now became clear that one of them should go to Moscow to make a final check with the authorities there, before they wrote the last chapter of *Soviet Communism, A New Civilisation*. Beatrice was not strong enough and so Barbara Drake, her sister Georgie's eldest daughter, and Stafford's son, John Cripps, accompanied Sidney on his second trip to Russia. He was gratified by his reception in Moscow. He was a new kind of ikon, he told his niece. Soviet Communism was their Co-operative Commonwealth put into practice, and he whispered to her, "It works." He returned with his manuscript checked. There had been little to alter.

1935 was a gloomy year for the whole of Europe. In Great Britain the National Government had failed to deal with unemployment and the crisis in India was still unsolved. Even the brilliantly staged jubilee celebrations of King George V's reign, and the popularity of the Royal family, could only soften the harsh reality. The shadow of Hitler had already fallen over Europe. But for Sidney and Beatrice, exhausted and breathless, it was the end—a thrilling moment. *Soviet Communism, A New Civilisation*—the question mark triumphantly dropped—was published in the autumn. An edition at five shillings a copy had been sold to the Workers' Educational Association before publication. Shaw, as ever, was delightfully appreciative. "It is now plain that providence was equipping you for that colossal work on Russia. Nobody else could have done it, and you would not have done it but for your clinical practice in live social organisations,"[5] he said. M. Maisky also approved. "You write so well. I like your last sentence." The last sentence was:

Will this new civilisation with its abandon of the incentive of profit-making, its extinction of unemployment, its planned production for community consumption, and the consequent liquidation of the landlord and the capitalist, spread to other countries? Our reply is: "Yes, it will." But how, when, where, with what modifications, and whether through violent revolution or by peaceful penetration, or even by conscious imitation we cannot answer.

On the twelfth anniversary of Lenin's death, there was a telephone call from Moscow inviting Sidney to pay a tribute to the glorious founder of the Soviet Union. His message, incoherent and long-winded, was not understood at the other end. It did not matter. *Soviet Communism, A New Civilisation* had come out in time to celebrate a "bumper harvest". The message was, "It will endure." Beatrice called it their last will and testament.

16

"V.W.L."
1935–1943

MANY BOOKS ABOUT RUSSIA were written during the 1930s, some by authors who had lived there for a number of years. The Webbs' was one of the biggest. It did not matter that they had only visited Russia for three weeks because their bulky volume, hailing Soviet Communism as a new civilisation, was compiled from material and statistics supplied to them by Soviet Government officials rather than from first-hand experience of the régime which had turned out to be a most cruel reign of terror. Beatrice attributed their unbounded admiration for Soviet Russia to senility. She said, "Old people often fall in love in extraordinary and ridiculous ways—with their chauffeurs for example: we feel it more dignified to have fallen in love with Soviet Communism." And at the very outset, in the preface to their book, they qualified their extravagant claims for it. "Why did two aged mortals both nearing their ninth decade undertake a work of such magnitude? We fear our presumption must be ascribed to the recklessness of old age."

Their account of the Soviet constitution was an immediate success. They were brilliant "publicists"—a word Beatrice liked to apply to herself and Sidney—and with their broadcasts, articles and lectures they soon established themselves as experts on the subject. People came to them for their opinion and advice about Russia. The wife of the Cambridge atomic fission scientist, Kapitza (who had been kidnapped by the Russians during a reckless visit to his native land), begged them to intercede with the Russian Government on his behalf. His letters seemed to Beatrice to have been written by a neurotic, spoilt egotist. However, although she usually refused appeals of this kind, she promised to do her best to prevent "unnecessary martyrdom". Kapitza, she had heard, was a genius and on the eve of some great discovery (in fact, splitting the atom). Apart from everything else, she found the problem of how far a scientist could be compelled to discover or invent an intensely interesting sociological question. For the state to insist on a right which it could not enforce seemed to her mere "Marxist pedantry".

Another example of Beatrice's Russian expertise was in a letter she wrote to her brother-in-law Henry Hobhouse, whose cousin had made some misguided assumptions about Russia:

> Citrine, who seems to be her favourite authority . . . is not a skilled sociologist and he only knows the U.S.S.R. through three weeks' tour. What amused us was your cousin's assumption that the nicotine, which has been discovered in certain grasses in Siberia, is used to make poison gas. I'm afraid it is used for a fraudulent kind of tobacco which, when the tobacco plant was too expensive to import, was imposed on lovers of tobacco in the Russian cigarettes. But it is always interesting to see intelligent persons' reactions to the facts they know, or think they know, about another country.[1]

The Webbs, like everyone else in the late thirties, were horrified by Stalin's purges. Sidney believed that a scientific sociological explanation would, in the end, be forthcoming, though they themselves might not live to see the mystery solved. Beatrice was less sanguine. She never doubted that the trials were genuine, and the more she listened to the verbatim reports the more she was pained and bewildered by what was happening in the U.S.S.R. She wondered how those intelligent men, some of whom she had met, could get involved in such a crazy conspiracy at the risk of their lives. The accusation and conviction of all who disagreed with Kremlin policy, and the fear of innocent citizens, struck her as a serious social disease.

When Beatrice King, the editor of the *Anglo-Soviet Journal*, begged her to contribute an article on the absence of dictatorship in Russia, she overcame the difficulty of making her argument convincing with comparative ease (constitutionally Stalin was not a dictator), but felt bound to point out in the last paragraph the infantile disease of the U.S.S.R. She referred to the "disease of orthodoxy" and drew attention to the fact that "Lenin and Stalin were idolised and idealised by the Russian people." Anxious editors hurried down to Passfield Corner to try to persuade Beatrice to omit the final critical paragraph. She refused to alter a word. Then they sent the corrected proof, signed by her, with the offending paragraph missing. She would not pass it for publication. Irritated by the Communist Party's display of "primitive passion for conformity",

Beatrice withdrew her article and used it instead as an introduction to the new edition of *Soviet Communism, A New Civilisation*. This episode was never referred to by either Beatrice or Maisky in any of their subsequent meetings. The Russians had yet to learn good manners, concluded Beatrice, as she compared the suppression of free opinion in the Soviet Union with events taking place in Great Britain, the "fort of capitalism", where an abdication and an accession had just been engineered in six days "without a ripple of abuse", and where Leonard Woolf was broadcasting eloquent pleas for the old "Liberal creed of Freedom of Thought".

It was a creed which belonged to an age gone by, when she and Sidney and Shaw and their friends had dedicated their young lives to social betterment, and to the days of the Fabian Society's growing influence. She was now president of the Society, but she reminded Shaw that it had begun to lose its impact as long ago as 1914. (Shaw at this time was helping her with proofs in return for Sidney's draft of how the Shaws could endow culture with their respective fortunes.) Beatrice told him, "You and we are on the bank and we can only notice what is happening in the raging river." Whether she was visiting her old house in Grosvenor Road, listening to the "old, old gossip about the Labour world", or embracing old friends, some of whom were over ninety (kissing Shaw for the first time in her eightieth year), lunching with H. G. Wells (who said "Let's all live to a hundred") or reviving childhood memories at Standish, she felt like a ghost creeping about, haunting "this mad century". Reading through her diaries she began to wonder whether all their efforts and intrigue to bring about reforms had really been worthwhile, and a depressing glimpse she caught of the meaningless mechanised society of the future, as visualised by Wells, when she and Sidney went to see his film *The Shape of Things to Come*, did nothing to reassure her. Then, as always, her happiness with Sidney and the work they had in hand and his sturdy faith in its usefulness to the community dispelled her misgivings and, in the summer of 1937, she was able to summon up sufficient energy and high spirits to assemble, on the lawn at Passfield Corner, a great party of friends, Fabians and family. A hundred descendants of Richard and Laurencina Potter gathered in memory of their ancestor, the income of whose fortune Beatrice had spent on trying to destroy the society on which it had been founded and which it had built up (leaving, in true Victorian financial tradition, the capital untouched to pass on to the next generation). None of her nephews or nieces would make revolutionaries, Beatrice realised, but they were a cultivated lot and some of them even public-spirited. Shaw and Beveridge were there, and she was proudly able to number among her guests three peers, four privy councillors, two cabinet ministers, two baronets, and a couple of F.R.S.'s. Appropriately, greetings were sent from both her father's old firm—Price, Potter & Co.—and the Soviet Embassy.

1938 began, for Beatrice, with a personal calamity. She had just celebrated her eightieth birthday. Bouquets, articles, letters and a "grand display of kindly remembrance" from her friends had greatly pleased her. Two days later, on January 24th, when she took in his morning tea at 6,30, she found Sidney standing by his bed looking puzzled, his hand twitching, and only able to make grim sounds when he tried to speak. He had had a stroke.

When she saw him lying there helpless, so still and silent, tended by nurses night and day, Beatrice realised that never again would they "march together in work and recreation". How could she face marching alone? If only he could express himself, and they could communicate! He tried again and again to say something. There would come a strange sound and then a silence and a pained expression. Beatrice watched tenderly over her old man. He could nod his head when she kissed his hand and held it in hers. She read to him and talked to him about the past and told him news of the present, and she was always able to bring a smile to his face by saying, "we have written the book." As he grew better they took little turns up and down the landing, and when she could not understand the meaning of the sounds he uttered they laughed and kissed and Beatrice told him to wait until he was stronger. These were her happiest hours. When she was alone writing or wandering over the common where they had walked together, or listening to threats of war over the radio, she was apt to relapse into gloom. Barbara Drake's visits were her one great comfort.

By late spring Sidney was well enough for Beatrice to take him to Eastbourne for a change of air. They returned refreshed, Sidney apparently happy and now in charge of Mrs Grant (Beatrice called her his valet-nurse), whom she had engaged to look after him. For a time life took on a more cheerful aspect. Beatrice was working away again on *Our Partnership* and their children, as she was fond of calling the Fabian Society, the *New Statesman*, the London School of Economics and their latest book on Russia were all prospering. The weather was glorious and only the constant roar of planes overhead reminded them of the inevitability of warfare.

Hitler had annexed Austria and politicians were growing impatient with Chamberlain's appeasement policy. Some of them were turning to the Soviet Union as a possible ally. Maisky informed Beatrice that Stalin had received flattering messages from Lloyd George and that even Churchill, at the risk of offending his constituents, had made friendly overtures. Beatrice did her bit too. She sent a rousing message over the air to the German workers via the Freedom station:

Fellow workers ... keep up your energy for the fight. ... We are confident that Hitler's brutal tyranny is rousing the people from their torpor. ... Hitler's Germany, like Tzarist Russia, is a rotten structure. When the crisis comes it will fall to pieces. Be ready to rise against it and establish a classless society. ... We have fervent faith in the success of your persistent and heroic endeavour to destroy what is evil and create what is good.[2]

But the horror of war crept nearer. The Webbs had scarcely recovered from the shock of the Nazi-Soviet Pact when Chamberlain made his declaration of war against Hitler. It was immediately followed by an air-raid warning which made many people scuttle for shelter. Beatrice went at once to Sidney. She found him sitting with his gas-mask on. She told him to take it off. The valet-nurse protested. "I am his wife," Beatrice insisted. "It's damned nonsense putting on gas masks out in the countryside. ... The Germans won't use their gas on us." This was the first of many disagreements Beatrice had with Mrs Grant. The warning turned out to be a false alarm and there was no further sign of active warfare in England for the next nine months, though friends of the Soviet Union received a further shock when the Red Army attacked Finland. Beatrice began to fear that the new civilisation was only a dream of hers, and although she was agreeably surprised that Maisky continued his friendly visits and their talks, it seemed to her that they were now like "little ants creeping about a shattered hill".

Christmas, 1939, was the darkest for Beatrice since her marriage in 1892; and when she was invited to contribute to "What I Believe" (described on the cover as "the inner voice of our age, the private counterpart of its public controversies"), she gladly turned from the spectacle of human failure to the affirmation of her own beliefs. All her life she had thought about God as persistently as an impotent man thinks of "what Venus did to Mars". The faith she held was

> ... that Man is related to the universe by an emotional as well as by a rational tie, that there is a spirit of love at work in the universe, and that the emotion of prayer or aspiration reveals to man the ends he should pursue if he desires to harmonize his own purpose with that of the universe. ...

"I am a religious outcast", she continued:

> I cannot enjoy, without sacrificing intellectual integrity, the immeasurable benefit of spiritual comradeship ... Men of science ... are today re-interpreting the mystical meaning of the universe; and it is they who may bring about a new synthesis between our discovery of the true and our self-dedication to the beautiful and the good.[8]

A journalist from the *Daily Telegraph*, who visited her towards the end of her life, wrote:

> Mysticism which, like hers, finds no horizon beyond earthly life is bound to degenerate into the mere worship of power. Benevolence becomes contempt, and the furtherance of the interests of others a form of arrogance. The pilgrim turns back from the Delectable Mountains and all the trumpets sound for him in the city of Destruction.
>   She had it in her to become a saint—another St. Theresa, and fierce, but sublime. Instead, she took the stony, desolate path of those who believe that the salvation of the individual lies in the exaltation of the collectivity. There was only one possible destination and in the end she found it. The last time I saw her she took me upstairs to see a portrait of Lenin. ... The lighting, arranged from below, exaggerated the cruel mouth, the mongoloid eyes and the cheekbones. It seemed a perfect symbol of the age—this product of Victorian uplift, of Fabian endeavour; this architect of the Welfare State and proponent of 'ethical' religion, now, on the threshold of death, abasing herself before one of the most ruthless and bloody tyrants of history, who had held up to scorn everything she had ever purported to believe in.

By the summer of 1940 Sidney could talk and walk again. He even insisted on going up to London to lunch with the Shaws in order to see that Charlotte fulfilled her promise to endow the London School of Economics with £1,000 for the "teaching of culture and good manners". The routine at Passfield Corner was resumed, except that Sidney now took daily exercise with Mrs Grant who carried a camp-stool for him to sit on when tired, while Beatrice walked two or three miles in another direction with Mrs. Grant's dog, Peter. (Sandy had been put down.) They listened incessantly to the news together. England was actively at war, Winston had taken over and France had fallen. Beatrice was tired of living. Sleeplessness and "whizzing" in her brain prevented her from concentrating on serious writing—"scribbling" in her diary she treated as an indulgence which dulled the pain of existence. The state of the future, she thought, would surely provide facilities for the Voluntary Withdrawal from Life, V.W.L. she called it. (The use of initials for everything had just come into fashion.) "A painless death under pleasant circumstances without a sense of shame ought always to be open to any who desire it; a kindly experienced mental specialist might be provided for those who were anxious to discuss the question To be or not to be? ..." News of Virginia Woolf's suicide confirmed her opinion. Beatrice longed for her life to end, but Sidney was content with his present and pleased with his past. One afternoon when they were sitting in the garden, Beatrice asked him if he wished to go on living. After a long pause he eventually answered no. But he insisted that V.W.L. was out of the question. Beatrice could not go without him, so for his sake she put away thoughts of Voluntary Withdrawal, and settled down again to facing wartime preoccupations with slices of meat, pats of butter and lumps of sugar by day, and air-raids at night, during which she and Sidney stayed in their beds, writing and reading, while their two servants, Annie and Jean, and Mrs Grant with her dog Peter, sheltered under the stairs.

The entry of Russia into the war, and Stafford Cripps' rise to power—from ambassador to Moscow to Minister of Aircraft Production—were reflected in the life of the Webbs. Their prestige increased and articles by them were much in demand. The Ministry of Information commissioned one for a magazine published in Kubishev, *Our British Ally*, and arrangements were being made for another—"The Truth about Russia"—to be published in America.

The effort taxed her strength, but made her feel she could still be a useful citizen. In 1942, the Beveridge Report, with its sweeping proposals for cradle-to-grave social security was published. Reporters hurried down to Passfield for Beatrice's views on a plan which incorporated so much of what she and Sidney had striven for, all their working life. Beatrice was not altogether enthusiastic about it. She doubted whether capitalists would be willing or able to finance such large-scale reforms. Also, she disagreed with her old protégé's proposal for unemployment insurance. Unemployment, she persisted, was an inherent disease of the profit-making motive and "the sad fact is that the better you treat the unemployed, the worse unemployment will become." In her view, a new social order designed to eliminate poverty could only be achieved by following the bold experiments in Soviet Russia, which were "deliberately devised to carry out their new living philosophy of scientific humanism." The applause accorded to the Beveridge Plan astonished her. "One queer result of this strange and terrible war . . ." she observed, "is that Beveridge, whose career as a civil servant and a Director of the London School of Economics was more or less a failure should have risen suddenly into the limelight as an accepted designer of a New Social Order."

She rarely went to London now, but there was a continual flow of callers to Passfield. She used to say they came to worship at the shrine; Fabians, Labour Party representatives, old friends, and disciples who were now leaders of thought in their own right; the Coles, Kingsley Martin from the *New Statesman*, Professor Robson from the London School of Economics, and, most often of all, her sister Georgie's daughter, Barbara Drake, on whom the Webbs depended, in their old age, for the love and comfort they might have had from a daughter of their own. Beatrice's sister Rosy was a frequent guest, though a troublesome one due to her habits of scattering papers, paints, clothes, books and ideas about wherever she went. But the two surviving sisters clung together now, finding that the tie of Potter blood endured long after the complete contrast of their approach to life had ceased to matter. Beatrice had dedicated herself, sixty years before, to "a flight from the service of God to the service of man", All Rosy had ever asked was to love and be loved. Now, Beatrice remarked reflectively to a visiting nephew, "Sometimes, I think that after all Rosy was right." All Beatrice longed for was to disappear, while Rosy, with all passion spent, cheerfully continued to peck up what remained of her mortal existence and to keep a sharp look-out on the eternal horizon for any evidence of immortality. She irritated Beatrice by sitting in Sidney's chair, reading their newspapers and borrowing Beatrice's glasses (which were specially supplied by the Army and Navy stores and fastened to her dress), and tired the Webbs by arguing about the news. Beatrice took to putting Rosy up at the nearby Passfield Oak Hotel (or as she now called it, the P.O.H.), so that she could have her company without the exhaustion of entertaining her.

One day Beatrice's maid announced the Archbishop of Canterbury. Beatrice graciously greeted her august guest. He praised their book and spoke enthusiastically about the new civilisation and Beatrice began to congratulate herself on having, all unawares, actually converted the head of the Anglican Church to the communist faith. It was only when she introduced him to Sydney as "His Grace" that Dr Hewlett Johnson explained that he was not the Archbishop but the Dean of Canterbury. This disclosure brought the visit to an end. As the Red Dean, a communist sympathiser as notorious as Beatrice herself, departed, she puzzled over his outlook and wondered whether he believed in miracles.

Journalists also remained eager for interviews, which Beatrice was always willing to grant. One of them described meeting her when she was eighty-six. She marched him up and down the stairs, showed him every room in the house, and walked him all round the garden. When Sidney came back, tired from his walk, Beatrice, placing one hand on the sun-dial, beckoned him to join her. He complained that his legs ached and that he wanted to sit down. "*Come* along Sidney, *come* along",[5] she insisted and Sidney, "obedient to the beloved will", tottered over to within reach of her spare arm which she placed round his shoulder. Thus the famous pair posed together for their last portrait.

When Beatrice realised that her kidney disease, arrested by an operation ten years before, was now spreading, she knew that she would not have much longer to wait. She believed that the end of the war was already in sight, and she and Sidney were both confident that the scientific humanism of Soviet Communism would prevail, but she had no wish to live to see it. She called Barbara Drake to Passfield to discuss the disposal of the Webb property. Her jewellery was to be distributed among her relatives; Rosy was to have her clothes, and suitable legacies were to be given to her employees. Her home, with all the furniture and portraits and the rest of her money, she left to the London School of Economics. She invited its director, Professor Carr-Saunders, to Passfield Corner to tell him about her cherished dream of her little home as a haven where tired sociologists could rest and discuss, pointing out that there was even a field for cricket. She was delighted when he seemed impressed with the idea and the place.

At the beginning of 1943, she wrote to the secretary whom she had found, long ago, for Shaw, and who was still devotedly serving him.

> Dear Miss Patch,
>
> I do hope the tribunal on Friday exempted your housemaid from being called up ... I can't believe that any authority will deprive such distinguished and aged persons of a servant upon whose presence depends their comfort. We are singularly fortunate in our warm and comfortable little house; all our four employees who have been with us for many years are still here ... I am rather an invalid ... and a very tired brain which adds to my chronic sleeplessness ... If it were not for my beloved partner I should be glad to quit life. We have lived the life we liked and done the work we intended to do, what more can a mortal want but a peaceful and painless death?[6]

In the autumn of 1942 Beatrice had at last given in. She felt too ill to live. She could only just manage to crawl over to the wireless set to listen to the news at nine, which she had already heard at six, and that was generally a repetition of the news at midday. The rest of the time she lay, with her feet up, in a comatose condition. One evening the following spring, she was sitting as usual with Sidney and Mrs Grant and Annie and Jean when all of a sudden it seemed to her that everything had ceased to exist and she had a vision of the painless and unafraid death she had longed for. That night as she lay in pain, unable to go to sleep, she took up her pen to scribble the last confused sentences in the diary she had kept for seventy years.

> To-night when we were listening to the wireless, the BBC broadcast and the electric fire suddenly ceased. Sidney and Mrs Grant and Annie all asserted that it was accidental. But presently ... the BBC ceased its activity and my cup of tea went

cold and so did Sidney's glass of sherry. Ann came to tell me that the two British air machines had passed low over our house and they suddenly disappeared ... I could not for the next few hours get my feet warm and comfortable ... but I suddenly ceased to exist. So did Annie and Jean and Mrs Grant and Sidney. For if my reasoning is right, we shall all disappear including the Germans themselves from the territory they have conquered. There will be no Jews, no conquered peoples, no refugees. The garden will disappear and all our furniture, the earth and the sun and the moon. God wills the destruction of all living things, man and even a child ... we shall not be frozen or hurt. We should merely not exist ... It all seems incredible. ... Even Churchill and Roosevelt, Stalin and kingdoms would disappear. No one would fear, it would be sudden and complete, and so no one needs worry. ... It is as ridiculous as it is terrifying. Annie, as she left me, said she would bring me my breakfast and even offered to stay with me during the night, so that I should not be lonely. So I kissed her and said good-night. I thought it kinder not to tell Sidney and Mrs Grant. We shall none of us suffer, it will be sudden, complete, as the wireless set was in its broadcast and the fire and the electric light, the chairs and the cushions and the kitchen, the sitting-room, the study and the dining-room. What an amazing happening and well worth recording in my diary. But that also will suddenly disappear even if I went on with this endless writing. As I turn out the light and turn over onto the hot-water-bottle so my stomach may no longer pain me, I feel that this is inconceivable and that therefore it will not happen, and we can go on as long as we are conscious that we do exist.

Beatrice died on the eve of Labour Day, 1943.

Rosy went over to Passfield to attend the burial of her ashes. The evening before, she and Sidney sat sadly together in the room where Beatrice had talked and worked and where her presence was strongly evoked by the smoke from the herbal cigarettes which still lingered in the air as though she had only just blown it from her nostrils. Suddenly Rosy was startled by a voice saying, "That's Beatrice you know." It was Sidney calling her attention to the casket which rested precariously on the low bookshelf among the piles of blue-prints, Soviet propaganda and copies of the *New Statesman*.

It was all he had to say. As he had told Beatrice when she had wondered at Henry Hobhouse's composure after the death of Maggie, "Everyone has their own peculiar manner in the face of death of loved ones; you cannot tell how much or how little they are actually feeling." The next morning they buried her in the glade at the bottom of the garden.

In 1944, Sidney was awarded the Order of Merit, "for eminent services to social and political science". He died in 1947 and his ashes were laid with those of Beatrice, as they had wished—but not for long.

Westminster Abbey

AFTER SIDNEY'S DEATH, Shaw, himself ninety-one years old, launched a campaign to reverse their cherished plans. He wrote to *The Times*:

Sir,

It has been objected to the claim for Sidney Webb of a place in the Abbey that he himself directed that his ashes should lie beside those of his wife in a glade at Passfield Corner. The objection is not valid. No man, however eminent, can confer a national tribute on himself by directing or suggesting that he shall be buried in the Abbey. His direction must be within the ordinary competence of his executors.

But in Webb's case there is a point on which his wishes should be respected. The ashes of his wife are not in the Abbey: but they should be. Equally with himself, she was a great citizen, a great civiliser, and a great investigator. There can be no difficulty in transferring her ashes along with his from the Passfield glade to Westminster, where they will not only repair the oversight, but commemorate an unparalleled partnership.

I am not urging this because the Webbs were my personal friends and colleagues. What are earthly honours to them now? It is to the Abbey that their ashes are due; for it owes its secular sanctity not to its stones but to the mighty dead enshrined. The time has come to open its doors to greet world-betterers and to famous women as widely as to kings and captains, novelists and actors. The Dean and Chapter are fully as responsible as the Cabinet. The initiative belongs to either and both. In the present case a disagreement is hardly conceivable.[1]

His plea succeeded with the Dean and Chapter. And so it came about that on December 12, 1947, in the third year of the Welfare State, with 229 Fabians in the House and ten in the Cabinet, Barbara

Drake took the Webbs' ashes from Passfield Corner to Westminster, leaving the stone slab which Sidney had erected in memory of his Beatrice to gather moss. The house was never used for week-ends of discussion and cricket by the "students of narrow means not so privileged as we have been" for whom they had intended it.

It was the first time in 900 years of history that a man and his wife had been buried together at the same ceremony in Westminster Abbey. The Dean had to prepare a special re-interment service.

The congregation assembled, the Government on one side, the relatives on the other. No one noticed a late arrival strolling slowly up the aisle. Beatrice's grey costume with velvet facings hung awkwardly on her spare frame. "Well, here I am," she announced, taking her seat among the family. It was Rosy.

G. K. Chesterton's hymn "O God of earth and altar" was sung and the address was given by another Fabian, Clement Attlee, the Prime Minister, who said, "Millions are living fuller and freer lives today because of the work of Sidney and Beatrice Webb."

Senior members of the Government and family moved over to the grave which was at the foot of the flamboyant tomb of the great Whig parliamentarian Charles James Fox and near to the bust of Joseph Chamberlain. The solemn moment arrived. The Dean was committing the caskets to their final place when there was a hoarse whisper from Rosy. "Which is Sidney and which is Beatrice?"

No one answered her. In the silence after the final prayer she made her last (and audible) protest. "They should have left them where they were."

Notes

The first number refers to the page on which the note appears
the second is the note number

1   Youngest But One

19.1. Herbert Spencer, *Autobiography*
20.2. Laurencina Potter's Journal
21.3. Letter from Richard Potter's father, 1817
22.4. Laurencina Potter, *Laura Gay*, published 1856
25.5. Laurencina Potter's journal
25.6. Letter. Passfield Papers
26.7. Laurencina Potter's journal
27.8. Laurencina Potter's journal
28.9. *My Apprenticeship*
29.10. *My Apprenticeship*
31.11. Laurencina Potter's journal

2   Philosopher on the Hearth

33.1. Stephen Hobhouse, *Margaret Hobhouse and Her Family*
33.2. Letter from Margaret Potter, 1870. Family papers
33.3. Letter from "X", 1870. Family papers
33.4. Letter from "X" 1867. Family papers
34.5. Letter from "X", 1860. Family papers
34.6. Letter from Beatrice, undated. Passfield Papers
35.7. Letter from Beatrice, undated. Passfield Papers
35.8. H. Taine, *Notes on England*, 1872
35.9. *My Apprenticeship*
36.10. *Margaret Hobhouse and Her Family*
38.11. Letter to Robert Holt's mother, from his sisters. Family papers
40.12. "Two", *Home Life With Herbert Spencer*
43.13. Herbert Spencer, *Autobiography*
43.14. Letter from Margaret Potter to Beatrice, 1872. Family papers
44.15. *My Apprenticeship*

3 "Only a Schoolroom Girl"

45.1. Colonel Richard Meinertzhagen, *Diary of a Black Sheep*
45.2. *Gloucester Journal*, September 1873
46.3. Letter from Margaret Potter, August 1872. Family papers
46.4. Letter from Margaret Potter. Family papers
47.5. Letter from Margaret Potter, September 1872. Family papers
55.6. Letter from Georgina Meinertzhagen, January 1875. Family papers
55.7. Herbert Spencer, *Synthetic Philosophy*

4 Coming-out

57.1. Letter from Georgina Meinertzhagen, April 1876. Family papers
58.2. Letter from Margaret Potter, December 1878. Family papers
59.3. *My Apprenticeship*
59.4. Letter from Margaret Potter, Spring 1878. Family papers
60.5. Letter from Margaret Potter, 1871. Family papers
60.6. Letter from Margaret Potter, 1875. Family papers
61.7. *My Apprenticeship*
61.8. Letter from Margaret Potter, 1878. Family papers
61.9. Letter from Margaret Potter, 1876. Family papers
62.10. Letter from Margaret Potter, 1875. Family papers
65.11. Margaret Potter's journal
66.12. George Eliot, *Middlemarch*
67.13. Kate Potter's journal
67.14. *My Apprenticeship*

5 Dutiful Daughter

71.1. Journal of Rosy Dobbs
72.2. Journal of Rosy Dobbs
73.3. Journal of Rosy Dobbs
75.4. Letter to Richard Potter. Passfield Papers
77.5. *My Apprenticeship*
77.6. *My Apprenticeship*
79.7. *My Apprenticeship*
81.8. Letter to Richard Potter. Passfield Papers
81.9. Letter to Margaret Hobhouse. Family papers
84.10. Letter from Richard Potter. Family papers

6 Joseph Chamberlain

87.1. Herbert Spencer, *Autobiography*
92.2. Letter from Maggie Harkness. Family papers

95.3. Journal of Rosy Dobbs
95.4. Medical Bill. Amendment to the Medical Act of 1858
96.5. Letter from Beatrice, February 1886
96.6. Letter from Chamberlain, February 1886
97.7. Letter from Beatrice, March 1886
98.8. Letter from Chamberlain, March 1886
98.9. Letter from Beatrice, March 1886
99.10. Letter from Chamberlain, 1887 (?)
99.11. Letter from Mary Booth. Family papers
100.12. Letter from Kate Courtney. Passfield Papers
100.13. Letter from Kate Courtney. Passfield Papers

7 The Investigator

101.1. Letter from Kate Potter. Family papers
102.2. *Life of Canon Barnett, Vol 2*
102.3. *Life of Canon Barnett*
103.4. *My Apprenticeship*
103.5. *My Apprenticeship*
103.6. *My Apprenticeship*
104.7. *My Apprenticeship*
104.8. *My Apprenticeship*
105.9. *My Apprenticeship*
105.10. *My Apprenticeship*
107.11. *Life of Canon Barnett*
109.12. *Life of Canon Barnett*
110.13. *Life of Canon Barnett*
111.14. Mary Booth, *Charles Booth: A Memoir*
112.15. *My Apprenticeship*
112.16. Work-Girl's Diary. *Nineteenth Century*

8 Sidney

119.1. Letter from Bernard Shaw, 1889
119.2. Emma Brooke, *Transition*
120.3. Letter from Sidney Webb to Sidney Olivier, 1885
121.4. Letter from Sidney Webb to Graham Wallas, July 1885
122.5. Letter from Sidney Webb to Graham Wallas, July 1885
122.6. Letter from Sidney Webb to Graham Wallas, November 1882
122.7. Sonnet by Sidney Webb to "W.D.F.", May 1883. Passfield Papers
128.8. Letter from Kate Courtney, January 1892. Passfield Papers
128.9. Letter from Mary Playne, January 1892. Passfield Papers
129.10. Robert Holt's Journal, July 1892

9 Young Fabians

132.1. Doris Langley Moore, *Life of Edith Nesbit*
133.2. Doris Langley Moore, *Life of Edith Nesbit*
134.3. Shaw, *Early History*
134.4. Shaw, Letter to Ellen Terry
135.5. Shaw, Letter to Ellen Terry
135.6. Shaw, *Collected Letters*
136.7. *Our Partnership*
137.8. Hesketh Pearson, *Bernard Shaw*
138.9. Shaw, *Sixteen Self-Sketches*
139.10. Shaw, *Collected Letters*
140.11. Shaw, *Collected Letters*
140.12. Shaw, *The Webbs and Social Evolution*

10 Wily Webb

143.1. Webb, *History of Trade Unionism*
148.2. *History of Trade Unionism*
149.3. *The London Programme*, 1891
150.4. Sidney Webb, Address to the Association of Technical Institutes
154.5. Shaw, *Collected Letters*

11 Salon on Grosvenor Road

161.1. Letter from Shaw. Passfield Trust collection
161.2. Francis Galton, *Webbs and Their Work*
163.3. E. Pease, *History of the Fabian Society*
165.4. Broadcast by Bertrand Russell
167.5. Wells, *Experiment in Autobiography*
170.6. Wells, *The New Machiavelli*
171.7. Letter from Shaw. *Collected Letters*
172.8. R. K. Ensor, *The Webbs and Their Work*

12 Poor Law

176.1. Beveridge, *Power and Influence*
176.2. Shaw, *Major Barbara*
177.3. Webb, *The Prevention of Destitution*
177.4. Webb, *The Prevention of Destitution*
178.5. Shaw, *Major Barbara*
181.6. Charles Loch Mowat, *The Charity Organisation Society*
183.7. Webb, *Minority Report*
184.8. Webb, *Minority Report*

185.9. Beveridge, *Power and Influence*
185.10. Beveridge, *Power and Influence*
188.11. *The Charity Organisation Society*
191.12. Mary A. Hamilton, *Sidney and Beatrice Webb*
193.13. Beveridge, *Power and Influence*
194.14. *The Charity Organisation Society*
195.15. *The Charity Organisation Society*
196.16. Webb, *Minority Report*
196.17. Shaw, *New Statesman*, 1914

13   Middle-aged Fabians

199.1. Shaw, Letter. Passfield Trust
200.2. Shaw, Letter. Passfield Trust
202.3. G. D. H. Cole, *The World of Labour*
205.4. Leonard Woolf, *Beginning Again*
205.5. Leonard Woolf, *Beginning Again*
206.6. Leonard Woolf, *Beginning Again*

14   The Twenties

224.1. Letter from Shaw. Passfield Trust

15   In Love With Russia

234.1. D. H. Lawrence, Letter
236.2. Kingsley Martin, Obituary of Beatrice Webb in *New Statesman*
242.3. Letter from Maisky. Passfield Papers
243.4. Letter from Malcolm Muggeridge. Passfield Papers
244.5. Letter from Shaw. Passfield Papers

16   "V.W.L."

246.1. Letter from Beatrice Webb to Henry Hobhouse. Family papers
249.2. Broadcast of Freedom Station.
250.3. *What I Believe* (Allen and Unwin)
250.4. Malcolm Muggeridge in the *Daily Telegraph*
253.5. Allan Chappelow in *John Bull*
254.6. Letter from Beatrice Webb to Blanche Patch. Miss Patch's collection

Epilogue

257.1. Shaw, Letter to *The Times*

Bibliography

Asquith, Herbert, *Memoirs and Reflections*, Cassell, 1928
Asquith, Margot, *Autobiography*, Bodley Head, 1920
Barnett, Henrietta, *Canon S. Barnett*, John Murray, 1918
Balfour, Arthur, *Chapters of Autobiography*, Cassell, 1930
Bell, E. A. C. Moberley, *Octavia Hill*, Constable, 1942
Beveridge, William, *Power and Influence*, Hodder and Stoughton, 1953
Brooke, Emma, *Transition*, Heinemann, 1895
Cole, G. D. H. *World of Labour*, Bell and Sons, 1913
Cole, Margaret, *Beatrice Webb*, Longmans Green, 1945
——, *The Webbs and Their Work*, Muller, 1949
——, *The Story of Fabian Socialism*, Heinemann, 1961
——, *Growing Up Into Revolution*, Longmans Green, 1949
Cooke, Colin, *Life of R. S. Cripps*, Hodder and Stoughton, 1957
Copleston, Frederick, *Herbert Spencer, Progress and Freedom. Ideas and Beliefs of the Victorians*, Sylvan Press, 1949
Creighton, Louise, *Life of Bishop Mandell Leighton*, Longman's Green, 1906
Cripps, Hon. F., *Life's a Gamble*, Odhams Press, 1957
Cruikshank, R. J., *Charles Dickens*, Pitman, 1949
——, *Roaring Century*, Hamish Hamilton, 1946
Dalton, Hugh, *Call Back Yesterday*, Muller, 1953
Dunbar, Janet, *Mrs. G. B. S.*, Harrap, 1963
Eliot, George, *Middlemarch*, Dent, 1871
Elliott, Hugh, *Life of Herbert Spencer*, Constable, 1917
Elton, Lord, *Life of James Ramsay MacDonald*, Collins, 1939
Ervine, St. John, *Life of Bernard Shaw*, Constable, 1956
Estorick, Eric, *Stafford Cripps, Master Statesman*, Heinemann, 1949
Farrington, Benjamin, *What Darwin Really Said*, Macdonald, 1966
Freemantle, Ann, *This Little Band of Prophets*, Mentor Books, 1960
Galton, Francis, *Memoirs of My Life*, Methuen, 1908
Gardiner, A. G., *Prophets, Priests and Kings*, Alston Rivers, 1908
Garvin, J. L., *Life of Chamberlain*, Macmillan, 1932
Gooch, G. P., *Life of Lord Courtney*, Longmans Green, 1920
Haldane, R. B., *Autobiography*, Hodder and Stoughton, 1929

Hamilton, Mary A., *Sidney and Beatrice Webb*, Sampson Low, 1933

Harris, S. Hutchinson, *Auberon Herbert, Crusader for Liberty*, Williams and Norgate, approx. 1880

Hassel, Christopher, *Rupert Brooke*, Faber, 1966

Henderson, Archie, *George Bernard Shaw*, Apple-Century-Crofts, 1956

Hewins, W.A.S., *Apologia of an Imperialist*, Constable, 1929

Hill, Octavia, *Letters*, Allen and Unwin, 1928

Hobhouse, Stephen, *Margaret Hobhouse and Her Family*, Stanhope Press, 1934

Kagarlitski, J., *H. G. Wells*, Sidgwick and Jackson, 1966

Kent, William, *John Burns; Labour's Lost Leader*, Williams and Norgate, 1950

Letvin, Shirley Robin, *Pursuit of Certainty*, Cambridge University Press, 1966

Martin, Kingsley, *Father-Figures*, Hutchinson, 1966

McCarthy, Desmond, *Autobiography*, MacGibbon and Kee, 1953

Meinertzhagen, Dick, *Diary of a Black Sheep*, Oliver and Boyd, 1964

Meinertzhagen, Georgina, *Ploughshare to Parliament*, John Murray, 1908

Moore, Doris Langley, *Life of Edith Nesbit*, Ernest Benn, 1933

Mowat, Charles Loch, *The Charity Organisation Society*, Methuen, 1961

Nineteenth Century Magazine, 1888

Pearson, Hesketh, *Bernard Shaw*, Methuen, 1961

Pease, Edward R., *History of the Fabian Society*, George Allen and Unwin, 1924

Postgate, Raymond, *Pocket History of the British Working Class*, N.C.L.C., 1963

Potter, Laurencina, *Laura Gay*

Raymond, E. T., *Mr Balfour*, Collins, 1920

Robson, William, *The Government and Misgovernment of London*, George Allen and Unwin, 1939

Rodgers, W. T. and Donoghue, B., *People Into Parliament*, Thames and Hudson, 1966

Samuel, Viscount, *Memoirs*, Cresset Press, 1945

Shaw, George Bernard, *Collected Letters*, Bodley Head, 1966

——, *Letters to Ellen Terry*, Reinhardt & Evans, 1949

——, *Sixteen Self-Sketches*, Constable

——, *Widowers' Houses*, Constable

——, *Mrs Warren's Profession*, Constable

——, *Major Barbara*, Constable

——, *Man and Superman*, Constable

——, *The Apple-Cart*, Longmans Green and Constable

——, *The Millionairess*, Constable

——, *The Intelligent Woman's Guide to Socialism and Capitalism*, Constable, 1928

——, *Everybody's Political What's-What*, Constable, 1944
Simey, T. S., *Life of Charles Booth*, Oxford University Press, 1960
Spencer, Herbert, *Autobiography*, Williams and Norgate, 1904
——, *First Principles*, Williams and Norgate, 1880
Strauss, P., *Cripps, Advocate and Rebel*, Gollancz, 1942
Tawney, R. H., *Beatrice Webb*, British Academy, 1943
Trevelyan, G., *Life of John Bright*, Longmans Green, 1913
——, *British History in the Nineteenth Century*, Longmans Green, 1922
——, *English Social History*, Longmans Green, 1944
"Two", *Home Life with Herbert Spencer*, J. W. Arrowsmith, Bristol, 1906
Webb, Beatrice, *My Apprenticeship*, Longmans Green, 1926
——, *Our Partnership*, Longmans Green, 1948
——, *Diaries*, 1912–24, Longmans Green, 1952
——, *Diaries*, 1924–32, Longmans Green, 1956
——, *Minority Report*, Longmans Green, 1909
——, *Prevention of Destitution*, Longmans Green, 1911
——, *Constitution for the Socialist Commonwealth of Great Britain*, Longmans Green, 1920
——, *Soviet Communism. A New Civilisation*, Longmans Green, 1935
——, *History of Trade Unionism*, Longmans Green, 1894
Wells, H. G., *Experiment in Autobiography*, Gollancz, 1934
——, *Ann Veronica*, Harper Bros., 1909
——, *The New Machiavelli*, Bodley Head, 1911
Williams, Francis, *Fifty Years March*, Odhams Press, 1949
Winsten, Stephen, *Salt and His Circle*, Hutchinson, 1951
——, *Shaw's Corner*, Hutchinson, 1958
Wingfield-Stratford, Esme, *Victorian Tragedy*, Routledge, 1930
Woolf, Leonard, *Sowing*, Hogarth Press, 1960
——, *Growing*, Hogarth Press, 1961
——, *Beginning Again*, Hogarth Press, 1964

Index

[i]

A Note About the Authors

Kitty Muggeridge

is the wife of the noted British journalist and critic
Malcolm Muggeridge and the niece of Beatrice Webb (her
mother was Beatrice's younger sister, Rosy). She was educated privately and at the London School of Economics.

Ruth Adam

has published eight novels and is also well known in Eng-
land as a journalist and broadcaster. She was educated at
Nottingham School for Girls and St. Elphin's School for
Daughters of the Clergy. She is married to Kenneth Adam,
Director of BBC Television.